T0326297

*The Ri-me Philosophy
of Jamgön Kongtrul the Great*

The RI-ME PHILOSOPHY

of Jamgön Kongtrul the Great

A STUDY OF THE BUDDHIST
LINEAGES OF TIBET

Ringu Tulku

Edited by Ann Helm

SHAMBHALA
BOULDER
2007

Shambhala Publications, Inc.
4720 Walnut Street
Boulder, Colorado 80301
www.shambhala.com

Printed in the United States of America

⊗This edition is printed on acid-free paper that meets the
American National Standards Institute z39.48 Standard.
♻Shambhala Publications makes every effort to print on recycled
paper. For more information please visit www.shambhala.com.
Shambhala Publications is distributed worldwide by
Penguin Random House, Inc., and its subsidiaries.

Designed by Gopa & Ted2, Inc.

The Library of Congress catalogues the previous edition of this title as follows:
Ringu Tulku.
The ri-me philosophy of Jamgon Kongtrul the Great / Ringu Tulku;
Edited by Ann Helm.
p.   cm.
Includes bibliographical references and index.
ISBN 978-1-59030-286-6 (hardcover: alk. paper)
ISBN 978-1-59030-464-8 (paperback)
1. Kon-sprul Blo-gros-mtha'-yas, 1813–1899.   2. Buddhism—
China—Tibet—Doctrines.   I. Helm, Ann, 1949–   II. Title.
BQ968.057R56 2006
294.3'923'092—dc22
2005021272

CONTENTS

HOMAGE

With many profound and vast discussions of the dharma
You show the excellent path to permanent happiness
For the limitless beings of this degenerate age.
I pay homage to Shakyamuni Buddha, who is unequalled and
    utterly courageous.

The scriptures of the Buddha's and the bodhisattvas' fine
    explanations
Were brought to the Land of Snow without corruption.
I bow down to the holders of the teaching lineage, who are like
    great pillars
Maintaining the strength and upholding the house of the
    Buddha's teachings.

The heart essence of all the good paths of sutra and tantra
Is the boat that takes us to the island of full liberation in
    one life.
Those who drive the chariots of the eight practice lineages—
The lineage holders and their students—are the objects of my
    homage.

Hundreds of streams of the teaching and practice lineages of the
    dharma in Tibet
Flowed into the deep and wide ocean of his understanding.
In turn, he impartially showered the dharma upon all beings.
May the Jamgön lama, Lodrö Thaye, be victorious.

His powerful intelligence contained the marvelous *Five
  Great Treasuries,*
Which arose from the secret of his lordly speech
And flowed forth like the great Brahmaputra River.[1]
Although I lack even a fraction of his ability to hold all of that,

From the oceanlike qualities of the three secrets of his body,
  speech, and mind,
A little drop of knowledge has trickled into my ears.
This caused the flower of devotion to open in my heart,
And with that inspiration, I have endeavored to write this book.

By starting with these verses, I would like to express the greatness of
the Tibetan Ri-me master, the bodhisattva Lodrö Thaye, or Kongtrul Yönten Gyatso. A scholar learned in all the five branches of learning—language, craftsmanship, medicine, logic, and philosophy, he is so
special that I take his name with utmost reverence. The secret of his
enlightened speech is so profound and vast that his *Five Great Treasuries* are like the ocean; they contain innumerable teachings. From this
vast ocean I can extract only a tiny drop.

Through these verses I also want to emphasize that the precious
Buddhadharma that spread in Tibet was kept intact without degeneration. Jamgön Kongtrul was instrumental in showing that among the
great charioteers who hold the various Tibetan lineages there is a single ultimate understanding, that all their teachings arrive at the same
essential point, and there is no need for sectarianism. Showing this single understanding is the essence of the Ri-me approach, and the way in
which Kongtrul established this is the main thrust of this book.

PREFACE

THE FIRST CHAPTER, "The Meaning of Ri-me," describes the nonsectarian understanding and the manner in which Jamgön Kongtrul and other masters show that there are no fundamental contradictions among the Buddhist teachings that came to Tibet. The Ri-me approach is an inclusive one, recognizing the distinctions of the various lineages and teachings, while seeing them all as valid instructions that lead to the same ultimate understanding. This approach is not a new one. It is the foundation of all the teachings of the Buddha. Jamgön Kongtrul and Jamyang Khyentse Wangpo reiterated and highlighted this principle and lived it themselves.

This impartial appreciation of all schools of Tibetan Buddhism is exemplified in the life story of Jamgön Kongtrul the Great, which is the subject of chapter 2. Jamgön Kongtrul was a living example of a Ri-me master, and just by reading his biography one can come to understand the Ri-me philosophy. Jamgön Kongtrul, along with his teacher and colleague Jamyang Khyentse Wangpo, are especially renowned for the way that they received, practiced, and preserved the teachings of all the main practice lineages of Tibet. Their collaboration in this effort is a highlight of this biography. With Khyentse's urging and support, Kongtrul compiled over ninety volumes in five large collections known as the *Five Great Treasuries:* the *Treasury of Instructions,* the *Treasury of Kagyu Vajrayana Instructions,* the *Treasury of Knowledge,* the *Treasury of Precious Terma,* and the *Treasury of Vast Teachings.* The most important of these collections for the Ri-me movement, the *Treasury of Instructions,* has eighteen volumes of teachings, which include all eight practice lineages. Not only did Kongtrul and Khyentse collect and preserve these teachings, but they practiced them and transmitted them to their students.

Although Jamyang Khyentse was a great source of inspiration and encouragement, it was Jamgön Kongtrul who compiled the *Five Great Treasuries,* taught them many times, and got all of them published. The information in chapter 2 is drawn from Kongtrul's own autobiography, and from the account of Kongtrul's passing and funeral observances by his student Tashi Chöphel.[1] This chapter gives a clear overview of Kongtrul's most important relationships, writings, and activities.

Chapter 3 covers the history of the teaching lineages of sutra and tantra in India and Tibet, and chapter 4 covers the history of the eight practice lineages and their introduction into Tibet from India. The sutra teachings focus on the Vinaya, Abhidharma, Pramana, Prajna-paramita, and Madhyamaka; the tantra teachings, as well as those of the eight practice lineages, cover a vast array of vajrayana scriptures and practices. Each of these lineages has its own authoritative texts, seminal founders, and representative masters, who continue to be revered in the Tibetan tradition. These chapters are presented in chronological order. One reason for giving these lineage histories is to show that the teachings of Shakyamuni Buddha are the sole source of Tibetan Buddhism, and that the Tibetans also inherited the clarifications of the Buddha's teachings by great Indian masters whose knowledge and realization are undisputed. All the great charioteers who brought these teachings to Tibet were predicted by the Buddha; without question they were realized beings who had reached the level of the bodhisattva bhumis.

A second reason for presenting the history is to make it clear that the Buddhist teachings brought to Tibet have not degenerated or been defiled or distorted in any way. And third, I have endeavored to show that the individual traditions which continue to this day are unbroken lineages, that the noble scholars and meditation masters who hold these teachings have continued to maintain and spread them in a very pure way. The lineage histories also show that although all the schools of Tibetan Buddhism stem from Shakyamuni Buddha, each of them contains a variety of lineages that are interconnected and intermingled.

Next, chapter 5 introduces the main teachings of the eight practice lineages. It is very helpful for students of a particular lineage to have an overview of the practices and important texts of not only their own lineage but also the other main lineages. In chapter 5 I have highlighted the particular methods and paths used by each of these spiritual traditions in order to bring an individual to enlightenment. When all these teachings are seen side by side, it becomes evident that there are no discordant elements among them; the essence of their understanding is ultimately the same. In fact, one could say that the whole of Tibetan Buddhism can be categorized within these eight practice lineages, and when one understands their teachings, it becomes evident that they have no basis for dispute.

Of course, there have been disagreements among proponents of the various schools, and the final chapters focus on two areas that have been widely debated. It could be said that the topics in these chapters subsume and deal with all the major disputes between the different schools of Tibetan Buddhism. Chapter 6 discusses the controversy concerning Rangtong and Shentong Madhyamaka. According to Kongtrul, their basic disagreement is whether or not the dharmata, or true nature, is there, and whether or not primordial wisdom is truly established. Aside from exploring this debate, this chapter covers Madhyamaka history, logic, and key figures such as Chandrakirti, Tsongkhapa, Shakya Chogden, and Taranatha.

Chapter 7 discusses some of the misunderstandings and allegations that some followers of Sarma tantras levied on the Nyingma masters. The Nyingma tantras appeared in Tibet before the tenth century, while the Sarma tantras were brought from India after that time. Many scholars questioned the validity of the Nyingma tantras to the extent that they were omitted from the early versions of the Kangyur, the translated words of the Buddha. Both chapters 6 and 7 include the main points used by each side for affirmation and refutation in the debates, and show how some of the most brilliant scholars have displayed their skill in using scripture and reasoning. These debates also point out how their views ultimately arrive at the same essential point.

TRANSLATION NOTES

Ann Helm and I have translated into English almost all of the Tibetan text titles mentioned in this book. A few titles were put into Sanskrit rather than English, such as the *Kalachakra Tantra* and the *Prajnapara-mita Sutra,* because the Sanskrit names are already more familiar in English-speaking countries. At the end of the book there is a Sources section that gives all the text titles in English alphabetical order, along with the Tibetan transliteration, the Sanskrit title if originally written in Sanskrit, and the author's name if known. We made this list so that readers can read without being distracted by clumps of foreign syllables in parentheses and so that the original titles are available for those who know the Tibetan or Sanskrit names.

Although there are many quotations in this book, there may arise some questions about the relatively small number of specific citations. Tibetans seem to have a much looser attitude than Westerners about quoting, copying, and citing others' texts. Before 1960, there were no copyrights in Tibet, and it was enough to merely state, "As Chandrakirti says," without giving a book title, chapter, or page reference. Sometimes writers did not even do that much, and freely incorporated passages into their own texts without saying they were quoting someone else. This is done because one never claims that what he writes is his own but that all dharma comes from an authentic source. In my 1985 Tibetan edition of this book, there are only about thirty citations with page numbers from the works of Kongtrul and other scholars. But the fact is that the whole book is based on the works of Kongtrul and some of his lineage holders, and there is nothing here that I invented on my own. Moreover, since the Tibetan edition was completed twenty years ago and my notes are no longer available, it does not seem feasible to reconstruct all the references.

THE RI-ME PHILOSOPHY OF
JAMGÖN KONGTRUL THE GREAT

1

THE MEANING OF RI-ME

WHILE DOING RESEARCH WORK on the Ri-me movement in the 1970s, I had the opportunity to meet and interview a number of prominent Tibetan lamas, including His Holiness the Dalai Lama and the heads of the four main schools of Tibetan Buddhism. I prepared a questionnaire, and one of the questions I asked was whether they believed that the other schools of Tibetan Buddhism showed the way to attain buddhahood. I have never been so rebuked in my life as when I asked that question! All of them, without exception, were shocked and insulted, feeling deeply saddened that I, a monk, could ever have such doubts. They would not speak with me until I persuaded them that this was one of those unimportant, procedural questions that are part of the modern university system.

"How can you say such a thing?" they rebuked me. "All the schools of Buddhism practice the teachings of the Lord Buddha." They went on to discuss how all four Tibetan schools share the same monastic code, the Sarvastivada Vinaya, and practice the Mahayana way of training the mind. All of them investigate the ultimate truth through Madhyamaka philosophy, and follow the two great charioteers, Nagarjuna and Asanga. On top of that, all the Tibetan Buddhist schools one-pointedly take the Anuttarayoga tantras as their main, heart practice. Therefore, there is no actual basis for sectarianism, and all the schools essentially follow a Ri-me approach.

What is Ri-me?

Ri or *chok-ri* in Tibetan means "one-sided," "partisan," or "sectarian." *Me* means "no." So, *Ri-me* means "not taking sides," "nonpartisan," or "nonsectarian." It does not mean "nonconformist" or "noncommittal," nor does it mean forming a new school or system that is different from the existing ones. Followers of the Ri-me approach almost always follow one lineage for their main practices. Although they respect and learn from other traditions, they would not dissociate from the school in which they were raised. One can take, for example, the founders of the Ri-me movement, Jamgön Kongtrul (1813–1899) and Jamyang Khyentse Wangpo (1820–1892). Kongtrul was educated in the Nyingma and Kagyu traditions, and Khyentse was raised in the Nyingma and Sakya traditions. Although these two scholars and meditation masters received, collected, practiced, and transmitted the teachings of all eight practice lineages, they never failed to acknowledge their affiliation to their own schools.

One of the unique features of Buddhism is the acceptance that different paths are appropriate for different types of people. Just as one medicine cannot cure all diseases, so one set of teachings cannot help all beings—this is a basic principle of Buddhism. One chooses the most appropriate sutras and/or tantras from the Buddhist canon and makes them the basis for one's practice. This is how different schools of Buddhism begin. There are no "sects" in Buddhism because there are no groups that break away from the main school. Different lineages have come into being even among those who practice the same teachings.

In Tibet, like other places, the different schools practiced and studied in rather isolated environments, without much contact with other schools and lineages. A lack of communication breeds misunderstanding. Even where there was no misunderstanding or disrespect to other schools, some practitioners, in their enthusiasm to keep their own lineages pure and undiluted, went so far as to refuse teachings from the masters of other lineages, and would not study the texts of other schools. Ignorance is the most fertile ground for growing doubts and misconceptions.

Jamgön Kongtrul on Sectarianism

Jamgön Kongtrul disagreed so thoroughly with a partisan approach that he asserted that those with sectarian views cannot uphold even their own tradition. Kongtrul says:

Just as a king overpowered by self-interest
Is not worthy of being the protector of the kingdom,
A sectarian person is not worthy of being a holder of the dharma.
Not only that, he is unworthy of upholding even his own tradition.

And again:

The noble ones share a single ultimate view,
But arrogant ones bend that to their own interests.
Those who show all the teachings of the Buddha as without
   contradiction can be considered learned people,
But who would be foolish enough to think that those who cause
   discord are holders of the dharma?

Ri-me is not a way of uniting different schools and lineages by emphasizing their similarities. It is basically an appreciation of their differences and an acknowledgment of the importance of variety to benefit practitioners with different needs. Therefore, the Ri-me teachers always take great care that the teachings and practices of the different schools and lineages, and their unique styles, do not become confused with one another. Retaining the original style and methods of each teaching lineage preserves the power of that lineage experience. Kongtrul and Khyentse made great efforts to retain the original flavor of each teaching, while making them available to many.

Kongtrul writes about Khyentse in his biography of the latter:[1]

Some people are very fussy about the refutations and affirmations of the various tenets, becoming particularly attached to their own versions, such as Rangtong or Shentong Madhyamaka. There are many who try to pull others over to their own side, to the point of practically breaking their necks. When Jamyang Khyentse teaches the different tenet systems, he does not mix up their terminology or ideas, yet he makes them easy to understand and suitable for the students.

In general, the main point to be established by all the tenets is the ultimate nature of phenomena. As the *Prajna-paramita Sutra* states:

The dharmata is not an object of knowledge;
It cannot be understood by the conceptual mind.

In addition, Ngok Lotsawa, who is considered the crown jewel of Tibetan intellectuals, agrees with this understanding when he says:

The ultimate truth is not only beyond the dimension of language and expression, it is beyond intellectual understanding.

So, the ultimate nature cannot be established by the samsaric mind, no matter how deep that mind may be.

The scholars and siddhas of the various schools make their own individual presentations of the dharma. Each one is full of strong points and supported by valid reasoning. If you are well grounded in the presentations of your own tradition, then it is unnecessary to be sectarian. But if you get mixed up about the various tenets and the terminology, then you lack even a foothold in your own tradition. You try to use someone else's system to support your understanding, and then get all tangled up, like a bad weaver, concerning the view, meditation, conduct, and result. Unless you have certainty in your own system, you cannot use reasoning to support your scriptures, and you cannot challenge the assertions of others. You become a laughing stock in the eyes of the learned ones. It would be much better to possess a clear understanding of your own tradition.

In summary, one must see all the teachings as without contradiction, and consider all the scriptures as instructions. This will cause the root of sectarianism and prejudice to dry up, and give you a firm foundation in the Buddha's teachings. At that point, hundreds of doors to the eighty-four thousand teachings of the dharma will simultaneously be open to you.

The Ri-me concept was not original to Kongtrul and Khyentse, nor was it new to Buddhism. Shakyamuni Buddha forbade his students to criticize others, even the teachings and teachers of other religions and cultures. This directive was so strong and unambiguous that in the *Entrance to the Middle Way,* Chandrakirti felt compelled to defend Nagarjuna's Madhyamaka treatises by saying:

> If, in trying to understand the truth, one dispels misunderstandings, and therefore some philosophies cannot remain intact, that should not be considered as criticizing others' views.

Rongzom Pandita's Clarification of Higher and Lower Views

We need to realize that all the Buddhist traditions ultimately arrive at the same point, and that, in general, the Buddha's teachings do not contradict themselves. True followers of the Buddha cannot help but be Ri-me, or nonsectarian, in their approach. This view is elaborated by Rongzom Pandita Chökyi Zangpo in his *Points to Remember about the View:*[2]

> In the treatises of the Buddhist teachings, one can make distinctions of higher and lower views, where the higher ones clarify points in the lower ones. Other than that, they do not improve on the lower ones or go against them. In clarifying what needs to be clarified, they do not undermine the basic principles or repudiate the lower teachings. Therefore, all the teachings of the Buddha are of one taste; they are seeking the nature of suchness and they end up with the nature of suchness. All of them are like that.
>
> There are no differences in the basic teachings, like there being one tenet that asserts the self does exist and another that asserts the self does not exist. By discussing selflessness, all the yanas, lower and higher, examine the root of phenomena and teach the nature of things more and more deeply. They are not discussing different bases. Since the Hinayana and Mahayana and the higher and lower views have no separate bases or separate paths, that means they have no separate results. This needs to be understood.

Some traditions discuss slightly different ways of entering the path, but these can easily be joined into one system. For example, the Shravaka system clears away all doubts about the selflessness of the person within the aggregates, sense fields, and consciousnesses. The Mahayanists do not say they have a different understanding of personal selflessness, and that it is higher or an improvement on the Hinayana understanding. Nor do the Mahayanists say that the Hinayana understanding is wrong.

The Mahayanists see a need to clarify further that the aggregates, sense bases, and consciousnesses are not substantially existent dharmas. However, they do not undermine the basis of the Hinayana understanding by asking questions about the aggregates, consciousnesses, and sense bases, like where they exist, to whom they are known, what their characteristics are, and so forth. They do not undermine the basic understanding by statements like "the self and the world do exist, but the aggregates, sense bases, and consciousnesses do not exist." If that were the case, then the higher Buddhist tenets, like Yogachara, might say something completely different. But it is not like that; all the Buddhist teachings have the same basis.

All the Buddha's teachings are of one taste and one way; nothing is excluded within the state of vast equality. For example, all the small streams flow into large rivers and then accompany the large rivers to flow into the ocean. Within the vast ocean, all the rivers have the same taste of salt. Similarly, all the small entrances of the lower yanas are small rivers of understanding personal selflessness, which wash away the dirt of the belief in substantial entities. They join the large rivers of the Mahayana sutras and all of them end up in the great ocean of Dzogpa Chenpo. There is not even a particle of dust that does not become of one taste with this great, vast equality.

Accordingly, within the yanas, the lower views have certain points that need to be clarified by the higher views, and certain points that do not need to be clarified. The higher views do not repudiate nor try to improve whatever is already clear in the lower views. In relation to what is unclear in the lower views, the higher views do not repudiate their basis nor undermine their basis. In these four ways all the Buddha's teachings should be understood as being of one taste and one way. We need to understand the differences between the higher and lower views, and this is one aspect of knowing the various views. However, the heart of the matter is that even with their differences, all the Buddhist traditions are fundamentally of one taste. Please hold this as the highest and most essential understanding.

Those are the words of Rongzom Pandita. There are many other teachings that similarly clarify this point, such as the *Scripture of the Embodiment of the Realization of All Buddhas,* which states:

Manjushri, the karmic obscuration of rejecting the noble dharma is a subtle one. When one thinks that some of the Tathagata's teachings are good and others are bad, then that is rejecting the dharma. By rejecting the dharma, a person is criticizing the Tathagata and expressing negativity toward the sangha. If someone says, "That is right and this is not right," then that is rejecting the dharma. If one says, "This is taught only for the bodhisattvas," or "This is taught only for the shravakas," or "This is taught only for the pratyekabuddhas," then that is rejecting the dharma.

Khenchen Kunpal on Clarifying Misunderstanding

So, does this mean that the treatises written by the great, learned masters of the past that criticize certain views and establish other views are useless? No, it is not like that. Those treatises were not just criticizing each other; they came from unbiased minds in order to show how ordinary beings can have misunderstandings. If you thoroughly examine their main points, their clarifications become a source of deep understanding. It is as Khenchen Kunpal says:[3]

Those who are very learned from their study of the five branches of knowledge and other topics, and those who have reached the stage of warmth in their meditative experience, receive predictions and are directly cared for by their lamas and special deities. These learned and accomplished masters truly benefit the teachings and beings through their activities of teaching, debating, and writing. Those who use reason and debate meaningfully to refute misunderstanding and establish right understanding are great masters, whether they come from our tradition or another tradition. If we look deeply to find their real intention and do not look in a wrong way, their presentations strengthen our understanding. Rather than causing harm, they are highly beneficial.

If you do not approach other traditions with an open mind, and you criticize them by exaggerating and denigrating their views just because of hatred, then you will cause great harm. Those who are ignorant, from the cowherds upwards, will be like the storybook animals who were alarmed by a rabbit running scared at the sound of a branch falling in the river. Like those forest animals, they will join the panicking crowd and have wrong views about the genuine dharma. They will make baseless allegations, and that is a serious fault. Your criticism will bring others to disaster, and you will be a long way from the liberated lifestyle of a noble being. Devastated from the desire to talk too much, you will expose your dirty guts for all to see. You will stray far from the teachings of the buddhas and bodhisattvas, and that is highly inappropriate.

What Khenchen Kunpal says is true. That is why the two emanations of Manjushri, Khyentse and Kongtrul, together with their students and lineages, have the conviction that all the great tenets of Buddhism arrive at the same ultimate point. They do not act in sectarian ways; they do not try to bring people over to their side, nor are they attached to their own traditions and hateful toward others. They instruct us to hold all the teachings within our mindstreams without contradiction, and when it is our turn to teach the dharma to others, we should explain it and emphasize the main points just like the great charioteers of the past. We should not change the teachings or corrupt them even the tiniest bit.

Doctrinal Disputes

Then why are there so many debates and criticisms among the different schools of Buddhism? There is an old saying in Tibet:

> *If two philosophers agree, one is not a philosopher.*
> *If two saints disagree, one is not a saint.*

It is accepted that all realized beings have the same experience, but the question is how to describe it to others. Almost all debates are concerned with ways of using language. For example, the main debate between the schools of Svatantrika and Prasangika Madhyamaka comes down to whether to include the word "ultimately" or not. For example, whether to say, "Form is empty" or "Form is ultimately empty."

The legendary, ten-year debate between Chandrakirti and Chandragomin is a good example. Both of these masters are regarded as realized beings by all sides, so why did they debate? Their debates rested on how to phrase the teachings to have the least danger of misinterpretation.

Rangtong and Shentong

In particular, there has been a great deal of heated debate in Tibet between the exponents of Rangtong and Shentong Madhyamaka. The lineages, philosophies, and debates of these two schools are discussed later in this book. In relation to this discussion of nonsectarianism, here is a quote from Jamgön Kongtrul summarizing the relationship of these two systems:[4]

> For both Rangtong and Shentong Madhyamaka, all phenomena included in the relative truth are emptiness, and

there is the cessation of all fabricated extremes in meditation. Their views do not differ on these points. However, in
relation to post-meditation, to clearly distinguish the tenet
systems, merely in terms of the way they use terminology,
Shentong says that the dharmata, or true nature, is there,
and Rangtong says the dharmata is not there. In the ultimate analysis, using the reasoning that examines the ultimate, Shentong says nondual primordial wisdom is truly
established, and Rangtong says primordial wisdom is not
truly established. These two statements delineate their main
differences.

So, their difference lies in the words they use to describe the dharmata
and primordial wisdom. Shentong describes the dharmata, the true
nature, as ultimately real, while Rangtong philosophers fear that if it is
described in that way, people might understand it as the concept of a
soul or atma. The Shentong philosophers think there is a greater chance
of misunderstanding if the enlightened state is described as unreal and
void. Their debates rest on how to phrase the teachings to have the least
danger of misinterpretation. Kongtrul finds the Rangtong presentation
best for dissolving concepts, and the Shentong presentation best for
describing the actual experience.

Nyingma and Sarma

Kongtrul deals in the same way with the problems between the
Nyingma and Sarma, or the Early and New Translation traditions, concerning the validity of the Nyingma tantras and the Dzogchen practice
of Thögal. Kongtrul says there are two reasons why the Nyingma
tantras are genuine. First, the original Sanskrit versions were eventually
found, and second, both the earlier and later translations of the tantras
have the same perspectives and understanding. Kongtrul makes this
very clear in his *Informal Discussion of the View*:[5]

The natural state, the Mahamudra,
Is clearly taught in all the sutras and tantras.

The Ri-me position is that although the various Tibetan lineages have evolved different emphases and practices, they have a single ultimate understanding, and their teachings all arrive at the same essential point. Kongtrul Rinpoche bases his discussion on the instructions in the *Sutra of the King of Concentrations*, the Anuttarayoga tantras, the teachings of Maitripa, and the teachings of Marpa and his followers. For example, Kongtrul says the Mahamudra teachings of the Kagyu lineage arrive at the same point as the Dzogchen teachings of the Nyingma lineage. He says about the Mahamudra instructions:

> These teachings correlate with the Semde teachings of Dzogchen.

He also proclaims the convergence of the Sakya and Kagyu lineages in their understanding of the ultimate:

> *The five Sakya forefathers asserted*
> *The tenet system of subtle Madhyamaka*
> *And the view of Mahamudra.*

One might question Kongtrul's understanding of this because of Sakya Pandita's criticism of the Kagyu Mahamudra in his book *Differentiating the Three Vows*. Kongtrul says about Sakya Pandita:

> *Because it was necessary in that context,*
> *In* Differentiating the Three Vows *he refutes*
> *The Dagpo Kagyu, the Mahamudra, and others.*
> *But in his book the* Commentary Praising Selflessness,
>   *he personally accepts the view of Mahamudra.*

In Jamgön Kongtrul's *Informal Discussion of the View*, he states that the Gelugpa lineage also shares the same understanding, and that Tsongkhapa's presentation does not contradict the Dzogchen view. He says:

> *The real point of Je Tsongkhapa's understanding*
> *Is indisputably the same as the tenets of Dzogchen.*

> *This is clear in his text the* Sublime Medicine, the Amrita of
> Questions and Answers.

Kongtrul also says:

> *When the Gelugpas explain the Six Yogas of Naropa*
> *They teach meditative absorption beyond concepts.*
> *Also, in practicing Guhyasamaja, they mainly follow the system*
> *of Marpa.*

Further on, he says:

> *There is a commentary written by the first Panchen Lama,*
> *Called the* Geluk-Kagyu Tradition of Mahamudra.

These quotations should make Kongtrul's perspective on nonsectarianism apparent.

When we examine the lives of the great Tibetan masters of the past, we find that they studied with many teachers of different traditions and lineages, and had great respect for them. The conflicts between lamas and monasteries, and sometimes between regions of Tibet, have sometimes been presented as religious or doctrinal conflicts. However, almost none of them had anything to do with doctrinal or philosophical disagreements. Most of these conflicts were based on personality problems or mundane political rivalries.

The Ri-me movement of Kongtrul and Khyentse was not a new concept, but it was a timely and unique movement with great consequences. A great portion of Buddhist literature would have been lost but for the efforts of these two luminaries to preserve it. Although Khyentse was the source of inspiration and greatly contributed toward this effort, it was Kongtrul who actually put together the gigantic collection of the *Five Great Treasuries.* The compilation and transmission of the *Five Great Treasuries,* together with the *Compendium of Sadhanas* and the *Compendium of Tantras,* broke the isolation of single lineage teachings in the majority of Tibetan Buddhist schools.

These collected works made possible a tradition that has developed in the twentieth century of receiving the teachings of various lineages and schools from a single teacher in a single place. Take, for example, the *Treasury of Instructions,* one of the collections of Kongtrul's *Five Great Treasuries.* This compendium of most of the essential teachings of the eight practice lineages is now preserved and transmitted as one lineage. Transmitting teachings of this kind has become not only common but popular among the masters of all schools of Tibetan Buddhism.

The great success in this field goes back to the fact that Kongtrul gave these teachings himself, many times over, to a wide range of students, from the heads of schools to the humblest of lay practitioners. Many among his wide range of students spread these teachings in their own schools and monasteries. Also, Kongtrul was able to have almost all of his major works carved into wood blocks and published while he was still alive. When the Tibetans started coming out of Tibet in 1959, the entire *Five Great Treasuries* of Kongtrul were available. From 1960 onward, His Holiness Karmapa and His Holiness Dudjom Rinpoche started giving transmissions of these collections in India. It is well known that the only Tibetan books that Chögyam Trungpa and Akong Rinpoche brought when they first came to England in the early 1960s, besides their daily practices, were the volumes of Jamgön Kongtrul's *Treasury of Knowledge.*

His Holiness the fourteenth Dalai Lama has been strongly influenced by several great Ri-me teachers such as Khunu Lama Tenzin Gyaltsen, Dilgo Khyentse Rinpoche, and the third Dodrupchen, Tenpe Nyima. Due to the efforts of nonsectarian teachers like these great lamas, in recent years there has been more interchange of teachings among different schools of Tibetan Buddhism than ever before. Following the tradition of Ri-me, the Dalai Lama has been receiving and giving the teachings of all schools in their respective traditions and lineages.

At this time we Tibetans have little good fortune and little power. The only area in which we are fortunate is that the fourteenth Dalai Lama, Tendzin Gyatso, is still alive. The Dalai Lama is a proponent of nonsectarianism, and his views accord with those of Jamgön Kongtrul. For example, the Dalai Lama publicly proclaimed in a recorded talk:

> The slight understanding I have of the Dzogchen view has come from Je Tsongkhapa's notes called the *Secret Explanation*

of the Forty Letters, which is a commentary on the *Guhya-samaja Tantra.*

So, there is no reason to doubt that all the Buddhist views are without contradiction. I would like to close this introduction to the Ri-me philosophy by composing a small verse:

> The noble ones are like bees who enjoy the nectar of instruction
> In the garden of blooming flowers of impartial treatises;
> While the sectarian ones with bad intentions are like caterpillars
> Whose spit merely binds them inside their cocoons.

2
THE BIOGRAPHY OF KONGTRUL YÖNTEN GYATSO

Early Years

THE GREAT RI-ME MASTER renowned as Jamgön Lodrö Thaye, or Kongtrul Yönten Gyatso, was born in Kham, the area of the six mountain ranges divided by four great rivers. His birthplace was in the Dridza Zalmogang mountain range, which is located between the Drichu River and the Shardza River, which is also known as the North Dzachu River. In the hidden valley known as Röngyap, close to Padma Lhatse Mountain, Jamgön Kongtrul was born into a middle-class family, in 1813, the Female Water Bird year of the fourteenth sixty-year cycle, at sunrise on the tenth day of the tenth month. His father was named Yungtrung Tendzin and his mother was named Tashi Tso. His mother gave birth painlessly and easily.

His mother was gentle and good-natured—she was happy to give away anything she owned, and she was filled with devotion and pure perception. She recited 150 million MANI mantras during her life. She married a Bön lama named Sönam Phel, but they did not have any children. Jamgön Kongtrul's natural father was the Khyungpo lama, Yungtrung Tendzin, who came from the Khyungpo clan, the same family line as Jetsun Milarepa.

From the time he was small, Jamgön Kongtrul was awake to his noble nature. For example, he did not like wearing laymen's clothes. His games consisted of nothing but pretending he was reading scriptures, building Bön shrines to the local gods and Buddhist temples, making tormas of mud, offering the tormas, and performing smoke offerings. It made him happy to see ritual vases, bells, and dorjes, and he spent all his time on virtuous activities.

When he was three years old, the khenpo Sönam Lodrö, who was

from Menri in the province of Tsang, came to his district. Jamgön Kongtrul's parents requested him to perform the haircutting and naming ceremony for their son. Jamgön Kongtrul received the name Tendzin
Yungtrung, which was the name everyone called him until much later.
At the age of five, he learned the alphabet by merely looking at it. From
the age of eight his reading ability outshone older readers.

The people of his area were Bönpo, and since there was a Bön monastery nearby, that was where he went for group practices. He became
very knowledgeable about the Bön rituals, learning how to play the
music and make the tormas. However, he had faith in Buddhism in
general and Padmasambhava in particular. Just like a thirsty man longs
for water, he was eager to meet the lamas who were known as emanations of Guru Rinpoche, such as Situ Padma Nyinje Wangpo,
Dzogchen Padma Rigdzin, and the Bön lama Möngyal Padma Gyalpo.
When little Jamgön Kongtrul was playing games, he said that he was
also a tulku of Padmasambhava. While still young, he obtained knowledge from his dreams; for instance, he could tell who would be coming to visit the next day. He saw the face of Guru Rinpoche and other
masters in dreams, in meditative visions, and in actual experience.

In his youth he was good at making things with his hands and he
enjoyed learning craftsmanship, medicine, and the other sciences. At
the age of sixteen, he learned the techniques of painting, sculpting, and
sketching from the master sculptor in Chamdo. From the time he was
young, Kongtrul was humble and gentle. Because he was so well-
behaved, people always liked him and were kind to him. In the late summer of his sixteenth year, he became the secretary of Khangsar Tsephel,
the chief of the Chö-de district. Jamgön Kongtrul became one of the
chief's favorites, and because he was intelligent and articulate, the chief
insisted he should study the traditional arts and sciences. The chief sent
Kongtrul Rinpoche to Shechen Monastery to study with Shechen
Öntrul Gyurme Thutop Namgyal, a great scholar of the five sciences.

Kongtrul's Studies

Jamgön Kongtrul learned from Shechen Öntrul how to write Tibetan
poetry through texts such as the *Mirror of Poetry in Three Chapters,*

Situpa's great commentary on the Tibetan grammar texts, and the Chandrapa Sanskrit grammar. Kongtrul learned the root texts and commentaries by heart, and took an examination on them all. He knew the main Sanskrit grammar texts—the Kalapa grammar and the Sarasvata grammar—after merely hearing them. Kongtrul learned how to compose poetry according to complicated rhythms, and he also learned Tibetan mathematics.

During his late teens, he studied all the tenets of the Buddhist and non-Buddhist philosophical schools. In breaks between his studies, he received from Lama Gyurme Tenphel the empowerments and reading transmissions of the *Embodiment of the Sugatas,* an Avalokiteshvara practice of the Mindroling tradition; and the *Embodiment of the Precious Ones,* or *Könchok Chidu.* The *Könchok Chidu* is Jatsön Nyingpo's terma for practicing on Guru Rinpoche in three aspects: peaceful, wrathful, and in the female form of Sengdongma. Jamgön Kongtrul also received the reading transmission, practice, and instructions for doing the Northern Terma Vitality Practice, in which one obtains all one's nutrition from stalagmites. For a week he did this practice and lived on nothing but extracted essences.

During this time he also studied with teachers such as the Vajrayana scholar Kunzang Sang-ngak, from whom he received Minling Terchen Gyurme Dorje's instructions on the three vows. From Gyurme Tendzin he received Longchenpa's *Seven Treasuries.* From the lord guru Shechen Öntrul he learned the two styles of Sanskrit calligraphy called *lentsa* and *vartu,* and from Lama Padma Kalzang he learned to refine those writing styles, as well how to write Tibetan in the Mindroling style. From the chant master Gyurme Chödar he learned the techniques for making three-dimensional mandalas, and the calligraphy styles called old *zabdri* and *tsukchen.*

Shechen Öntrul impressed upon him the importance of maintaining the monastic tradition, so when Jamgön Kongtrul was twenty he took full ordination from Shechen Öntrul. On New Year's Day in the Water Dragon year [1832] he took the three monastic vows all at once, according to the tradition of the Lower Vinaya. Shechen Öntrul used his own notes to give him detailed instructions on performing the three main monastic rituals: the summer retreat, the confession liturgy, and the retreat-conclusion ceremony.

Then, on the eighth day of that month, Shechen Öntrul began the reading transmissions and oral instructions of the main Buddhist scriptures, the foremost being the precious collection of the Kangyur, the Buddha's own words. He also gave the empowerments and reading transmissions of the *Eight Sadhana Teachings, the Assembly of the Sugatas;* Karma Lingpa's terma of the Peaceful and Wrathful Deities; and the Mindroling *Excellent Vase That Satisfies All Desires,* which contains many different practices. Shechen Öntrul also gave Jamgön Kongtrul all the instructions and explanations needed to perform the rituals. He told Kongtrul, "Do not forget these. Who can say who might be of benefit to the teachings in the future?"

Kongtrul's Study and Practice at Palpung

When he was twenty-one, in the second month of the Water Snake year [1833], the chief Khangsar Tsephel insisted that Jamgön Kongtrul should leave Shechen Monastery and move to Palpung Monastery. When he left for Palpung, Shechen Öntrul gifted him with his own personal monastic robes, a pair of vases, and an auspicious verse that embellished upon Kongtrul's ordination name, Yönten Gyatso. He told his student, "This is an auspicious link for consecrating you as a lama. As a general rule, I advise you to keep your expectations small, maintain mindfulness, and don't be sectarian."

Kongtrul began his studies at Palpung Monastery by learning how to make astrological calculations. He studied the *Excellent Vase Filled with Necessities* with the very learned lama, Tashi Namgyal, and then calculated and wrote down the calendar of one year.

In the tenth month of that same year, Situ Padma Nyinje Wangpo returned to Palpung Monastery from a trip to the central Tibetan province of U. As the Situ incarnation, he was the presiding lama of Palpung Monastery. At this time, Jamgön Kongtrul wrote a complex praise in the kunzang khorlo style and offered it to him. This is a diagrammatic poem that can be read forward, backward, vertically, and diagonally. That night Situ Rinpoche dreamed of the sun rising. Later he said, "This is a sign that Kongtrul will greatly benefit the teachings," and he was very happy with Jamgön Kongtrul.

Chief Khangsar Tsephel told him, "Mainly, I educated you so you would benefit this monastery, so I want you to stay here indefinitely." This is how Palpung became Kongtrul's home. At this time, Situ Rinpoche insisted that Kongtrul also take the vows of full ordination in the Upper Vinaya tradition. So, on the sixth day of the tenth month, in the great assembly hall of Palpung Thubten Chökorling, Kongtrul Rinpoche received the precepts from Situ Rinpoche, whose full name was Jamgön Tai Situ Palden Tendzin Nyinje Thrinle Rabgye Chok-le Namdröl Padma Nyinje Wangpo. Situ Rinpoche acted as both the khenpo and the loppön for the ceremony. The others of the five officials needed for ordination were Öngen Karma Thegchok Tenphen acting as the personal consultant on the Vinaya, the doctor Karma Tsepal as the scheduler, the umdze Karma Khentsun as the instructor, and Je Ön Karma Thogme as the extra monk needed. It is said in a place central to the dharma, ten monks are needed for ordination, but in an outlying area, only five monks are needed. Kongtrul took full ordination, and as before, he took the three levels of vows all at once. His ordination name was Karma Ngawang Yönten Gyatso Thrinle Kunkhyap Palzangpo. He was also named as the incarnation of Kongpo Bamtang Tulku, who had been a student and attendant of the previous Situ in the early part of Situ's life. So, from that time onward he was known as Kongtrul, the "Kongpo tulku."

At this time Jamgön Kongtrul was twenty-one. He began to receive from His Eminence Situ Rinpoche a great number of empowerments, transmissions, and instructions, primarily the reading transmissions of the Kangyur and the Collection of the Nyingma Tantras. These transmissions took many months. During breaks in the main transmissions, he received many empowerments, transmissions, and instructions from the visiting lamas of their own special lineages. In particular, from the very learned Tenphel of Lhalung, Kongtrul received the texts of Rangjung Dorje called the *Profound Inner Meaning, Distinguishing Consciousness and Wisdom,* and the *Treatise on Buddha Nature.* This lama also explained in detail the *Sole Intention of the Drigung.* In return, Kongtrul taught Tenphel the Chandrapa Sanskrit grammar.

During the winter of the Horse year [1834] and continuing through the Sheep year [1835], Jamgön Kongtrul studied medicine. The very learned doctor Karma Tsepal transmitted to Kongtrul three of the four main medical tantras: the *Explanatory Tantra,* the *Root Tantra,* and the *Instruction Tantra.* Kongtrul took the *Root Tantra* and the *Yuthok Tantra* as part of his daily practice. The *Yuthok Tantra* is part of the writing of Yuthok Yönten Gönpo, who was a renowned doctor of eighth-century Tibet. During this time Jamgön Kongtrul also memorized the Mahakala Sadhana.

In the first month of the Wood Sheep year [1835] he did a retreat on White Manjushri, and afterward had no difficulty in composing any type of writing. Around this time, according to the general custom, he asked His Eminence Situ Padma Nyinje Wangpo for a prediction of which yidam would be best for him. Situ Rinpoche told him to take White Tara as his special deity and do a retreat on her practice, so he did that. During Kongtrul's retreat of the White Tara practice according to the Jonang tradition, he experienced signs of spiritual accomplishment.

At various times he received from Situ Rinpoche, Öngen Rinpoche, and other masters all the main empowerments and reading transmissions of the long and short sadhanas practiced in the Karma Kagyu tradition, including Vajravarahi, the Five Deities of Chakrasamvara, the All-Knowing Nine Deities of Jinasagara, Akshobya, the Nine Deities of Amitayus, and the Guru Yoga of Karma Pakshi. All these empowerments included their condensed and extensive mandalas. He received the appropriate transmissions for the daily prayers, and instructions for doing the sadhanas and practicing Mahamudra in its three versions— expanded, medium, and condensed. He also received the complete oral instructions for the Six Yogas, like one vase being filled from another.

In doing the practices of the Kagyu lineage, he started with the four hundred thousand preliminaries for Mahamudra, and then did the recitation practices of the mandalas of Chakrasamvara and the other yidams. After that he practiced the Six Yogas and Mahamudra meditation. In general, he actualized the mandala of every deity he practiced, and he himself said that for each practice he did, he experienced at least one of the signs predicted in the texts. Especially, he received the teachings of Six Yogas of Niguma three times from the spiritual master Karma Norbu, and he accomplished all these practices.

Kongtrul Begins to Teach

In the year of the Fire Monkey [1836], Gyalwa Karmapa Thegchok Dorje took his encampment and entourage to Karma Gön Monastery in Kham. He insisted that Jamgön Kongtrul come there to teach him Sanskrit language. Kongtrul closed his retreat and went to Karma Gön. On the first day of the first month of the Fire Bird year [1837], when Kongtrul was twenty-four, he began teaching the Karmapa the Kalapa grammar, the Sarasvata grammar, and the *Precious Source for Composing Prosody*, one after another. He also gave the Karmapa an annotated version of the root text of the Kalapa grammar and a word-by-word commentary on the Sarasvata grammar. It was during this period that Kongtrul perfected the practice of using mercury as medicine.

In the Earth Pig year [1839] the two doctors, Mendrön Tsepal and Karma Tsewang Rabten, gave him detailed explanations on the *Last Tantra*, the last of the four medical tantras. They also gave him practical instructions on formulating and dispensing medicines and using herbs.

For the next three years he taught various subjects at Palpung Monastery, particularly Sanskrit language. He taught Sanskrit grammar, poetics, prosody, calligraphy, and astrological calculations. He also taught philosophical texts such as Rangjung Dorje's two small treatises and the *Profound Inner Meaning*. Throughout this time he studied and contemplated a great number of texts of the causal vehicle, primarily those connected with Madhyamaka, Prajnaparamita, Vinaya, the *Treasury of Abhidharma*, and the five books of Maitreya.

While he was in the service of the Gyalwa Karmapa, Jamgön Kongtrul received gold and precious gifts, which he later presented to the master Situ Rinpoche as gifts to formally request the bodhisattva vow. At this time Situ Padma Nyinje Wangpo performed the elaborate form of the bodhisattva vow and bestowed on Kongtrul the name Bodhisattva Lodrö Thaye.

It was during the Iron Mouse year [1840], when he was twenty-seven years old, that he first met Jamyang Khyentse Wangpo, who was then twenty years old. At that time Kongtrul taught Khyentse by giving him teachings on the Chandrapa grammar and other texts.

Kongtrul Begins His Retreat

In the Water Tiger year [1842], he moved into the upper mountain hermitage above Palpung, which had belonged to Situ Padma Nyinje Wangpo. During the time of the previous Situ Rinpoche, Chökyi Jungne, there had been an upper retreat center. Later, Palpung Öntrul Wangi Dorje started a lower retreat center, and the upper house fell into disuse. Jamgön Kongtrul fixed it up and lived there for the rest of his life. He gave it the new name Kunzang Dechen Ösal Ling.

Kongtrul Rinpoche asked permission to practice for a good length of time, and he was given permission to stay for three years. Before going into retreat, he disposed of everything he had, both large and small. As the body support for his retreat, he painted eleven thangkas of good quality and good size, depicting the deities of the *Embodiment of the Master's Realization,* or *Lama Gongdu,* including the protectors. As the speech support, he calligraphed in gold ink a book of the *Prajnaparamita Sutra in Eight Thousand Stanzas.* As the mind support, he formed a hundred thousand tsa tsas. He offered all these to his guru, Situ Padma Nyinje Wangpo. He took into retreat only one set of old clothes, one brick of tea, and five measures of barley.

When he was twenty-nine, on the fifteenth day of the ninth month, the month that commemorates Buddha's descent from Tushita Heaven, Kongtrul Rinpoche began his retreat with the very profound Guru Rinpoche practice called the *Könchok Chidu.* From then on he remained in strict retreat—he did not go anywhere, except to bring special benefit to the teachings and sentient beings by doing things like mediating in wars and disputes, giving or receiving teachings, or joining drupchens, which are intensive and elaborate group retreats. Otherwise, he remained in retreat and firmly planted the victory banner of meditation.

Kongtrul and Khyentse

When he was thirty-six years old, he gave Khyentse Rinpoche many teachings of the Karma Kagyu lineage, principally the Seven Mandalas of Ngok and the *Kalachakra Tantra.* Following that, they gave each other many empowerments and transmissions, and this strengthened the connection between them. Although previously Kongtrul Rinpoche had pure perception of the unbiased Ri-me tradition of the dharma, this exchange of empowerments completely eliminated sectarianism from his mind. He himself said:[1]

> These days even the well-known lamas and geshes concentrate on their own traditions. Other than knowing a few texts, their pure perception of the impartial teachings of the Buddha is very small. Most lamas, whether high or low in rank, have studied very little and lack extensive knowledge of the dharma. Especially these days, lamas are not straightforward and do not have the eye of the dharma, so they impose their views through their personal power and authority. They talk a lot about whether a particular tradition is good or bad, or a particular lineage is pure or impure. Many of them denigrate others' traditions in favor of their own school. Like a one-eyed yak who startles himself, they become unsteady, and without any reason they are full of doubts and lack pure vision, even about their own tradition.
>
> When I was younger, although I had a deep longing for the dharma, I lacked strength in my convictions and was too timid to accomplish my wishes. But gradually the lotus of devotion has opened in me toward all the doctrines and the doctrine holders of the unbiased teachings of the Buddha, and my understanding of the dharma has increased. It is due to the kindness of the precious guru, Khyentse Rinpoche, that I have not accumulated the serious karmic consequence of rejecting the dharma.

Jamyang Khyentse Wangpo was renowned as the master who held the Seven Transmissions. He gave Kongtrul Rinpoche all the teachings he had, starting with the transmissions of the Nyingma school and including all of the eight practice lineages. Khyentse Rinpoche enthroned Jamgön Kongtrul as the holder of his teachings, and he repeatedly urged Jamgön Kongtrul to write his *Five Great Treasuries*. Kongtrul's writings were based on the encouragement and positive circumstances that Jamyang Khyentse provided.

One example of this occurred when Kongtrul gave Khyentse the empowerments and reading transmissions of the Seven Mandalas of Ngok, according to the writings of Karma Chagme. Khyentse Rinpoche told him, "Although Ngok's tantras have an uncorrupted continuity of blessings, Karma Chagme's scriptures are unsuitable for intensive group practice. Therefore, you should compile these practices into a usable format."

Also, on a trip to Lhasa, Khyentse Rinpoche had two predictions from the deities and lamas, and he wrote Kongtrul again and strongly urged him to reorganize those texts. He asked other people to urge Kongtrul as well. Kongtrul Rinpoche said:

> I have no choice but to do this, since I have been urged again and again, but I don't know how good my succession of lives and my aspirations were in the past. If they were negative, then by writing this I will be closing the door of liberation for others and I could harm the teachings. So far I have left this work undone, as I have not dared to start it. If I really need to do this, then I must be certain about it.

So, he asked Dawazang Tulku and Khyentse Rinpoche to examine his past lives, and they agreed that he was an incarnation of the great translator Vairochana.

In addition, Khyentse Rinpoche had a dream in which he read Kongtrul's life story in a book of detailed biographies of great teachers, which contained stories of their previous lives. The first verse about Jamgön Kongtrul said:

> *He abandoned his retinue of followers, and savored solitude like nectar.*
> *He discarded duplications, omissions, and errors in mantra recitation as if they were poison.*
> *He exerted himself in meditation, just like a flowing river.*
> *He saw the face of the yidam and attained the supreme siddhi.*
> *He was freed from the naga sickness that arose from his residual karma.*

The last line refers to the translator Vairochana contracting a naga disease as a karmic consequence of his role in Queen Margyen's getting leprosy, and it was prophesied that Kongtrul Rinpoche would contract the same eye disease and later be liberated from it. All this appeared clearly in Khyentse Rinpoche's dream.

The Treasury of Kagyu Vajrayana Instructions

Another factor that led to the composition of the *Five Great Treasuries* was the need to do the Hevajra and Guhyasamaja sadhanas at the death ceremonies of Situ Padma Nyinje Wangpo. In connection with that occasion, Kongtrul compiled the complete practice texts of the Hevajra mandala, using the writings of Chenga Chökyi Dragpa and Jonang Taranatha as the basis. This was the beginning of his compilation called the *Treasury of Kagyu Vajrayana Instructions.* By assembling some tantras he found from the Kagyu lineage of Marpa with tantras that were already well known, he compiled entire sadhana cycles for thirteen different mandalas. These sadhana cycles include the empowerments, the creation stage practice mandalas, the completion stage instructions, the additional requisite parts, and their specific dharmapala practices. He began this collection in the Water Ox year [1853] and finished it in the Wood Hare year [1855]. As supportive teachings for the *Treasury of Kagyu Vajrayana Instructions,* he wrote medium-length commentaries on three texts: the *Sublime Continuum,* the *Profound Inner Meaning,* and the *Hevajra Tantra.*

When he was thirty-five or thirty-six years old, even though he was very poor, he sponsored a handwritten copy of the thirteen volumes of the *Lama Gongdu,* a terma of Sangye Lingpa. This is another example of how Jamgön Kongtrul gave whatever wealth he acquired to the dharma.

When he was thirty-seven, which is an astrologically inauspicious year, he did long-life practice. One night he saw in his dream a pleasant meadow with a throne in it. Guru Padmasambhava was sitting on the throne, which was made of a boulder of white stone and had many Sanskrit and Tibetan letters naturally appearing on it. Kongtrul bowed down respectfully in front of Guru Rinpoche and supplicated the guru to clear the obstacles to his life. Guru Rinpoche blessed him and said, "Because I am blessing you now, from now until you are forty-four years old, nothing will harm you. At that time you will meet me in person." Later on, when he was forty-four, he received the profound terma, the *Heart Practice That Dispels All Obstacles,* from the great tertön Chogyur Dechen Lingpa. Kongtrul Rinpoche said later that he realized that this was the occasion Guru Rinpoche was referring to.

From this time onward, Kongtrul gradually became more and more famous. His groups of students grew larger, since many people wanted him to teach them Sanskrit language, Tibetan grammar and poetry, medicine, and the other inner sciences. The King of Derge and others also showed him great respect.

Around the fourth month of the Water Ox year [1853], he went to meet His Eminence Situ Padma Nyinje Wangpo. Upon greeting his teacher, while doing prostrations, Kongtrul Rinpoche felt he was receiving the four empowerments from Situ Rinpoche, and he had a boundless experience of bliss-emptiness. At this meeting Situ Rinpoche gave Jamgön Kongtrul his own full jade cup and some personal instructions. Three months later, on the seventh evening of the fifth month, Situ Rinpoche passed away without having any particular illness. His death was marked by auspicious signs, such as earthquakes, and at his cremation, his skull came out intact, with self-appearing images on it. The activities connected with Situ Padma Nyinje Wangpo's passing, such as the after-death rites and the construction of a golden stupa, were done principally by Kongtrul Rinpoche.

Just after these activities were finished, Jamgön Kongtrul got the naga disease on his eyes, as predicted. Also around this time, Dazang Rinpoche, who had been the retreat master at Palpung Monastery, moved to Karma Gön Monastery, so from this time onward Kongtrul Rinpoche was the main instructor at the Palpung Monastery retreat center. He carried out this responsibility for eight three-year retreats.

Kongtrul and Chogyur Lingpa

Around this time, when he was forty years old, he began his reciprocal dharma relationship with the great tertön Chogyur Lingpa, who was known at that time as Kyater. Following Khyentse Rinpoche's advice, Kongtrul gave Chokling (Chogyur Lingpa) the empowerment and all the instructions on the *Guhyagarbha Tantra*. After Chokling discovered his terma, the *Barche Kunsel*, or *Heart Practice That Dispels All Obstacles*, Chokling went to Dzongsar Monastery where Jamyang Khyentse helped him to write it down. Chogyur Lingpa was practically illiterate and needed assistance to write down his treasure findings.

After that, Chokling went back to Kongtrul Rinpoche and told him about his terma discovery. Kongtrul asked if it would be possible to receive at least the blessing for these teachings. Chokling told him, "You needed to receive these teachings earlier, but you didn't say anything to me. Since you are my teacher, I couldn't very well say that I should give them to you, and it remained that way. Yes, it is very important that I give them to you now."

As an auspicious connection, he started by giving Jamgön Kongtrul the empowerment for the Vitality Practice of *Könchok Chidu,* and then he gave Kongtrul all his terma teachings.

Chokling explained how he had received his terma and how Kongtrul appeared in his terma prophecies. Jamgön Kongtrul was considered to be the incarnation of Vairochana, and he had contracted the eye disease that was a karmic consequence of Vairochana inflicting leprosy on Queen Margyen. Chokling told Kongtrul Rinpoche that if he would do the Vajrapani recitation and meditation of the Vajra Club, a branch practice of the *Heart Practice That Dispels All Obstacles,* then his eye disease would clear up. That is how Kongtrul and Chokling became close friends. Although no one understood the medical basis for it, after doing that practice, Kongtrul Rinpoche's eye disease went away.

The Treasury of Precious Terma

Around the time of the Wood Hare year [1855], Kongtrul thought that it would be very helpful for the continuity of the teachings to make a collection of the many important but small Nyingma terma teachings that he had received at various times. Since many of the terma of the minor tertöns were helpful but not vastly important, he thought it would be good to assemble them with the terma of the major tertöns, including all the short and rare teachings and their lineages and empowerments.

Kongtrul Rinpoche asked Khyentse Rinpoche about this idea, and in reply Khyentse gave him about four volumes worth of terma from the minor tertöns that he himself had already collected and written down. He encouraged Jamgön Kongtrul by saying, "Now, in accordance with your wishes, use these as the basis for compiling the complete teachings found by the great tertöns, with their Guru Yoga, Dzogchen, and Avalokiteshvara practices as the main part of the collection. This will be excellent." At this point, Kongtrul and Khyentse compiled a list of contents for the collection.

In order to be able to accomplish this and to obtain permission to compile these texts, he did a retreat of the recitation practice and the supplications of the *Terma Treasury of Spontaneous Wish-Fulfilling Qualities*. When he had completed it, definite signs of accomplishment and auspicious omens appeared. He asked Chokling Rinpoche to make a stringent examination of whether compiling the terma texts would be appropriate for him to do. Chokling had a vision of Guru Rinpoche around New Year's Day in the Fire Dragon year [1856]. In that vision Guru Rinpoche told Chokling that because of Kongtrul's karmic connections and past aspirations, whatever Kongtrul wanted to do in forming this collection would be all right, and that is what Chokling told Kongtrul.

Kongtrul Rinpoche engaged three scribes to help write the texts, and by the middle of the Fire Dragon year [1856] he had completed about ten volumes of the new compilation of terma. He called these ten volumes the *Branch Terma Teachings*. However, that name was changed, because in the Iron Bird year [1861], when he received many empowerments and reading transmissions from Khyentse Rinpoche, Khyentse had a pure vision connected with these texts. In this vision Khyentse saw a large stupa with four doors, plus an additional door on the vase portion of the stupa. Khyentse Rinpoche went inside, where he saw many images and books. He asked the person showing him the stupa which books these were, and the guide said that they were the *Five Great Treasuries*, talking about them at length. After that vision, Khyentse Rinpoche said, "Kongtrul Rinpoche, it seems that you are destined to write the *Five Great*

Treasuries." So, from then on, the collection they had previously called the *Branch Terma Teachings* was renamed the *Treasury of Precious Terma.* Kongtrul Rinpoche gradually compiled the sadhana manuals, empowerment manuals, practice instructions, and other necessary parts of these teachings. Twelve years later, in the Earth Dragon year [1868], when he was fifty-five, Kongtrul gave the first teaching of the *Treasury of Precious Terma.* This included all the empowerments and reading transmissions, and they were given to many lamas, tulkus, and other students, headed by the great master, Dzogchen Rinpoche Thubten Chökyi Dorje. The teachings began with a weeklong drupchen practice of Vajrasattva, and then Jamgön Kongtrul gave the empowerment of Nyangral Nyima Özer's terma, the *Eight Sadhana Teachings, the Assembly of the Sugatas.* Since Kongtrul Rinpoche considered the *Excellent Vase That Satisfies All Desires,* a collection of terma by Minling Terchen Gyurme Dorje, as the source material for the *Treasury of Precious Terma,* he put that text together with the *Treasury of Precious Terma,* and bestowed their empowerments, blessings, knowledge entrustments, life-force entrustments, explanations, and the four volumes of secret teachings. It took five months to bestow all of them.

During his life, Kongtrul gave the whole teaching of the *Treasury of Precious Terma* five times. Over the years he gradually added to this work to make it complete. Eventually, when he was seventy-six years old, in the Earth Ox year [1889], he finalized the table of contents and lineage history of the *Treasury of Precious Terma.*

Kongtrul's Middle Years

In the Fire Dragon year [1856], when he was forty-three years old, he gave the entire teaching of the *Treasury of Kagyu Vajrayana Instructions,* which he had just finished compiling. He gave all the empowerments, transmissions, and instructions to about twenty lamas and tulkus, including the omniscient Khyentse Rinpoche, Gönchen Shar Lama, Dzogchen Padma Rigdzin, and others. In addition, he gave them the thirteen volumes of the *Lama Gongdu;* a reading transmission of scriptures on the peaceful and wrathful deities; the great precepts of Kalachakra; the Infinite Chakrasamvara; the Infinite Yamantaka; and the practice instructions on *Possessing the Six Transmissions*, using the new translation by Shiwa Bepa. In return, Kongtrul received many profound and vast teachings from the lamas who were there.

Throughout this time Kongtrul Rinpoche continued to look after Palpung Monastery. During the same year, while he was making his customary winter trip to gather alms, he recognized the sacred place of Dzongshö. When he traveled through the caves there he found medicinal substances from India like bamboo manna and sindura powder, and pills that had arisen spontaneously from the earth. The next day, when he went to Terlhung, an unbearably bright white rainbow appeared at sunrise. The end of the rainbow came down near Kongtrul, and there was a snowfall in the shape of flowers. On both sides of him were round rainbows of five-colored light, which remained visible for a long time. So, many amazing signs appeared on that occasion.

Around this time, Chokling Rinpoche received the terma of the Three Sections of Dzogchen from the Crystal Cave of Padmasambhava in Dzam, and Kongtrul acted as the scribe to write it down. Chokling also discovered a terma of White Amitayus, which was destined for Jamgön Kongtrul, but Chokling was the one who revealed it and brought it to Kongtrul. Kongtrul helped him to write down the text, and during the period when he was writing the Amitayus empowerment text, he dreamed of living into his eighties, which was a good omen. Chokling also offered Kongtrul the terma he discovered in the Yel Cave, which included an image of Mahakala amid flames, which Nagarjuna himself had carved on black stone in the Cool Grove Charnel Ground in India.

At that time, a list of twenty-five sacred places in Tibet, which he would later reveal, came into the hands of Chokling Rinpoche. Then, Kongtrul Rinpoche received all of Chokling's terma teachings from Chokling himself. When Chokling was revealing terma at Sengphu, both Khyentse Rinpoche and Kongtrul Rinpoche went to assist him. After he received that terma, Chogyur Lingpa was elaborately enthroned and honored by both Khyentse and Kongtrul.

At this point, Situ Rinpoche's reincarnation had been born in the area of Namtso and recognized. The child was living at Tsurphu Monastery when Palpung Monastery insisted that Kongtrul Rinpoche should go get the little Situ Rinpoche and bring him to Palpung. On the twenty-second day of the sixth month of the Fire Snake year [1857],

Kongtrul left for Tsurphu in central Tibet. On the way he met Chokling Rinpoche, and they exchanged many teachings. Kongtrul traveled to central Tibet on the middle northern route, and he arrived in Tsurphu on the twenty-second day of the twelfth month of that year.

After he arrived in Tsurphu, Jamgön Kongtrul offered the empowerments and transmissions of all the *Chokling Tersar*, the new treasure findings of Chogyur Lingpa, to His Holiness the Karmapa, Drugchen Rinpoche, the young reincarnation of Situ Rinpoche, and others. He visited Lhasa, Samye, and all the other sacred places in central Tibet, where he did whatever meditation practices he could, such as drupchens or three-day sessions, to establish spiritual connections with those holy places. Then, he went to Mindroling Monastery, where he received many empowerments and transmissions, and while he was there he gave many empowerments, transmissions, and instructions in return. He also exchanged empowerments and transmissions with Nenang Pawo Rinpoche. While he was in central Tibet he met the Dalai Lama's regent, Radreng Rinpoche, and became friends with him. Radreng Rinpoche sent a white scarf to Chokling Rinpoche, requesting a prophecy of what would benefit the whole of Tibet.

Gradually, Kongtrul Rinpoche moved his encampment in the direction of Kham, taking the Situ incarnation to Palpung. He was very busy along the way, managing the many receptions and Red Crown ceremonies of the young Situ Rinpoche, as well as giving all the empowerments and transmissions that people requested of him. Finally, on the morning of the tenth day of the tenth month of the Horse year [1858], they reached Palpung Monastery. During the same year Kongtrul also gave the reading transmission of the entire *Nyingma Kama* and its empowerments to Jamyang Khyentse Rinpoche, Chokling Rinpoche, and the queen and prince of Derge.

At the new year of the Earth Sheep year [1859], there was a prediction that a new monastery should be built in Tro Mendral Thang in order to benefit the teachings and the area of Derge. When Kongtrul went to see that place, there was a snowfall with layers of white, red, and black snow. This snowfall was seen as a bad omen when not long afterward, the rebel army of Nyarong caused a lot of destruction to the religious and secular welfare of Derge.

Before the beginning of the next year, His Holiness the fourteenth

Karmapa, Thegchok Dorje, came to visit Palpung. He enthroned the young Situ Rinpoche on the fifth day of the first month of the Iron Monkey year [1860]. For this ceremony, Kongtrul did the explanation of the long mandala offering, and the explanation of the *Guhyagarbha Tantra*. Kongtrul also gave the *Treasury of Kagyu Vajrayana Instructions* and many other teachings to the Karmapa and the others there.

In accordance with a prophecy made by Chokling Rinpoche, Kongtrul constructed a temple of Palchen Heruka in the upper retreat center of Palpung. He also established a new retreat center that would accommodate six retreatants and one Mahakala practitioner for three-year periods. According to instructions from Khyentse Rinpoche, on the northern side of the retreat center Kongtrul Rinpoche constructed a stupa of the Two Immaculate Mantras. In between these activities, as was his custom, he fulfilled everyone's requests for teachings—whether they were lamas or tulkus, or of high or low status. Kongtrul's fame spread in all directions like the wind, and more and more students came to him from all parts of the country. He continued to give the instructions, empowerments, and transmissions at the Palpung retreat center, and he also gave the empowerments and instructions of the Shije, or Pacification lineage, and rekindled that practice lineage.

On the fourteenth day of the first month of the Water Dog year [1862], the three-year retreatants performed their first cloth-drying ceremony. This ceremony tests the degree to which the retreatants have mastered the yoga of Inner Heat. In the cold winter weather the practitioners remain all night wearing one layer of cotton cloth. In the morning they walk in a procession and many spectators come to watch them. On this occasion there was a lot of heat, so the people felt very blessed and joyful.

During this period there was continuous fighting and war in Kham because of the Nyarong warlord Nyagke. Jamgön Kongtrul was summoned to Derge to do prayers and rituals, and an atmosphere of fear and turmoil pervaded the whole area. Throughout this time, Kongtrul never felt the slightest bit nervous or disturbed. He continued busily working on his construction projects and teaching the dharma. During this time he constructed another stupa of the Two Immaculate Mantras in a place called Dongpo-me. In order to establish the summer retreat for the monks in Palpung, Kongtrul wrote down the Vinaya procedures for two of the main monastic practices—the summer retreat and the ceremony for ending the summer retreat. He taught these procedures to the practice leaders of Palpung, and then they started the summer retreat in Lhasar, the new temple in Palpung. In order to dispel obstacles to the Buddha's teachings in general, Kongtrul initiated an annual Vajrakilaya drupchen in Palpung. For this retreat he gave the monks the practice instructions on Vajrakilaya, and he acted as the vajra master.

When he was not too busy with these kinds of activities, he continued compiling the *Treasury of Precious Terma*. He spent his time putting together the empowerments, instructions, and other required parts of the terma. Despite the fact that there was a war going on in his area, he did not waste a single minute, which is clear from reading his autobiography.

The Treasury of Knowledge

Then, in the Dog and the Pig years [1862–63], when he was fifty years old, Kongtrul wrote the *Treasury of Knowledge*, both the root text and the commentary. He wrote the root text in the second month of the Water Dog year [1862], when he did a seven-day retreat on the hearing lineage teachings. Earlier, Lama Ngedön had said that Kongtrul should write a treatise on the three vows, and when that was done Lama Ngedön would write a commentary on it. However, Kongtrul thought that several texts on the three vows were already available, and that if he had to write something, it should be more comprehensive in scope and helpful for people who had not studied very much.

With that in mind, during the breaks between sessions of a one-week retreat, he wrote the root text of the *Treasury of Knowledge*, a treatise on the three higher trainings of discipline, meditation, and wisdom. Later on, he showed this to Jamyang Khyentse, who told him, "When you wrote this you must have been inspired by the blessings of the lamas, and your channels opened by the power of the dakinis. You should place the *Treasury of Knowledge* at the head of the *Five Great Treasuries,* and you need to write a commentary on it."

To encourage him, Khyentse gave him many gifts along with these words. So, in only three months, from the fourth month until the seventh month of the Iron Pig year [1863], Kongtrul wrote the commentary to the *Treasury of Knowledge,* with Khenchen Tashi Özer acting as the scribe. The part that was left undone was finished during the warm weather of the following year.

Civil War in Kham

In the Iron Pig year [1863], the army of the warlord Nyarong took over the capital of Derge, and Nyarong controlled all the districts of the Kingdom of Derge. The government of Tibet sent General Shappe Phulungwa to drive away Nyarong's army. Many soldiers converged and there were big battles.

It was around this time that Kongtrul Rinpoche made a fervent request to Chokling Rinpoche to write down his terma called the *Heart Essence of Vajrasattva.* Chokling did so and also gave the empowerment and transmission for it. Around the same time, Kongtrul asked Khyentse Rinpoche to write a commentary on Longchenpa's *Quintessence of the Master.* Khyentse Rinpoche replied, "I have no such thing in mind. Undoubtedly, you are the right person to do it. I advise you to keep the Mindroling commentary as the basis, but the Mindroling commentary is a more general teaching and does not have the specific Quintessence teachings of Longchenpa. That makes it especially necessary for you to write it." Khyentse was emphatic about this, so Kongtrul wrote down the commentary on the *Heart Essence, Mother and Child.*

At that time the leader of the army of Dragyap, named Dongkam Tripa, became ill, so the Tibetan army invited Kongtrul to give him medical treatment. Kongtrul's visit was very helpful to the patient, and all the divinations they requested of Kongtrul showed accurate predictions. Because of that, the central Tibetan army came to regard Jamgön Kongtrul as their teacher. Kongtrul received a promise from the army that no damage would be done to Palpung Monastery or to any monastery in that area, whether large or small.

When the armies from the Dragyap, Gojo, and Richap areas of central Tibet captured Gönchen, the capital of Derge, they waged war on all the places in Derge that did not surrender. Accusations were made against Palpung Monastery and it was close to being destroyed, but Kongtrul was very helpful in saving it and the other Kagyu monasteries. After the Tibetan army won the war against Nyarong, both the Tibetan government and the Derge government thanked Kongtrul and awarded him large gifts, including gifts of land. Palpung Monastery also commended him for his assistance.

Around this time, at the request of the Tibetan governor, Kongtrul Rinpoche did many practices for the welfare of Tibet. During this period he also taught the Kalapa grammar to his very learned student, Lhagsam Tenpe Gyaltsen, and he received many lineage empowerments and transmissions from Shechen Lama Dönpal, which he had been unable to receive previously from Shechen Öntrul.

In the Fire Tiger year [1866] Jamgön Kongtrul gave the reading transmission of the Kangyur to Situ Rinpoche and many lamas and tulkus. He also preformed the medicine-making ritual with Tertön Chokling, and he did retreat practice on White Umbrella and the Lord of Life practice from the *Seven Profound Practices*. Jamgön Kongtrul continued giving empowerments, transmissions, and instructions, and during this year he taught his commentary on the *Treasury of Knowledge* twice.

Collaboration between Khyentse, Kongtrul, and Chokling

This was an important time in the collaboration of Jamgön Kongtrul, Chogyur Lingpa, and Jamyang Khyentse. When Chokling sent a letter requesting Kongtrul to come, Kongtrul Rinpoche closed his retreat in the eleventh month of the year and went to be with Chokling. He helped to write down Chogyur Lingpa's terma, such as the *Four Doctrines of the Dharma Protectors,* the *Five Heart Essence Cycles,* the *Six Root Sadhanas,* and the *Shvana Teachings.* They also performed the practice of throwing torma in the four directions for the *Four Dharma Protectors.* Then, Kongtrul requested and received the new terma teachings from Chokling that he had not already received. Jamyang Khyentse Wangpo also came at that time, and he gave the root empowerment for the terma, the *Heart Essence of the Great Siddhas.* They also performed a drupchen of this heart practice in Khangmar Gön Monastery.

Then, Khyentse Rinpoche gave a detailed explanation of the *Gradual Path of the Wisdom Essence*, an explanation of the *Stages of the Vajrayana Path*, and the empowerment of the *Heart Practice of the Wrathful Guru* from the yellow terma scrolls. These yellow scrolls are the papers found in terma containers with coded dakini script written on them. The tertön is able to decipher the code and write down the full text for others to read. Tertön Chokling gave the empowerment for the root sadhana of the *Heart Practice of the Wrathful Guru*, and a deep and extensive explanation of it. Also during this year Kongtrul wrote down the terma *Teachings on Interdependence*, and performed the ceremony to empower and enthrone the King of Derge.

In the second month of the Fire Hare year [1867] of the fifteenth sixty-year cycle, Khyentse, Kongtrul, and Chokling came together in the place called Dzongshö and wrote down teachings from yellow scrolls of terma, such as the remaining *Shvana Teachings* and the *Secret Predictions*. They also did a drupchen of Khyentse's newly discovered terma, the *Eight Sadhana Teachings, the Embodiment of the Sugatas*. Then, at Dzongshö, Kongtrul pointed out the five sacred places connected with enlightened body, speech, mind, qualities, and activities. Khyentse and Chokling asked Kongtrul to sit on a throne made of stones, and they enthroned him as a tertön, formally giving him his tertön name. Both of them wrote long-life prayers for Kongtrul Rinpoche. All three of them discovered terma at Dzongshö during that time.

In the eleventh month of that year, Khyentse Rinpoche came to Palpung on a teaching visit. He acted as the vajra master for the Vajrakilaya drupchen, and then gave teachings on the *Vajrakilaya Piece of the Root Tantra*. Following that, he gave the empowerment, transmission, and detailed teachings of the Vajrakilaya hearing lineage to Kongtrul and others. Khyentse also went to Kongtrul's retreat place and gave teachings on the root *Chakrasamvara Tantra* and the *Nyingma Kama*. He also gave the transmission of the *Collected Works of the Great Tertön*, which are the writings of Minling Terchen Gyurme Dorje, as well as other teachings requested of him. In thanksgiving, Kongtrul Rinpoche offered many long-life practices, feasts, and mandala offerings for Jamyang Khyentse, and then Khyentse Rinpoche went back to his own place.

In the Earth Snake year [1869], when Kongtrul Rinpoche was fifty-six, he wrote his commentaries on the *Profound Inner Meaning*, the *Hevajra Tantra*, and the *Sublime Continuum*, and he also gave teachings on them. From Lama Karma Salje he received many rare empowerments and transmissions, including the transmission of the *Collected Works of Dölpopa*, and from Dzogchen Rabten he received the transmission of the nine volumes of the second Shechen Rabjam. It was during this year that Kongtrul finished giving the first transmission of the *Treasury of Precious Terma*, and that Tertön Chogyur Lingpa passed away.

On New Year's Day of the Iron Sheep year [1871], Khyentse Rinpoche showed Kongtrul Rinpoche his mind terma text, the *Embodiment of the Three Roots' Realization*, and he made Jamgön Kongtrul the holder of this lineage. Jamyang Khyentse also gave him many other teachings at this time.

The Treasury of Instructions

When they were together at this time, Kongtrul asked Khyentse what he thought of their collecting the most important instructions they had received from the eight practice lineages, in order to keep these teachings from fading away. Khyentse Rinpoche replied that he had already written down about twenty volumes of explanations and commentaries, but his writings were unorganized and there were some missing parts, like the empowerments. He told Kongtrul it would be very good for him to do that and that they should call it the *Treasury of Instructions*. Khyentse listed the order for the contents of the ten volumes of the *Treasury of Instructions*, and then he gave Kongtrul the transmission of the Red and Black Volumes of the Lamdre, which are Sakya lineage teachings of the Path with Its Result.

Khyentse told him, in particular, to write a commentary on the Sakya lineage teaching called the *Eight Cycles of the Lamdre Teaching*, and Kongtrul agreed to do that. On the ninth evening of that month, Khyentse Rinpoche had an auspicious dream in which he was in a beautiful forest in India, full of sandalwood and teak trees. He saw the Ngorpa Sakya lama, Khenchen Dorje Chang Jampa Kunga Tendzin, sitting on a throne made of teak wood. He was wearing monks' robes and looked radiant, warm, and smiling. Khyentse prostrated to the khenpo, who said to him, "It is very good that you and Kongtrul Rinpoche are writing a book about the Lamdre teachings."

Khyentse said to him, "Oh, we are not composing a book about the Lamdre teachings. Since last year we have been merely collecting the existing empowerments, transmissions, and instructions that are part of the Lamdre."

The khenpo pretended he had not heard that and said again, "It is so excellent that you are writing a book on the Lamdre teachings. Previously, the great lama Sönam Gyaltsen wanted to make a commentary on all nine of the Lamdre teachings, but he finished commentaries on only the first four great root texts. He was unable to write commentaries on the eight later Lamdre teachings. So, your doing that will fulfill his intentions. Here is the text called the *Hearing Lineage of the Path with Its Result*. We should also give this to Kongtrul."

Saying this, Khenchen Kunga Tendzin took out from under his arm a medium-sized red book and gave it to Khyentse. Khyentse was astonished because he had never heard of a text by that name. He thought to himself, "Why should this be given to Kongtrul?"

The khenpo smiled and said, "Of course, you realize that Kongtrul belongs to us."

Khyentse asked out loud, "Who do you mean by 'us'?"

The khenpo replied, "But of course, Kongtrul is Muchen Sangye Rinchen."

Muchen Sangye Rinchen had been one of the greatest Sakya lamas, and Khyentse thought to himself, "Muchen Sangye Rinchen was the teacher of Jamgön Kunga Drölchok, a great Jonangpa lama. In fact, Muchen Sangye Rinchen gave Jamgön Kungpa Drölchok the Chakrasamvara teachings at the age of eleven or twelve. Jamgön Kunga Drölchok later reincarnated as Taranatha, and Taranatha reincarnated as Kongtrul. Unless Muchen Sangye Rinpoche and Jamgön Kungpa Drölchok are of one mind, one could not be the reincarnation of the other."

Again the khenpo knew his thoughts and said, "That's right. Muchen Sangye Rinchen and Jamgön Kunga Drölchok are of one mind." That was Khyentse's dream, which he later told to Kongtrul.

To encourage this particular composition, Khyentse Rinpoche offered Jamgön Kongtrul five very special representations of enlightened body, especially an image of Tara that spoke. This image had belonged to

Nagarjuna and was discovered by Khyentse Rinpoche at the place called Shang Zabulung. As representations of enlightened speech, he gave Kongtrul twelve volumes of pith instructions, and there were also two gifts representing enlightened mind. While making these offerings, Khyentse Rinpoche made an elaborate and auspicious speech. Kongtrul took all those things back to his own retreat place, and there began writing his commentary on the Lamdre teachings.

During this time he also continued writing the *Treasury of Instructions*. He began this compilation in 1871, and put the finishing touches on it eleven years later, in 1881. In the Water Horse year of 1882, he gave the first transmission of this work.

Making Medicine from Mercury

Around the beginning of 1872, the governor of Nyakhok, named Phuntsok Rabten, invited Khyentse Rinpoche to his place to begin the ceremony for making medicine from mercury. Khyentse Rinpoche said, "From now on, I am not going out; I am not crossing my doorstep. And other than me, there is no one except Kongtrul who knows the practice of making medicine from mercury." In this way, Kongtrul was given an invitation he could not refuse.

Jamgön Kongtrul left his retreat on the twelfth day of the second month of the Water Monkey year [1872] to go to Nyakhok. At this time he was fifty-nine years old. On the way, he stopped at Dzongsar, where Khyentse Rinpoche offered him long-life prayers and the five offerings. Khyentse Rinpoche told him, "This is the time for you to write down clear instructions on how to make this medicine from mercury. In addition, as a branch teaching of the *Treasury of Knowledge*, you should write some books on general Tibetan language and literature, including a commentary on the *Precious Source for Composing Prosody*."

After he arrived at Nyakhok, on the first day of the third month, Jamgön Kongtrul performed smoke and tea ceremonies, and did the feast offering of the *Yuthok Innermost Essence*. These particular Nyingtik teachings were discovered by the great eighth-century Tibetan doctor Yuthok Yönten Gönpo. After offering prayers to the dharma protectors,

Kongtrul started making the medicine, and many auspicious signs appeared, such as rainbows and rain. All the preparations went well for making the different kinds of mercury medicine, such as *tsotrung* and *mental.* After he finished making the tsotrung, he did an elaborate consecration ceremony, using the sambhogakaya form of the Medicine Buddha. He wrote down the instructions for making the medicine and how it should be dispensed, including notes from his own experience. At this time he also wrote the instructions for making and dispensing the medicine called *dashel.*

While in Nyarong, he also gave teachings to over a thousand lamas and monks. He gave the bodhisattva vows from the two traditions of Nagarjuna and Asanga, as well as the *Eight Sadhana Teachings, the Assembly of the Sugatas,* the Kalachakra empowerment of Entering as a Child, the *Queen of Great Bliss,* and much more.

This year he taught the *Treasury of Precious Terma* for the second time, and the assembly was headed by Palpung Öntrul, Kathok Getse Tulku, and others. Palpung Öntrul made a commitment to have woodblocks carved for all the volumes of the *Treasury of Precious Terma.* Although Palpung Öntrul passed away not long afterward, he had already collected the funds for this project, so the woodblocks were made and kept in Palpung Monastery.

Around this time the King of Ling invited Jamgön Kongtrul for a visit. When he went to Ling they honored him with great respect, and he gave them many different teachings. From this time onward, Wangchen Tendzin Chögyal, the King of Ling, became one of Kongtrul's main patrons. Later on, it was this king who constructed the great golden stupas in memory of Khyentse and Kongtrul. These two stupas are called the Ornaments of Dokham.

Teaching and Practice in His Later Years

In the Bird year [1873], when he was sixty years old, some of the monks of Palpung Monastery made baseless allegations against Jamgön Kongtrul and Palpung Öntrul, and actually sued them. Kongtrul Rinpoche was deeply saddened by this, and he did not return to Palpung Monastery for the next fourteen years. During that time, when Situ Rinpoche and other students from Palpung wanted to receive teachings from him, they had to come to his retreat place.

In the Wood Dog year [1874] he completed his commentary on the *Gradual Path of the Wisdom Essence,* and he went to Kathok Monastery, where he did a pilgrimage and gave many teachings. In the Wood Pig year [1875] the project began of forming woodblocks for the *Treasury of Knowledge* and the *Treasury of Precious Terma.* Again, he gave many teachings, including the *Treasury of Precious Terma.* He gave the teaching on the *Treasury of Knowledge* to about twenty lamas, tulkus, and geshes, particularly Khyentse Rinpoche and the Ngorpa khenpo, Khangsar Khen Rinpoche. These lamas and tulkus promised to spread the study of this text by Jamgön Kongtrul by teaching it in their own monasteries or residences. Around this time Jamgön Kongtrul exchanged teachings with the Sakya Jetsunma, Tamdrin Wangmo. The Sakya Jetsunma is the highest-ranking woman in the Sakya lineage. During this year he taught the Chandrapa grammar and its approach to the learned master Mipham Jamyang Gyatso, who was then twenty-nine years old. Throughout this time, as usual, Kongtrul Rinpoche continued his meditation practice, including doing several drupchens.

In the Fire Mouse year [1876] he started giving the empowerments and transmissions in Dzongsar Monastery for the *Treasury of Precious Terma.* Many important lamas and tulkus received this teaching, including Khyentse Wangpo, Palyul Gyatrul, Kathok Mogtsa, Shechen Rabjam, Shechen Gyaltsap Padma Namgyal, Ling Jedrung, Dzogchen Khenpo Akön, Rabjampa Kunzang Sönam, and the two Lhatrul emanations. In particular, Nenang Pawo Rinpoche, a high-ranking Kagyu lama; Kushap Khampa Rinpoche, the Drugpa Kagyu Khamtrul; and Chagla Khentrul came to receive teachings from him, and he gave them everything they asked for. He gave the great empowerment of Kalachakra to Thartse Pönlop Loter Wangpo, a high-ranking Sakya lama; Dzogchen Rinpoche; and others. This year he also did more building, including the stupa in Tse Sildor called the Very Powerful Stupa.

Previously, Khyentse Rinpoche had told Kongtrul it would be good to recite the *Seven-Line Prayer* a hundred thousand times, so at this point Kongtrul traveled to several places which were sacred to Guru Rinpoche and did retreats there. He visited famous sites such as Padma Shelphuk, Dagam Wangphuk, and Padma Shelri, and he recited the

Seven-Line Prayer more than a hundred thousand times. Excellent auspicious signs appeared. In particular, when he was in Dagam Wangphuk, one night in a dream Guru Padmasambhava appeared to him in the form of Khyentse Rinpoche. Khyentse opened a book containing many yellow scrolls with dakini script written on them, and he gave Kongtrul complete instructions on reciting the *Seven-Line Prayer.* During the daytime, every day there were clouds of white rainbows appearing in the sky. Later, when he visited Dzongsar, Khyentse Rinpoche told Kongtrul he should definitely write down those instructions on the *Seven-Line Prayer,* so Kongtrul wrote them down as mind terma. Later that year, a large number of students came from all over the country to study with him, and Kongtrul satisfied all their wishes.

In the Earth Tiger year [1878], he went back to visit Jamyang Khyentse at Dzongsar. During this visit the lord guru Khyentse Rinpoche said to him, "In both Kham and Tibet I have about two hundred lamas from whom I have received teachings, and among them I have four root lamas. If it was possible to see them, I would offer them my understanding, but three of them are no longer alive. Now you are the only one left, so I must offer you my understanding." Then, Khyentse Rinpoche briefly expressed his experience of the completion stage practice, both with and without characteristics. Kongtrul found out that Khyentse had developed complete control over the channels, winds, and essence element, and his winds were almost completely purified within the central channel. According to Mahamudra, he had the realization called One Taste, and according to Dzogchen, he had completely transcended any dualistic perception of his own manifestations. This is what Kongtrul reported that Khyentse told him. In return, Kongtrul offered his experiences to Khyentse, who said, "You have reached the stage in Trekchö practice called Awareness Reaching Its Full Measure."

During this visit, in the ninth month they did a drupchen of Jinasagara, which came from Khyentse's *Rediscovered Terma of Tri-me.* When the lord guru Khyentse Rinpoche gave the empowerment, transmission, and instructions on this practice, Kongtrul Rinpoche experienced unchanging great bliss and other signs of great blessing. At this time Jamyang Khyentse said to Jamgön Kongtrul, "This time I could do you a great service. I assure you that from now until you are seventy-three years old, no obstacles or harm will come to you. After that, your life span will depend upon the merit of the beings."

Also in 1878, Jamgön Kongtrul was invited to come to his own birthplace of Rongyap by the Tertön Tsewang Dragpa, who was a Bönpo tertön. There he did individual and group retreats, and gave many empowerments, transmissions, and instructions, and performed feasts, fulfillment offerings, and dharmapala practices. While he was there he went to the mountain of Padma Lhatse, which is sometimes called Karyak. It is connected with a terma prediction of one of the twenty-five great pilgrimage places, which says:

> A rock mountain, named Karlung, in the form of Padma's hat,
> Has a cave of Ugyen on the peak of the hat.

On Padma Lhatse there was a white boulder with three faces, and since the central face was very hard to reach, no one knew of a cave being there. However, Kongtrul made people go up there with ropes and ladders and search for it. In the middle there was a flat rock on which they found a large, spacious cave. Inside the cave was a naturally occurring image of Padmasambhava, the size of a human being. On the right side was a cave called the Cave of the Spiritual Friend, and on the left side was a cave called the Cave of Deathless Life. The cave contained footprints left by Guru Rinpoche and many Buddhist and Bönpo lamas. They found seals and other objects that were immediately shown to everyone present. Kongtrul also took out several terma images and sacred substances.

Situ Rinpoche and Chokling Rinpoche had both asked Kongtrul Rinpoche to construct a temple in Dzongshö, and since the year of the Ox [1877] Kongtrul had been gathering donations and help from his supporters to accomplish this. Jamgön Kongtrul built the temple to the extent of being inhabitable, and in the Iron Dragon year [1880] he did a very strict retreat at Dzongshö, in accordance with a prediction of Khyentse Rinpoche. During this time he did not see anyone, although he had many pure visions. Gradually over time, he established a retreat center at Dzongshö.

He finished this retreat in the Iron Snake year [1881], when he was sixty-eight years old. During this year he offered his terma teaching on the *Seven-Line Prayer* to Dzogchen Rinpoche, and he wrote down the terma he had received on the Yeshe Tsogyal practice. He gave many teachings to Khyentse Rinpoche, Situ Rinpoche, Dzigar Chogtrul, and others.

In the Water Horse year [1882], he taught the *Treasury of Kagyu Vajrayana Instructions* and many other teachings to Thartse Pönlop Jamyang Loter Wangpo and others. For the fourth time he gave the empowerments and transmissions of the *Treasury of Precious Terma*, this time to the lamas and tulkus from Palpung, Dzogchen, Palyul, Gyarong, Adzom, and other monasteries. He also gave the empowerments, transmissions, and instructions of the *Treasury of Instructions* to Ngorpa Pönlop, Dzogchen Tulku, and others, but only to those who made a commitment to either teach these instructions or do substantial practice on them. He also gave teachings to Deshung Tulku and others explaining the *Hevajra Tantra* and the commentary he had written on the general meaning of the *Hevajra Tantra*.

Khyentse's Rediscovered Terma

Then, he went to Dzongsar and received transmission for many terma that had been previously lost and then rediscovered by Khyentse Rinpoche. At this time Kongtrul said to Khyentse, "The new terma must be profound since these are applicable for the times. But these days only the names remain of the undisputed terma of the past. Up to now no one has been capable of retrieving those teachings. But you are a great master, recognized as the lord of the Seven Transmissions through predictions as well as through our own direct perception. It would be most excellent if you would restore even one of the great terma of the past." In this way Kongtrul requested again and again that Khyentse Rinpoche retrieve the lost terma.

Then, Khyentse Rinpoche had a dream in which he saw Tertön Sangye Lingpa, who said to him: "Up to now, you and the one who is both our teacher and student, Baso Chözang, have reestablished many old terma teachings, and that is excellent. From this time on, if you can complete twenty-five more old terma, you will fulfill the wishes of Guru Rinpoche. And through this you two will accomplish your life and work. To prevent any obstacles for that, you should do many authentic drupchens." The reference to Baso Chözang concerns a Sakya lama at the time of Sangye Lingpa, who much later reincarnated as Jamgön Kongtrul.

Because of this prediction and because Kongtrul had already received similar predictions, in the years of the Water Sheep and Wood Monkey [1883–84], Jamgön Kongtrul completed thirteen great drupchens in the following sacred places:

1. In the cave of Dagam Wangphuk, the practice of the Heart Essence of Deathless Tara;
2. In Padma Shelri, the Sadhana of the Vidyadhara Lineage, from the Northern Terma of Rigdzin Gödem;
3. At Dzum Tsangkar, the practice of Guru Chakrasamvara, a terma of Gyatön;
4. At Dzing Trawo Ne, the guru sadhana, the Essence of Light, a terma of Tri-me;
5. At Dzongshö Deshek Dupa, the *Great Compendium of the Teachings,* discovered by Orgyen Lingpa;
6. In the rocky cave in front of Godavari, the Vajra Amrita Sadhana, including the medicine-making ceremony, fire offering, and celebration for the practicing yogins and yoginis;
7. In the practice hall in front of the mountain called Atri Ne Rameshari, the practice of Jinasagara, the red Avalokiteshvara;
8. In Tashi Ne, the sadhana and feast of the Black Wrathful Lady;
9. In front of Pawo Wangchen Drak, one of Chokling's *Seven Profound Practices* called the King of Perfect Realization of the Mamos;
10. In front of Lhamdo Bummo Padmakö, the Sadhana of the Embodiment of the Secret Dakinis, along with a large number of fulfillment offerings;
11. At Munang Dorje Drakmar, the practice of Hayagriva Who Liberates All Evils;
12. At Rongme Karmo Tagtsang, the Vajrasattva practice of the Mindroling tradition;

13. At Padma Shelphuk, the Sadhana of the Five Families of Amitayus, a section of the Profound Vitality of the Three Roots, from Chokling's *Seven Profound Practices.*

Along with these and in between them, he did a drupchen of *Lama Gongdu,* and continued to give many teachings to his devoted students. In relation to Khyentse Rinpoche's activities in rediscovering lost terma, Jamgön Kongtrul said in his autobiography:

> The supplications I made for this work have been partially fulfilled. It seems very fortunate that Khyentse Rinpoche could effortlessly find whatever teachings I desired. Although certain terma scriptures still exist, their teachings, empowerments, and transmissions have been lost. In order to retrieve those teachings, Khyentse Rinpoche prays to Guru Rinpoche, and immediately Guru Rinpoche appears to him in the form of the individual tertön, and gives Jamyang Khyentse the short lineage transmission. The new terma he receives come directly from the dakinis and terma protectors in the form of yellow scrolls. They are all complete, having the full text of the creation and completion stages, and the texts for supplementary activities like the feast offerings. All of them are pithy and profound, like melted gold. Even a small amount of these terma is greater than a large quantity of other terma.

Around this time Kongtrul received various teachings from Jamyang Khyentse, such as the empowerment and transmission of Nyang's Avalokiteshvara practice called the Great Compassionate Tamer of Beings, Dorje Lingpa's treasure findings, and many others. In return, Kongtrul gave to Khyentse Rinpoche and large groups of students the transmission of the Collection of the Nyingma Tantras; the nine volumes of the *Eight Sadhana Teachings, the Assembly of the Sugatas;* Longchenpa's *Seven Treasuries* and his *Trilogy on Natural Ease;* and the reading transmission of the eighteen volumes of the *Collected Works of Taranatha.* He also gave many empowerments, transmissions, and instructions to Thartse Shabdrung, Thrangu Tulku, Tertön Sögyal, Shugjung Tsulo, Drubwang Tsognyi, Kyodrak Drungtrul, and others.

By this time Kongtrul was famous, and he stayed very busy, teaching his students and directing his construction projects. He did not have any administrators, such as treasurers or secretaries; his affairs had always been overseen by his mother. After his mother passed away, his niece, Rigdzin Drölma, took care of these things for him. Then, in the Wood Bird year [1885], his niece died. From then on, her brother, Tsering Döndrup, took over her duties. In the year 1885, Situ Rinpoche Padma Kunzang also passed away.

In the Fire Dog year [1886], when he was seventy-three, Kongtrul Rinpoche finished writing the *Life Stories of the Hundred Tertöns.* He considered these stories to be superior to previous biographies. Also during this year, he received Mipham Jamyang Gyatso's teachings from Mipham Rinpoche himself, who was then forty years old. To fulfill their individual requests, Jamgön Kongtrul gave teachings to Öngen Rinpoche, Surmang Tenga Rinpoche, Nenang Pawo father and son, Chokling Tulku, Khamtrul, and Dodrupchen Tenpe Nyima. He also received many small terma teachings from Khyentse Rinpoche that he had not received before. During this year Kongtrul went to Palpung Monastery for the first time after fourteen years. When Karmapa Khakhyap Dorje came to Palpung, Kongtrul was there to receive him, and astonishing omens were seen by everyone. It was winter, during the twelfth month, but the sky became completely blue, the frozen ground thawed, and it became as warm as summer.

Teaching the Fifteenth Karmapa

In the Fire Pig year [1887], Jamgön Kongtrul gave teachings to the young Karmapa, Khakhyap Dorje, who was then sixteen years old. This began on New Year's Day of that year, when Gyalwang Karmapa and other lamas and tulkus offered Jamgön Kongtrul symbolic representations of enlightened body, speech, and mind, along with many long-life prayers and elaborate offerings, including a one-day White Tara longevity practice. On the tenth day, the Karmapa and a small retinue went to Kongtrul's hermitage, and the teachings began with a tenth-day feast offering using Kongtrul's terma, the *Secret Heart Essence,* and then Kongtrul Rinpoche gave them the empowerment for the mandala of the *Secret Heart Essence.* On the eleventh day, he did the preliminary empowerment for the Avalokiteshvara practice, the Nine Deities of Jinasagara.

Then, he started teaching the Karmapa both the *Jewel Ornament of Liberation* and the Mahamudra Ngöndro instructions within each session. Alternating teaching sessions with empowerments, Kongtrul gradually bestowed all the mandalas of the Kagyu lineage, as well as the empowerments, transmissions, and instructions for the *Treasury of Kagyu Vajrayana Instructions.* In addition, he gave to the Karmapa alone the great empowerment of Mamo and Mahakala in Union. This is a very rare empowerment, and it was given only to the Karmapa within the dharma protectors' shrine room.

After that, he continued giving instruction on the main practice of Mahamudra and the Six Yogas of Naropa. He gave the empowerments and transmissions together with all aspects of the mandalas and practices involved. By this time, there were so many lamas and tulkus there to receive these teachings that they could no longer fit inside his residence, so the teachings had to be moved to the monastery.

During this time he offered the bodhisattva vows from the two traditions of Nagarjuna and Asanga to Gyalwa Karmapa and the other lamas. On the ninth day of the second month, he began teaching the *Treasury of Instructions.* Starting with *Freedom from the Four Attachments,* he taught the *One Hundred Instructions on Supreme Liberation* along with the *Treasury of Instructions.* Then, he did the drupchen of the Eight Sadhana Teachings and the Vitality Practice. During this time he exchanged many teachings with the various lamas who had gathered there.

In the Earth Mouse year [1888] Jamgön Kongtrul gave the entire teaching of the *Treasury of Precious Terma* to the Karmapa and his retinue. He started with the drupchen of the *Secret Complete Eight Sadhana Teachings* and finished with the empowerment of the Guhyasamaja Vitality Practice. From Bakha Tulku he received the treasure findings of Padma Lingpa, and from Gyatrul Rinpoche he received all the terma of Migyur Dorje's *Sky Teaching* and the terma of Dudul Dorje. Then, Kongtrul gave even more teachings to these two lamas and many others.

In the Earth Ox year [1889], he asked the Karmapa to find the incarnation of Situ Rinpoche. When the Karmapa had done that, Kongtrul

Rinpoche and the secretary and representatives of Palpung Monastery went to Litang to search for the child and bring him back. Kongtrul also gave instructions on the *Profound Inner Meaning* and the *Sublime Continuum* to the Karmapa. He gave him many other teachings as well, including all the teachings of the Shangpa Kagyu lineage. Kongtrul Rinpoche also received teachings from the Karmapa, including the Karmapa's composition of his own Guru Yoga and the stories of the Karmapa's previous lives before becoming the Karmapa. Kongtrul also received from Karmapa Khakhyap Dorje the reading transmission for the Protectors' Enriching Practice.

During this year the little eleventh Situ, Padma Wangchuk Gyalpo, was brought from Litang, and Gyalwa Karmapa formally cut his hair, gave his name, and enthroned him. After the enthronement, the Karmapa moved his camp to Lokhok. Then, Kongtrul went into a Vajrakilaya retreat, and gradually added the practice of Mitra's Nine Deities of the Unchanging Root of the Mind.

The Activities of Kongtrul's Last Decade

In the Iron Tiger year [1890], Lhakhampa Tulku and several realized yogis from Gechak requested and received many teachings from Kongtrul, especially the empowerment, transmission, and instructions for the *Chetsun Nyingtik* of Chetsun Senge Wangchuk. Jamgön Kongtrul also gave several teachings to the young Situ Rinpoche, such as the great empowerment of Kalachakra. During this year, Kongtrul received from Dzarka Tulku Kunzang Namgyal the *Collected Works of Tsele Natsok Rangdröl,* and all the Longsal and Dudul termas that Dzarka Tulku had compiled. Also, from Khyentse Rinpoche he received many teachings on the twelve volumes that include the root text and commentary of the *Vajrayana Stages of the Path.*

In the Iron Hare year [1891], when he was seventy-eight years old, Kongtrul constructed a large image of White Tara that was one-story high. He did a drupchen of White Tara for the longevity of Khyentse Rinpoche, and made his guru a large offering of three silver bricks, fine cloth, and other valuable things. This was one year before Jamyang Khyentse passed away. Once again, Kongtrul Rinpoche gave teachings on the *Treasury of Kagyu Vajrayana Instructions,* this time to Taglung Machen Tulku and others. He gave the teachings on the *Lama Gongdu* to Dzarka Chogtrul. Kongtrul performed a drupchen of the Eight Sadhana Teachings and a medicine-making group retreat, as well as extensive practice for the welfare of the Kingdom of Derge. He requested from Khyentse Rinpoche the teachings of the First and Middle lineages of the Pacification teachings since those lineages had been broken, and Khyentse Rinpoche gave those to him. During this year Kongtrul also received teachings on Rongtön's commentary on the *Six Transmissions of the Prajnaparamita.*

In the Water Dragon year [1892], Khyentse Rinpoche became ill at Dzongsar Monastery, so Kongtrul Rinpoche went there and did many long-life prayers and practices for him. At that time Khyentse Rinpoche said, "This time there is no problem. Around the twentieth day of the second month I will be completely healed." On the morning of the twenty-first, Khyentse was just sitting there and then suddenly passed away. Jamgön Kongtrul performed Jamyang Khyentse's forty-nine-day ceremony and cremation. He also constructed the memorial stupa made of copper gilded with gold.

During that year, Kongtrul gave empowerments, transmissions, and instructions to various gatherings, headed by Palyul Kuchen and Karma Khenpo Rinchen Dargye. They did many group sadhana practices, and Kongtrul Rinpoche also gave many bodhisattva vows. In Dzongshö he gave the reading transmission for the Nyingma tantras and in Dzongsar he gave an explanation of the *Kalachakra Tantra* to Mipham Rinpoche and Ngorpa Pönlop.

In the Water Snake year [1893] he went to Trayap and participated in the *Lama Gongdu* drupchen and gave the empowerments and transmissions of all the mandalas of the Kagyu lineage. He also gave the reading transmission of seven volumes of his own writings. His own compositions are compiled in fifteen volumes and called the *Treasury of Vast Teachings.* This collection is the fifth of Kongtrul's *Five Great Treasuries.* It should have contained all the special terma teachings that Kongtrul discovered, but he did not make much effort to establish his own terma teachings, so there is very little of his terma there.

During the same year, at the age of eighty, he completed three hundred thousand dakini fire offerings, ten thousand recitations of the

Stainless Confession Tantra, and one hundred thousand feast offerings. He also wrote his *Biography of Jamyang Khyentse Wangpo,* and fulfilled requests for teachings from students who came from all over the country, such as Surmang Trungpa Tulku and others.

In the Wood Horse year [1894] he began writing his autobiography. For the next five years he was sometimes sick, so he did not travel far. He continued to give whatever teachings were requested by his students and those who came to study with him. He continued with his writing, adding the final touches to his *Five Great Treasuries.* Even this late in his life, he made great efforts to receive whatever empowerments, transmissions, and instructions he had not yet received, and he sometimes presided as the vajra master at drupchens and medicine-making retreats.

In the morning of New Year's Day of the Earth Pig year [1899], the monks did a White Tara practice for him, and he felt very well. He completely recovered from his illness, and in a joyful mood he said, "White Tara is an extraordinary deity, and by her blessings I see definite signs that I am not going to die for another year." In the second month of that year he wrote a commentary to Sakya Pandita's translation of the *Piece of the Root,* the Vajrakilaya root tantra. His commentary was the perfect length—not too long and not too short. During this time he instructed Lama Traphel on finalizing the list of teachings that Kongtrul had received throughout his life.

Thartse Pönlop Jamyang Loter Wangpo of Ngor Monastery came to see him, and he gave Kongtrul many empowerments and transmissions, including the explanatory Yoga Tantra called the *Vajra Pinnacle,* the branch tantra called *Victorious Over the Three Worlds,* the supporting tantra called *Embodiment of the Glorious Supreme Family,* the Vajra Garland of Abhaya, the Hearing Lineage Chakrasamvara of Ngam Dzong, and Thangtön Gyalpo's teaching on the Secret Practice. Kongtrul gave teachings to Thartse Pönlop Loter Wangpo and others from his newly composed *Commentary on the Piece of the Root.*

In the sixth month, Situ Rinpoche came with his summer encampment, so Kongtrul went to see him, and he gave Situ Rinpoche many general and specific instructions. He asked Situ Rinpoche to return around the tenth month of that year, saying he would still be alive to one extent or another, and they could meet again then. Also, during this year Kongtrul made a large offering to Thartse Pönlop Loter Wangpo, praising his qualities and supplicating for his long life. As a general rule, Kongtrul did not like it when people wrote flowery poetry, but this time he wrote an elaborate poem and offered it to Thartse Pönlop.

Kongtrul's Death

From the first day of the ninth month he developed several illnesses. On the twenty-first day, he told his attendant Tsering Döndrup that it would be good to collect blessed medicines. Tsering Döndrup asked him, "Is there a sign that you will not live any longer?"

Kongtrul Rinpoche replied, "It is nothing like that. When death really comes, it is nothing very difficult." When Khenchen Tashi Özer and other students supplicated him to remain for a long time, he said, "Oh, yes, you holders of the dharma are great beings who say this with good intentions. Similarly, I will make aspirations to live a long time." After that, he did not say anything further, but sat there silently moving the beads on his mala.

On the twenty-seventh evening of the eleventh month of the Earth Pig year [1899], Khenchen Tashi Özer went to Jamgön Kongtrul's room and said, "How are you feeling?" Kongtrul Rinpoche replied, "At this point I have no pain; I am very comfortable." He sat up very straight and remained there, fingering his mala. That evening he asked his attendant to put his mala up on the shelf. Then, about midnight, he passed into the samadhi of the clear light dharmakaya.

Immediately, Khenchen Tashi Özer offered him the reminder of the teachings. Since Kongtrul Rinpoche was sitting upright, Tashi Özer put a yellow robe and meditation hat on him. After three days, in the middle of the night, the earth shook three times and there were sounds and other signs mentioned in the tantras that Kongtrul was ending his samadhi. On a favorable date his body was cremated amid auspicious signs. In particular, his heart did not burn, but remained intact for the sake of his disciples. And so the activity of that body came to an end.

The way in which this great being received teachings is clear from the record of teachings he received. Although he received a huge number of teachings, there is hardly one that he did not reciprocate by later teaching it to others. He practiced to some degree each of the empowerments, blessings, and instructions he received during his life. For every practice he completed, he experienced at least one of the signs of accomplishment mentioned in the tantras.

In general, he was very good-natured and he never tired of teaching. He was a treasure-house filled with oral instructions. It was as if there was nothing in his mind except the activities of the dharma. Students came to him like bees coming to a flower. All the interested students from the various traditions, whether Sakya, Geluk, Kagyu, Nyingma, or Bön, came to him over the years and received whatever teachings they desired. He particularly loved humble students whose behavior was unaffected and natural. His conversation was direct and frank, and he gave from his own plate and cup whatever he had to the people around him. All the offerings he received he used only for dharma activities, such as making representations of enlightened body, speech, and mind, or sponsoring large group retreats. As mentioned earlier, his writings of the *Five Great Treasuries* added up to about one hundred large volumes. Without a doubt these writings have been of great benefit and contributed to the spread of the dharma. If those compilations had not been made, we can imagine how many of those texts would have been completely lost, especially considering the recent tumult in Tibet.

This biography tells only a little bit about his activities, which are described in more detail in his own life story. Anyone who wants to know more about Jamgön Kongtrul should read his autobiography.

3

THE HISTORY OF THE TEACHING
LINEAGES THAT CAME TO TIBET

THE WAY THAT THE BUDDHA'S TEACHINGS were brought to
Tibet and transmitted can be divided into two parts: the
teaching lineages and the practice lineages. In this chapter we will discuss
the teaching lineages, which also have two parts: the sutra lineages and the
tantra lineages. First, for the sutra lineages, I will briefly describe the
teaching lineages of Vinaya, Abhidharma, and Pramana, and then give
a fuller description of the lineages of Prajnaparamita and Madhyamaka.

The Teaching Lineages of the Sutras

VINAYA

The Vinaya Tradition in India

The Vinaya is the textual framework upon which the monastic community is built. It includes two sections of rules that apply to individuals,
and two sections of procedures and conventions that apply to the entire
monastic sangha.

As background for understanding the Vinaya teaching lineages, there
were four main schools of the Shravakayana in India, which expanded
into eighteen schools. Each of them had a slightly different version of
the root *Sutra on Individual Liberation,* or *Pratimoksha Sutra,* and the
four sections of the Vinaya scriptures. The Sarvastivada school was the
tradition that came to Tibet, and it brought the *Pratimoksha Sutra* as
well as the four sections of the Vinaya. These four are called the *Basic
Transmission of the Vinaya, Distinguishing the Transmissions of the Vinaya,*
the *Minor Transmissions of the Vinaya,* and the *Sublime Teachings of the
Vinaya.*

For all the Shravakayana schools, the main Vinaya shastra, or commentary, is the *Great Treasury of Detailed Exposition,* or *Mahavibhasha* in Sanskrit. This is a compilation of commentaries on the Vinaya and other topics written by seven great masters of the Shravakayana. It was the main scripture studied by the Vaibhashikas, who took their name from that text. This way of naming resembles the Sautrantikas, who took their name from their focus on the sutras rather than the shastras. The Kangyur has thirteen volumes of Vinaya texts, which deal with seventeen topics concerning the ordained sangha.

Even though the *Great Treasury of Detailed Exposition* is the main commentary, it was not translated into Tibetan. The main Vinaya text studied in Tibet is a commentary called the *Vinaya Root Discourse.* It is the primary Vinaya text held by both the Shravakayana and Mahayana schools, and it was composed by Gunaprabha, one of the four great disciples of Vasubandhu.

Vasubandhu had many great students, and four of them were considered to be better than himself; Gunaprabha was the one who was better in the Vinaya. Gunaprabha put the four sections of the Vinaya into the proper order, and condensed the seventeen topics of the Vinaya into a shorter format; this is called the *Vinaya Root Discourse.* He wrote another text called the *Discourse of One Hundred Actions,* which gives practical instructions on activities related to the Vinaya.

Other important Vinaya texts are the *Continuous Flower Garland* by the arhat Sagadeva, and the *Fifty Verses* by Gedun Zangpo of Kashmir. The *Fifty Verses* is a popular Vinaya text that is especially useful for beginners. The great Vinaya master Shakyaprabha wrote a Vinaya root text and commentary called the *Three Hundred.* Since that time, Gunaprabha and Shakyaprabha have been renowned as the two supreme holders of the Vinaya. Gunaprabha's and Shakyaprabha's students, including the teachers known as the Six Masters of the Vinaya, extensively taught and spread the Vinaya in India. It is through their lineages that the Vinaya teachings came to Tibet.

To insert some background on the designation of Gunaprabha and Shakyaprabha as the supreme holders of the Vinaya, they are among the eight Indian scholars who are especially revered in Tibet. These eight are known as the Two Excellent Ones and the Six Ornaments. There are two ways these groups are categorized. Some people consider the Two

Excellent Ones to be Nagarjuna and Asanga, and the Six Ornaments to be Aryadeva, Vasubandhu, Dignaga, Dharmakirti, Gunaprabha, and Shakyaprabha. Sometimes the Two Excellent Ones refer to the two supreme holders of the Vinaya, Gunaprabha and Shakyaprabha. Then, for the Six Ornaments, the great ornaments of the profound view are Nagarjuna and Aryadeva, the great ornaments of vast bodhisattva activity are Asanga and Vasubandhu, and the great ornaments of valid cognition are Dignaga and Dharmakirti.

The Vinaya Lineages in Tibet

The Vinaya teaching lineages first came to Tibet in the eighth century, during the time of the dharma king Trisong Detsen, when Chokro Lui Gyaltsen studied in Tibet with two great Indian masters, Danashila and Jinamitra. Chokro Lui Gyaltsen transmitted the Vinaya teachings to the three scholars Mar, Yo, and Tsang. These Vinaya scholars were the three renowned monks who fled to eastern Tibet at the time of King Langdarma in the ninth century. Their full names are Mar Shakyamune of Tolung, Yo Gejung of Potongpa, and Rabsal of Tsang. Mar, Yo, and Tsang gave the Vinaya teachings to Lachen Gongpa Rabsal. Then, all four of them gave the teachings to Lu-me. Lu-me took the teachings back to central Tibet and transmitted them to Zu Dorje Gyaltsen. This became the teaching lineage called the Lower Vinaya tradition. It is called "lower" because it was established in Kham, near the Chinese border, before it came back up to Central Tibet.

Another Vinaya teaching lineage, called the Upper Vinaya tradition, came through Shakyasena, who received these teachings from both Jinamitra and Danashila. From Shakyasena the teachings went to Dharmapala, who taught them to Lup Lotsawa and Kyok Duldzin, the first Tibetans in this lineage. Lup Lotsawa and Kyok Duldzin taught it to Zu Dorje Gyaltsen, so Zu received both the Upper Vinaya and Lower Vinaya traditions, and he combined them into one lineage.

This combined Vinaya lineage went to Zu's four sons: Dzimpa Sherap Ö and Neso Dragpa Gyaltsen, who are called the Two Sons from Tsang; and Pochung Tsultrim Lama and Len Tsuljang, who are called the Two Sons from U. These four masters caused the Vinaya teachings to extend throughout Tibet. Later on, the great master Tsonawa wrote commentaries on the Vinaya, the most famous being the *Rays of the Sun,* and he truly caused the Vinaya teachings to radiate like the sun over Tibet.

There were many more great Vinaya masters in Tibet, such as Gya Dulwa Wangchuk Tsultrim and Ja Dulwa Wangchuk Bar. Both of them composed commentaries on the *Vinaya Root Discourse.* Ja Dulwa Wangchuk Bar also started dharma colleges at Zulphu and other places, and his Vinaya text was one of the most important. The teaching lineage of Ja Dulwa Wangchuk Bar became so important that people used to say, "The Vinaya goes back to Ja." Ja's lineage went to Tsi Dulwa Dzinpa and continued through others until Sonam Dragpa gave this teaching to Butön Rinchen Drup, who was an important figure in many of the Tibetan lineages.

Another Vinaya lineage came through Kache Panchen, who taught the *Vinaya Root Discourse* and the *Continuous Flower Garland* to Sakya Pandita. This lineage came down to Butön through Senge Silnön, Shangpa Jotön, Tseme Che, and others. In short, all the Vinaya teaching lineages came to Butön Rinchen Drup. He wrote the *Great Vinaya Rituals* and the *Commentary on Difficult Points of the Vinaya Root Discourse.* He greatly benefited the Vinaya teachings in Tibet, and his teaching spread far and wide.

Another great Tibetan Vinaya master was Kunkhyen Rongpo, who received the Vinaya teachings from Panchen Nagyi Rinchen. Kunkhyen Rongpo compared the Tibetan translations of the Vinaya with the original Sanskrit texts, wrote several Vinaya textbooks, and established a teaching lineage that still exists.

As noted above, there are two practice lineages of the Vinaya in Tibet, the Upper Vinaya and the Lower Vinaya. However, there is only one teaching lineage. All four schools of Tibetan Buddhism maintain the unbroken teaching lineage of the *Vinaya Root Discourse,* and there are no disputes about the Vinaya among the various schools.

ABHIDHARMA

The Abhidharma Tradition in India

The Abhidharma, or "higher dharma," is called the Mother of the Holy Dharma. This collection of teachings on Buddhist philosophy and psychology is said to be the basis for teaching the dharma and the gateway for entering the dharma. It has two divisions: the Upper Abhidharma of the Mahayana, and the Lower Abhidharma of the Shravakayana. For the Mahayana, the main treatise is Asanga's *Compendium of Abhidharma*. Sthiramati, Acharya Jinaputra, and many others wrote commentaries on this text.

For the Shravakayana, the main treatises are Vasubandhu's *Treasury of Abhidharma* and its autocommentary. There are many Indian commentaries on the *Treasury of Abhidharma:* one by Sanghabhadra, who was Vasubhandhu's own teacher; and others by Dignaga, Sthiramati, Purnavardhana, Jinaputra, Vasubandhu, and many others who taught the Abhidharma in India.

The Abhidharma Lineages in Tibet

In Tibet, during the early spreading of the teachings in the eighth century, Pandita Jinamitra, Lotsawa Kawa Paltsek, and others translated the *Compendium of Abhidharma* and the *Treasury of Abhidharma* and their autocommentaries. They also translated much of the Abhidharma literature, including Jinaputra's commentaries, and taught these texts. Three of Kawa Paltsek's disciples were particularly connected with the Abhidharma: Nanam Da-we Dorje, Lhalung Palgyi Dorje, and We Yeshe Gyalwa. Later, We Yeshe Gyalwa went to Kham and taught the Abhidharma to Gyalwe Yeshe, and Gyalwe Yeshe brought these teachings back to the areas of U and Tsang in central Tibet.

During that period, the *Compendium of Abhidharma* was the main text studied. Later, several teachers, such as Drangti Darma Nyingpo, took this as their main Abhidharma text. Panglo Chenpo, the great translator from Pang, wrote a commentary on it called the *Explanation That Clarifies the Objects of Knowledge,* and Panchen Shakya Chogden wrote a commentary called the *Ocean Waves of the Meaning of the View.* Although a great deal of study was done of the *Compendium of Abhidharma* during the early spreading of Buddhism in Tibet, the *Treasury of Abhidharma* later became more popular, and the *Compendium of Abhidharma* was studied less.

As for the teaching lineage of the *Treasury of Abhidharma,* when Pandita Mitrijnana, who was a great student of Naropa, came to Tibet, he went to a place in Kham called Den Longthang, where he taught the *Treasury of Abhidharma* to many scholars and monks. His student Yechenpo Sherap Drak and other masters spread this teaching in U, Tsang, and Kham. This is how Drangti Darma Nyingpo received the main teaching lineages of both the Upper and Lower Abhidharma. Drangti Darma Nyingpo's main students were Rok Chökyi Tsöndru and Gowo Yeshe Jungne. Along with Gowo's student Ben Könchok Dorje, and Ben's student called Thogar Namde, or Tho Kunga Dorje, these masters spread the Abhidharma widely.

Then, Chim Tsöndru Senge wrote a commentary called the *Running Letters*, which was the first Tibetan commentary on the *Treasury of Abhidharma*. From there the lineage went to Chim Namkha Drak, Samten Zangpo, Chomden Rigral, Rendawa and his lineage holders, and others. All these great scholars wrote commentaries and spread the teaching of the *Treasury of Abhidharma*. In Tibet it is said that "the Vinaya goes back to Ja and the Abhidharma goes back to Chim," which refers to Chim Tsöndru Senge, the author of the first Tibetan commentary on the *Treasury of Abhidharma*.

A special teaching lineage of this text started with Sakya Pandita, who was taught the *Treasury of Abhidharma* by Khache Panchen Shakya Shri. In summary, the teaching lineages of the *Treasury of Abhidharma* continue to this day, and all the major schools of Tibetan Buddhism have commentaries on it.

PRAMANA

The Pramana Tradition in India

It is generally said that Pramana, or valid cognition, is a general subject of study and not an inner or spiritual subject. However, according to Khechok Ngawang Chödrak, the treatises of Buddhist valid cognition should be included in the spiritual teachings. Similarly, Tsongkhapa said that Buddhist valid cognition is a spiritual subject because it dispels wrong views and gives an unconfused understanding of the four noble truths.

In the Buddha's teachings, the valid cognition of direct perception is taught very clearly, and inferential valid cognition is taught indirectly through reasoning. Vasubandhu's *Dialectics* is considered to be the first scripture on Buddhist valid cognition in India. There are two views on the true identity of the author—some scholars say it was written by the famous Abhidharma master Vasubandhu, and others say it was written by a different person with the same name.

The master Dignaga wrote 108 different texts on valid cognition, such as *Examining What Is Observed*. When he found that his 108 texts did not contain the whole body of valid cognition, he wrote the *Compendium of Valid Cognition*, also known as the *Discourse on Valid Cognition*, which has six chapters.

The master Dharmakirti wrote seven commentaries on Dignaga's *Compendium of Valid Cognition*, and they are collectively known as the *Seven Texts on Valid Cognition*. There are three main commentaries of different lengths: the detailed *Commentary on Valid Cognition*, the medium-length *Ascertaining the Meaning of Valid Cognition*, and the condensed *Drops of Reasoning*. Then, there are four branch commentaries: *Examining Relationships*, the *Drops of Logic*, the *Treatise on Debate*, and *Establishing the Reality of Other Minds*. Through these seven commentaries Dharmakirti opened the great path of the study of Buddhist valid cognition.

Dharmakirti asked his main student, Devindramati, to write commentaries on his seven books. Dharmakirti had already written an autocommentary on the first chapter of his *Commentary on Valid Cognition*, so Devindramati used Dharmakirti's autocommentary as the first chapter of his own commentary, which is called the *Twelve Thousand Stanzas on Valid Cognition*. Then, Devindramati's student, Shakyamati, wrote a commentary on the *Twelve Thousand Stanzas*. Acharya Vinitadeva, another great scholar of that time, wrote a commentary on all seven of Dharmakirti's commentaries. Gyen Khenpo Sherap Jungne, who is usually just called Gyen Khenpo, wrote a commentary on the *Commentary on Valid Cognition*, which he called the *Eighteen Thousand Stanzas on Valid Cognition*. He explained the intended meaning of valid cognition as being Madhyamaka philosophy. The masters Acharya Jina, Ravigupta, and Jamari of Kashmir, who is known also as Tarkika Yamari, followed Gyen Khenpo in explaining Dharmakirti's writings from the point of view of Madhyamaka.

Acharya Dharmottara, who is known as Gyal Nga Sumpa in Tibetan, wrote several commentaries on the books of Dharmakirti. His commentary on the medium-length *Ascertaining the Meaning of Valid Cognition* is called the *Great Exposition of Reasoning,* and his commentary on the *Drops of Reasoning* is called *Beneficial for Students.* Then, the great khenpo Shantarakshita took the meanings of the earlier texts on valid cognition and wrote a text called the *Summary of Suchness.* Kamalashila wrote a commentary on that text, which he called the *Great Exposition of Valid Cognition.* This book still exists in the Sanskrit language, and contemporary Sanskrit scholars in Varanasi regard it as being even greater than the writings of Dignaga and Dharmakirti. A great number of small commentaries on valid cognition were also written in India by Chandragomin, Sangharakshita, Jetari, Ratnakarashantipa, Prajnakaragupta, Jnanamitra, and others. Many of these texts were translated into Tibetan.

The Pramana Lineages in Tibet

The study of valid cognition began in Tibet during the Early Translation period in the eighth century, when Kawa Paltsek, Drenpa Namkha, and others translated some of the smaller commentaries by Dharmakirti. During the later spreading of the teaching, which began in the tenth century, Shama Sengyal translated Dignaga's *Compendium of Valid Cognition.* Ma Ge-we Lodrö translated Dharmakirti's *Commentary on Valid Cognition* and Devindramati's *Twelve Thousand Stanzas on Valid Cognition.* Khyungpo Drakse and others spread this teaching lineage a little bit, and it was called the Nyingma Tsema, or Old Lineage of Valid Cognition.

After that, in the eleventh century, Ngok Lotsawa Loden Sherap made some changes in these translations, and retranslated Dharmakirti's *Ascertaining the Meaning of Valid Cognition* and *Drops of Reasoning.* Ngok Lotsawa also started to formally teach valid cognition, mainly according to the system of Gyen Khenpo and Dharmottara. His teaching lineage is called the Sarma Tsema, or the New Lineage of Valid Cognition. The main holder of the Sarma Tsema lineage was Chapa Chökyi Senge, who lived in the twelfth century. He wrote *Eliminating the Darkness of the Mind,* a book that condenses the teachings on valid cognition. Chapa started a school for studying valid cognition, and his text became the first debate manual.

Although many scholars translated the literature of valid cognition, the main teaching lineages were the Sarma Tsema lineage begun by Ngok Lotsawa, and the lineage stemming from Sakya Pandita. Sakya Pandita Kunga Gyaltsen and Khache Panchen Shakya Shri translated and edited a new version of Dharmakirti's *Commentary on Valid Cognition*. Sakya Pandita wrote an important root text and autocommentary called the *Treasury of Logic on Valid Cognition*, which condenses all seven of Dharmakirti's books on valid cognition. Sakya Pandita had a large number of students in India, Tibet, and other countries. The main holders of his experiential understanding were Tsok, Drup, and Ön. The holders of his pith instructions were Lo, Mar, and others. The main holders of his teaching on valid cognition were Shar, Nup, and Gung. These short names refer to Sharpa Sherap Jungne and his brother Dorje Özer, Nupa Uyugpa Rigpe Senge, and Gungpa Kyotön Tri-me. They and others spread Sakya Pandita's teaching on Pramana very widely.

Uyugpa's nephew, Nyithogpa Sangye Kunmön, also had many students, and among them are those called the Four Great Pillars: Khangtön Özer Gyaltsen, Nyen Darma Senge, Shang Do-de Pal, and Zur Khangpa Kar Shakya Dragpa. Their students spread this teaching even further.

Another of Sakya Pandita's main students, Lhopa Rinchen Pal, wrote several textbooks on valid cognition. His lineage and that of Uyugpa remained strong for a long time. Over time, these lineages produced many great masters, such as Jamyang Kyapo, Lochenpo, Chöje Lama Dampa, and Nya Ön Kunga Pal. Nya Ön was particularly good at valid cognition, so there is a saying in Tibet that "Pramana goes back to Nya."

Many great masters came from Nya's lineage, including his student, Yak Mipham Chökyi Lama, and then Rongtön Sheja Kunzik, Jamchen Rabjampa Sangye Phel, Gorampa Sönam Senge, and others. From Rongtön's student, Je Dönyö Palwa, came other great scholars such as Panchen Shakya Chogden. Chöje Lama Dampa's main student of valid cognition was Lochen Jetse, and his main student was Lochen Dragpa. From that tradition came Bodong Kunkhyen, a great scholar who wrote the *Light of Reasoning on Valid Cognition* and established another new teaching system.

Then, from Shang Do-de Pal the teaching went to Khepa Norzang Pal, from there to Nyak Ön, then to Rendawa Shönu Lodrö, and from there to Je Tsongkhapa. From Tsongkhapa it went to Gyaltsap Darma Rinchen and Khedrup Gelek Palzang. Their lineage of valid cognition has not diminished; it continues to resound like a lion's roar.

After that, in the fifteenth century, the seventh Karmapa, Chödrak Gyatso, wrote a book called the *Ocean of Texts on Valid Cognition,* which covers the meaning of all of Dharmakirti's seven books of valid cognition. The seventh Karmapa's teaching lineage also still exists.

In relation to the philosophical views expressed in the literature on valid cognition, Jamgön Kongtrul says there are three ways that valid cognition is categorized in Tibet. The Sakyapas describe it as Yogachara Madhyamaka, Ngok Lotsawa describes it as the Madhyamaka that expresses essencelessness, and most others describe it as the Madhyamaka that accords with the way ordinary people see things.

There are also three ways that the literature of valid cognition is taught. Gorampa says:

> *In the region of the snow mountains there are three ways of teaching*
> *The scriptures of the two crown ornaments of valid cognition:*
> *One is to consolidate Dharmakirti's seven books into one,*
> *Another is to extract the great points of various Indian commentaries,*
> *And the third is to teach from one's own analysis.*

The first of these was the teaching style of Sakya Pandita, who taught by consolidating the main points scattered throughout the *Compendium of Valid Cognition,* the seven books by Dharmakirti, and Dharmakirti's autocommentary on the first chapter of the *Commentary on Valid Cognition.* Most Tibetan scholars have taught the second way, condensing the best points of the Indian commentators such as Devindramati, Shakyamati, Gyen Khenpo, and Dharmottara. The third way is exemplified by Gyaltsap Je and Khedrup Je, who based their teaching on their own reasoning and analysis. These three ways of teaching the literature of Buddhist valid cognition continue to this day.

PRAJNAPARAMITA

The Commentaries and Teaching Lineages in India on the *Ornament of Clear Realization*

There are two ways of conveying the meaning of the *Prajnaparamita Sutra,* or the Perfection of Wisdom teachings, the second turning of the wheel of dharma by the Buddha. The experiential understanding, or the secret meaning, is explained by the Regent Maitreya in his text, the *Ornament of Clear Realization,* and the direct, literal meaning of the Prajnaparamita comes from the Madhyamaka teachings of Nagarjuna.

The *Ornament of Clear Realization,* or *Abhisamayalankara* in Sanskrit, is the main commentary on the Prajnaparamita. The way this teaching spread in India was that Arya Asanga understood this text to have the same meaning as the *Prajnaparamita Sutra in Twenty Thousand Stanzas,* and he wrote a commentary explaining this view, which is called *Ascertaining the Meaning of Suchness.* Asanga's brother Vasubandhu explained the *Ornament of Clear Realization* according to the Chittamatra school, and his commentary is called the *Three Mothers Who Overcome Harm.*

Vasubandhu's student, Arya Vimuktisena, is particularly noteworthy in this tradition. From among Vasubandhu's four students who were considered to be better than himself, Vimuktisena was the one more learned in the *Ornament of Clear Realization.* He and Acharya Haribhadra wrote famous commentaries on the *Ornament of Clear Realization,* which were so good that most of the later masters of this tradition followed them, and their teaching styles became very popular.

Arya Vimuktisena's commentary, the *Light of the Twenty Thousand,* combined the *Ornament of Clear Realization* and the *Prajnaparamita Sutra in Twenty Thousand Stanzas.* In it he described these texts according to the Madhyamaka that expresses essencelessness. From that time on, many commentaries were written that combined the *Ornament of Clear Realization* and the shorter and longer versions of the *Prajnaparamita Sutra* in various ways. One of the most famous was by Vairochanabhadra, and there were many others.

Acharya Haribhadra was the other especially great master of these teachings. His commentary that combines the *Ornament of Clear Real-*

ization with the medium-length *Prajnaparamita Sutra* is called the *Essential Meaning of the Eight Chapters*. His commentary that combines it with the *Prajnaparamita Sutra in Eight Thousand Stanzas* is called the *Great Commentary on the Eight Thousand*. His commentary joining it to the abridged *Prajnaparamita Sutra* is called the *Commentary Which Is Easy to Understand on the Abridged Prajnaparamita Sutra*. Finally, his commentary joining it to all three main lengths of the *Prajnaparamita Sutra* is called the *Commentary with a Clear Meaning*, and it is the most popular and important of Haribhadra's commentaries.

To give an idea of the three main lengths of the sutra, the extensive Prajnaparamita is a hundred thousand stanzas, the medium length refers to the version in twenty thousand stanzas, and the abridged sutra is about forty-five pages long. The even more concise *Heart Sutra* and *Diamond Sutra* are located somewhere within these, but they are also considered to be separate texts.

Translations and Teaching Lineages of the Prajnaparamita Literature in Tibet

In terms of the literature on the second-turning teachings, all the main texts that were available in India were brought to Tibet. During the Early Translation period, Lang Khampa Gocha went to India. He memorized the entire *Prajnaparamita Sutra in a Hundred Thousand Stanzas* and translated it into Tibetan. King Trisong Detsen, because of his great reverence for the Mahayana dharma, had the *Prajnaparamita Sutra* written down using his own blood mixed with white goat's milk. This text is called the *Red Draft* or the *Short Translation of the Lama*. It was said to have been placed in a large stone stupa above Lhasa. Then, the *Prajnaparamita Sutra* was brought to Tibet from India and translated by We Manjushri and Nyang Indraparo. This translation was written down using King Trisong Detsen's hair ground up in white goat's milk. This four-volume text is called the *Blue Draft*.

These two texts, the *Red Draft* and the *Blue Draft*, were not detailed; many repetitions were omitted. So, Pagor Vairochana edited these translations to make them more elaborate and readable. Vairochana then wrote these texts in his own handwriting, and they were put into bags made of deerskin and kept at Chimphu. This set of texts was called the *Elabora-*

tion on the *Hundred Thousand Stanzas* or the *Medium Translation of the Lama*. During the time of King Ralpachen, Pandita Surendrabodhi and others, together with the two translators Kawa Paltsek and Chokro Lui Gyaltsen, reedited the sixteen-volume version, and it is called the *Great Translation of the Lama*. Around this time the *Ornament of Clear Realization*, Dushtasena's commentary on the *Prajnaparamita in a Hundred Thousand Stanzas*, and many other books on this topic were also translated, and these teachings spread widely.

During the second spreading of the dharma in Tibet, Lochen Rinchen Zangpo went to India. He studied the *Ornament of Clear Realization* and its commentaries with Pandita Gunamitra, and later established a new way of teaching it. Atisha Dipankara also taught this text to his students Khuchenpo Lhadingpa and Dromtön Gyalwe Jungne. Atisha and Rinchen Zangpo together translated a commentary on the *Ornament of Clear Realization* called *Illuminating the Difficult Points to Teach and Understand*. They also corrected many of the earlier translations, such as the *Prajnaparamita Sutra in Eight Thousand Stanzas*, the *Light of the Twenty Thousand*, and the *Great Commentary on the Eight Thousand Stanzas*. The teaching lineage started by Atisha's student Dromtönpa was passed to Drom Tongtsen, who is also called Go Lama. After Atisha taught this topic to Chadar Tönpa, his way of teaching went to Kham, where it got the name of the Kham Luk, or the Khampa teaching lineage of the Prajnaparamita.

In particular, Ngoklo Chenpo Loden Sherap received all the teachings on the *Prajnaparamita Sutra* from Pandita Sthirapala, who is also known as Bumtrak Sumpa in Tibetan. Ngok based his work on the *Prajnaparamita Sutra in a Hundred Thousand Stanzas* found in Pamthing Monastery in Nepal, which he edited and filled in. Along with the Indian khenpo, Shri Amaragomin, he corrected some of the translations of the *Ornament of Clear Realization* and its commentaries. Ngok also did many new translations and started a new teaching lineage of the Prajnaparamita.

All of these teaching lineages connected with the *Ornament of Clear Realization* spread to Kham. In particular, the lineages of Atisha, Rinchen Zangpo, and Ngoklo Chenpo came down to Dre Sherap Bar, one of the four main students of Ngoklo Chenpo, and he started a new teaching lineage that combined all three traditions.

This teaching lineage was passed down to Butön Rinchen Drup through one of Dre Sherap Bar's students, Ar Jangchup Senge. Butön Rinpoche wrote several commentaries on the *Ornament of Clear Realization,* including the one called *Hearing the Scripture.* His student, Lotsawa Rinchen Namgyal, taught the Prajnaparamita to Yaktön Sangye Pal, who was very important in the teaching tradition of the *Ornament of Clear Realization.* Yaktön Sangye Pal wrote three commentaries on it—short, medium, and long—and he taught it extensively. So, the saying arose that "the teaching on the *Ornament of Clear Realization* goes back to Yak."

Yaktön's student, Rongtön Sheja Kunzik, wrote at least forty-three different texts on the *Prajnaparamita Sutra* and especially on the *Ornament of Clear Realization.* In particular, he wrote a commentary on the *Ornament of Clear Realization* called the *Great Essential Explanation by Rong,* and he started a new way of teaching this topic. The teaching lineage of Yak and Rongtön spread all over Tibet, and it still exists today. Another student of Ngok Lotsawa, Tolungpa Lodrö Jungne, had a way of teaching that was later used by Geshe Chapa to establish another teaching lineage.

There are twenty-one large, renowned Indian commentaries on the *Ornament of Clear Realization;* twelve that combine it with the *Prajnaparamita Sutra* and nine that do not. At the time of Khedrup Je, there were about 147 Tibetan commentaries on the *Ornament of Clear Realization,* which shows how widely this text has been taught. This is noted in Khedrup Je's book, the *Ornament of the Essence of the Teachings,* which was recently published in Varanasi. Khedrup Je lived from 1385 to 1438, so by now there must be many more than 147 Tibetan commentaries.

MADHYAMAKA

All four schools of Tibetan Buddhism agree that Madhyamaka is the highest philosophy. However, the various schools differ in the way they understand the relative and ultimate truths. Their views will be discussed in detail in chapter 6. In this chapter, we are simply looking at the lineages of teachers and texts to see how the Madhyamaka teachings were transmitted.

The Main Teachers and Texts in India

Madhyamaka is the direct, literal meaning of the *Prajnaparamita Sutra*, and it unerringly shows the way of emptiness. This tradition stems from the great master Arya Nagarjuna in his text, *Wisdom, a Root Text on the Middle Way.*

In India, eight commentaries on this text were particularly renowned, but only four of them were translated into Tibetan. These are called *Nothing to Fear from Anyone,* the *Buddhapalita* by the master Buddhapalita, Bhavaviveka's the *Lamp of Wisdom,* and Chandrakirti's *Clear Words.*

Some of the earlier lists of texts, and some later masters such as Jonang Kunkhyen Dölpopa, say the text *Nothing to Fear from Anyone* was Nagarjuna's own autocommentary on *Wisdom, a Root Text on the Middle Way.* However, Khedrup Je says it could not have been by Nagarjuna because it was not quoted by any of Nagarjuna's students. Another reason is that in the twenty-seventh chapter of this commentary there is a quotation from Aryadeva's *Four Hundred Stanzas,* so it must have been written later.

The two schools of Madhyamaka—Prasangika and Svatantrika— came from the writings of two important commentators on *Wisdom, a Root Text on the Middle Way,* Buddhapalita and Bhavaviveka. First, Buddhapalita wrote his commentary called the *Buddhapalita,* and then Bhavaviveka criticized that view and wrote his commentary, the *Lamp of Wisdom.* Bhavaviveka's commentary marked the beginning of Svatantrika Madhyamaka philosophy. When Chandrakirti read Bhavaviveka's commentary, he refuted it and supported the view of Buddhapalita. That marked the beginning of the Prasangika Madhyamaka school. According to Jamgön Kongtrul, the difference between the two schools is in the way a person goes about realizing the ultimate truth; there is no difference in their understanding of what the ultimate truth is.

The main upholders of the Prasangika philosophy are Chandrakirti and Shantideva, and there are others as well. The main Prasangika texts are Chandrakirti's *Entrance to the Middle Way* and Shantideva's *Way of the Bodhisattva.* The writings by the followers of Chandrakirti's two students named the Elder and Younger Rigpe Khuchuk, and Atisha Dipankara's root text and autocommentary called the *Entrance to the Two Truths,* are also principal Prasangika commentaries.

The main upholders of the Svatantrika Madhyamaka philosophy are Jnanagarbha, Shantarakshita, and Kamalashila. These three are called the Three Rising Suns of Svatantrika. The main texts of the Svatantrika school include Avalokitavrata's eighty-volume commentary on Bhavaviveka's *Lamp of Wisdom,* called the *Great Commentary on the Lamp of Wisdom.* It is said that there is no text in Tibetan more detailed than this in explaining the non-Buddhist views. Other particularly important treatises are Jnanagarbha's root text and autocommentary called *Distinguishing the Two Truths,* Shantarakshita's *Ornament of the Middle Way* and its autocommentary, and Kamashila's *Illuminating the Middle Way* and the *Stages of Meditation: The First Treatise, Intermediate Treatise, and Final Treatise.* There are many other Svatantrika treatises as well.

The Teaching Lineages of Svatantrika Madhyamaka in Tibet

These traditions first came to Tibet during the earlier spreading of Buddhism in the eighth century, when Pandita Jnanagarbha and Chokro Lui Gyaltsen translated *Wisdom, a Root Text on the Middle Way* and the *Lamp of Wisdom,* and Shantarakshita established a teaching lineage of the Svatantrika system. During the later spread of the teachings in Tibet, Ngok Lotsawa Loden Sherap studied and taught the *Lamp of Wisdom* and other Madhyamaka texts, and the Svatantrika Madhyamaka spread widely. This teaching lineage was especially upheld at Sangphu Monastery, especially by the fifth lineage holder of Sangphu, Chapa Chökyi Senge, and his students known as the Eight Lions, the Three Noble Sons, and the Three Wisdoms.

The Svatantrika school was very popular during this time. Later on, the great master Rongtön Chöje remembered his previous life as Kamalashila and he had deep confidence in this view. The Svatantrika system was upheld in the institutes established by these great masters and in some Nyingma institutes. In the nineteenth century, Mipham Jamyang Gyatso wrote a great commentary on the *Ornament of the Middle Way,* which continues to be studied widely by the Nyingmapas. However, outside the Nyingma lineage, as time went on, the Prasangika way of teaching Madhyamaka became so prevalent that the study of Svatantrika Madhyamaka declined.

The Teaching Lineages of Prasangika Madhyamaka in Tibet

The view of Prasangika Madhyamaka is the main view of all the schools of Tibetan Buddhism. It was firmly established in Tibet through the teaching of Patsap Lotsawa Nyima Dragpa, who lived in the eleventh century. Patsap went to Kashmir and studied with the two sons of Sajjana for twenty-three years. While there, he translated *Wisdom, a Root Text on the Middle Way*, the *Entrance to the Middle Way*, the *Four Hundred Stanzas*, Chandrakirti's commentaries, and other Prasangika texts into Tibetan.

Patsap had four main students: Gangpa Sheu, who was learned in the words; Tsangpa Dregur, who was learned in the meaning; Maja Jangtsön, who was learned in both the words and the meaning; and Shangthang Sagpa Yeshe Jungne, who was not learned in either. They and their students opened the great way of teaching, debating, and writing based on the texts of Chandrakirti and other masters of Prasangika philosophy. It is important to recognize that all the study of Prasangika Madhyamaka in Tibet started with Patsap and his students.

The students of Shangthang Sagpa were very great masters who upheld the main seat of this teaching lineage. From them it went to the Sakya masters and their followers, to Butön Rinpoche, to Rendawa, and from Rendawa to Tsongkhapa and his lineage. In the Karma Kagyu lineage, the main scholar of Prasangika Madhyamaka was Karmapa Mikyö Dorje; and among the Drugpa Kagyu, the foremost scholars were Padma Karpo and his students. Most of the greatest scholars of Tibet have kept the Prasangika Madhyamaka as the center of their philosophy.

The application of the Prasangika view in meditation came from Atisha Dipankara and his students, and through them it became prevalent in the Kadampa lineage. From the Kadampa it went to all the schools of Tibetan Buddhism, especially the followers of the Geluk lineage, who take the Prasangika Madhyamaka as their central philosophy.

The Literature of Shentong Madhyamaka in India

The third-turning teachings, those on buddha nature, are found in the twenty "essence sutras" of the Buddha, and their inner meaning is explained by the regent Maitreya and Arya Nagarjuna. This understanding, which is classified as Shentong Madhyamaka, is found in four of Maitreya's treatises—the *Ornament of the Mahayana Sutras, Distinguishing Phenomena and the True Nature, Distinguishing the Middle and the Extremes,* and the *Sublime Continuum*—and also in Nagarjuna's *Collection of Praises.*

To give a little background on Nagarjuna's writing, he has three sections of teachings: the *Collection of General Teachings,* the *Collection of Reasoning,* and the *Collection of Praises.* The *Collection of General Teachings* mainly focuses on Buddha's first-turning teachings; and the *Collection of Reasoning* contains five or six texts, such as *Wisdom, a Root Text on the Middle Way,* which focus on the second-turning teachings. Nagarjuna's *Collection of Praises* is based on the third cycle of teachings and includes the praise of conditioned things and their nature in the context of the ground, the praise of skillful means and wisdom in the context of the path, and praises of each of the three kayas and the quintessence of the view in the context of fruition.

These books were commented on and widely taught by Asanga, Vasubandhu, Chandragomin, and their followers. Later, Shantipa, who was a great master during the time that Buddhism had almost disappeared in India, also taught and wrote about these works. These masters and others taught and spread these teachings very widely in India. Although the term "Shentong" was not used in India, these texts form the basis of the Shentong Mahyamaka view.

The Teaching Lineages of Shentong Madhyamaka in Tibet

This tradition came to Tibet during both the earlier and the later spreading of Buddhism, when many of the third-turning sutras and Indian commentaries were translated. During the later dissemination of Buddhism, Ngok Lotsawa studied the four later books of Maitreya with the Kashmiri master Sajjana, and then established the teaching of these texts and their commentaries in Tibet. In particular, he taught the *Sublime Continuum* and other texts to Drapa Ngönshe's student Tsen Khawoche, who then taught it to Changrawa and many others. That teaching lineage flourished for a long time.

The *Sublime Continuum* was passed down in two ways. Earlier, the tradition of Ngok Lotsawa was transmitted as a teaching lineage, and later, the tradition of Tsen Khawoche was transmitted as a practice lineage. Some people say that these two traditions were explained according to both the Chittamatra system and the Madhyamaka system. They say this mainly because Tsen Khawoche's approach asserts nondual consciousness to be truly existent, self-illuminating, self-aware, and the real essence of a buddha.

The Shentong teaching lineages were passed down through various masters, such as Khepa Tsang Nagpa; Karmapa Rangjung Dorje; Jonangpa Kunkhyen, who is also known as Dölpopa, and his lineage; Longchen Rabjam; Jangpa Rigdzin Padma Thrinle; Minling Terchen Gyurme Dorje and his brother, Lochen Dharma Shri; Situ Tenpe Nyingche Chökyi Jungne and his followers, and many others. Their way of teaching was the great lion's roar of nonreturning, which went beyond the Chittamatra school and established the Shentong system of Great Madhyamaka, which they considered to be the ultimate, definitive truth.

In India, the great master Palden Chökyong wrote a commentary called the *White Manifestation,* in which he explained Nagarjuna's *Collection of Reasoning,* especially *Wisdom, a Root Text on the Middle Way,* according to the third-turning teachings. This shows that Nagarjuna's writings on Madhyamaka reasoning, as well as his *Collection of Praises,* were taught according to the Shentong understanding.

The main source of the Shentong Madhyamaka system is the *Sublime Continuum* by Maitreya, which states:

> *In brief, the body of this entire teaching*
> *Has seven vajra points:*
> *The Buddha, dharma, sangha, buddha nature, enlightenment,*
> *Enlightened qualities, and enlightened activities.*

The *Sublime Continuum* contains these seven vajra points of the ultimate truth, which are taught in four chapters and established in accordance with the relative truth and the ultimate truth.

The Teaching Lineages of the Tantras

The following overview of the development of the Tibetan teaching lineages of the tantras has three main sections: first, the teaching lineages of the Nyingma tantras; second, the teaching lineages of the Sarma tantras of the Anuttarayoga; and third, the teaching lineages of the other, lesser tantras of the Kriya, Charya, and Yoga.

THE TEACHING LINEAGES OF THE NYINGMA TANTRAS

In the seventh century, at the time of King Songtsen Gampo, the emanation of Avalokiteshvara, there were already Nyingma lineage teachings in Tibet on several tantric deities such as Yamantaka, peaceful Avalokiteshvara, and wrathful Avalokiteshvara, or Hayagriva. Especially in the eighth century, at the time of King Trisong Detsen, the emanation of Manjushri, there were many great translators and teachers of the tantras in Tibet, such as Guru Padmasambhava, Vimalamitra, Buddhaguhya, Shantigarbha, the emanated translator Vairochana, Namkhe Nyingpo, Nyak Jnanakumara, and Nupchen Sangye Yeshe. Although these masters translated and established the general tantras, they specialized in translating and teaching the inner tantras of the Nyingma tradition. Their translations include the sadhanas, pith instructions, and commentaries for the creation stage, completion stage, and Dzogchen practices, as well as the tantras themselves.

It is said that many tantras that were not commonly known at that time were brought forth by the miraculous powers of these great masters, and they were translated and established in Tibet. The original texts in the Indian languages were kept in Pekar Kordzöling, the library of Samye Monastery. Later, when Atisha Dipankara saw these texts, he said that the degree to which the Vajrayana had spread in Tibet was unparalleled, even in India. After saying this, he reverently folded his hands and praised the great dharma kings, translators, and panditas of the previous centuries.

During the first spreading of Buddhism in Tibet, the Vajrayana teachings were kept very secret. In general, the Mahayana sutras and shastras were taught in the shedras, or centers of higher study, and the tantras were revealed only in the meditation retreat centers. Some of the outer tantras of Kriya, Charya, and Yoga were taught in the shedras, but the three inner tantras of Maha, Anu, and Ati were not taught there.

All the special inner tantras of the Nyingma lineage were preserved in the Collection of the Nyingma Tantras, and those texts and transmission lineages still exist. One particular tantra contains the essential meaning of all eighteen of the great Nyingma tantras. This is the Guhyagarbha, or the Secret Essence, whose full title is the *Glorious Guhyagarbha Tantra, the Net of the Magical Display of Vajrasattva*. Both the empowerment lineages and the teaching lineages of this king of tantras continue to this day.

According to Minling Terchen, the eighteen great tantras are grouped into the root tantras, the practice tantras, the activity tantras, and the last tantras. The five root tantras are *Equalizing Buddhahood*, the tantra of body; the *Secret Moon Essence*, the tantra of speech; the *Assembly of Secrets*, or *Guhyasamaja*, the tantra of mind; the *Glorious Supreme Primal Tantra*, the tantra of qualities; and the *Activity Garland Tantra*, the tantra of activities.

The five practice tantras give the instructions for doing the practices. These are the *Heruka Practice Tantra*, the *Hayagriva Supreme Practice Tantra*, the *Compassion Practice Tantra*, the *Nectar Practice Tantra*, and the *Arising of the Twelve Kilayas Tantra*.

There are five tantras of the branches of action: the *Mountain Pile*, the *Awesome Wisdom Lightning*, the *Array of Samayas*, the *One-Pointed Samadhi*, and the *Rampant Elephant*.

The tantra that gives all the instructions on how to enter into the activities of the mandala is the *Vairochana Net of Magical Display;* and the tantra that provides the conditions for achieving siddhis is the *Noble, Skillful Lasso, the Concise Lotus Garland*. These two are called "the last tantras that complete whatever is incomplete." Then, the essential meaning of all of these is the *Guhyagarbha Tantra*. These comprise the eighteen Nyingma tantras.

The eighteen great tantras came into the hands of King Ja in India, and went from him to his son Kukuraja. Kukuraja then transmitted them to Lalitavajra and Buddhaguhya, whose commentaries include Buddhaguhya's well-known commentary on the *Guhyagarbha Tantra* called the *Commentary on the Distinctions*. These two masters gave these teachings to Vimalamitra, who wrote a commentary called the *Inner*

Scriptural Commentary. In India there were many other great commentaries on the *Guhyagarbha Tantra*, such as the *Great Knot Commentary* by Chandragomin, and the *Great Explanation of Padma* by
Padmasambhava.

The Guhyagarbha Teaching Lineages in Tibet

In Tibet, the pandita Vimalamitra taught the *Guhyagarbha Tantra* to
Ma Rinchen Chok, who translated this tantra into Tibetan. Vimalami-
tra and Guru Padmasambhava also taught the Guhyagarbha to Nyak
Jnanakumara. From Nyak the teachings went to Sogpo Palye, and from
him to Nupchen Sangye Yeshe. Nup Sangye Yeshe also received the
Guhyagarbha from Ma Rinchen Chok's lineage in the following way.
When Ma Rinchen Chok went to Kham, he gave these teachings to
Tsugtu Rinchen Shönu and Gyere Chogkyong, and the two of them
gave these teachings to Darje Paldrak and Shang Gyalwe Yönten. Then,
Shang gave these teachings to Nupchen Sangye Yeshe. Also during the
Early Translation period, the great master Vairochana translated
Suryaprabhasimha's commentary on the *Guhyagarbha Tantra,* and he
taught it in the temple of Öru Jamchen in Kham.

Many lineages started from Nupchen's teaching; for instance, it was
incorporated by the three Zurpas, whose lineage is called the Zur Luk,
or the Zur way of teaching the *Guhyagarbha Tantra*. The third Zur,
Lhaje Drophugpa, was particularly renowned for spreading the Guhyagarbha. His disciple, Dzom Drowe Gönpo, passed this teaching to
Gyalwa Kathogpa Dampa Deshek, who founded Kathok Monastery,
the first monastery in Kham. From there the teaching lineage of the
Guhyagarbha Tantra spread widely. Puborwa Yeshe Gyaltsen, who came
from that lineage, wrote commentaries on it and started a Guhyagarbha
teaching and practice lineage known as the Kham Luk, or Kham teaching lineage, which eventually went back to central Tibet.

Another lineage, called the Rong Luk, came through Rongzom
Chökyi Zangpo. He received this teaching from many lineages, including those of Guru Padmasambhava, Vairochana, and Vimalamitra.
Rongzompa wrote a commentary on the *Guhyagarbha Tantra* called
the *Jewel Commentary*. The teaching lineage of Longchenpa began with
his commentary on the *Guhyagarbha Tantra*, called *Eliminating the*

Darkness of the Ten Directions, which explained this tantra according to the Dzogchen view. Also, Rok Sherab Ö received the teaching lineages of So, Zur, Kyo, and many others, and he started a new teaching lineage called the Rok Luk. These are some examples of the many teaching lineages of this tantra.

Later on, some scholars of the New Translation schools criticized the *Guhyagarbha Tantra,* saying that it might have been created by the Tibetans. The great master Chomden Rigpe Raltri, who was the first person to publish the Kangyur, received a Sanskrit original of this text, which was said to be in the handwriting of Guru Padmasambhava. He asked Tharpa Lotsawa to translate it, and that book became known as the *Floral Ornament of the Guhyagarbha Practice.* From then on, there were no more disputes about its origin.

Of all these teaching lineages, the Zur Luk was especially great. Later on, that lineage became weak, and in the seventeenth century Minling Terchen Gyurme Dorje and his brother Lochen Dharma Shri revived and firmly reestablished the teaching of the Guhyagarbha in Tibet. Minling Terchen received this tantra and many other Nyingma teachings of the Kama oral tradition, and he compiled these teachings and taught them with great interest and diligence. The texts he compiled became known as the *Ngagyur Kama,* or *Nyingma Kama,* which is a collection of Nyingma lineage teachings transmitted through the oral tradition. Lochen Dharma Shri, who is also known as Lochen Chöpal Gyatso, wrote several commentaries on the *Guhyagarbha Tantra,* including a general explanation called the *Oral Instructions of the Lord of Secrets* and a word-by-word explanation called the *Ornament of the Wisdom Mind of the Lord of Secrets.* From that time onward, the Minling tradition continued through the twenty-one lineage holders with the title of Rabjampa. One of them, Orgyen Chödrak, also commented on this tantra in the *Precious Garland* and other texts. Based on these teachings, the teaching lineage of the *Guhyagarbha Tantra* is prevalent even now.

Styles of Teaching the *Guhyagarbha Tantra*

The Guhyagarbha is called the king of tantras, and it is superior by means of eight qualities. It is taught through four tantras and three types of valid cognition. The four tantras are the *Oceanlike Exposition Tantra*, the *Sound Consequence Root Tantra*, the *Wisdom Essence Tantra*, and the *Vajra Mirror Tantra*. The Guhyagarbha is part of the Mahayoga teachings, which are taught through what are called the Seven Ornaments. This tantra in particular is taught in three ways, which are called Teaching Like an Arrow Held at the Tip, Teaching Like a Spear Held in the Middle, and Teaching Like a Sword Held at the End. The first way of teaching, like an arrow held at the tip, explains the entire ground, path, and fruition by using only the title of the text.

In relation to the second way of teaching, like a spear held in the middle, the fifth chapter of the *Guhyagarbha Tantra* states:

> *Containing abundant characteristics of understanding and engaging,*
> *The cause and condition ripen to fruition.*
> *Those with power and ability*
> *Are renowned as vidyadharas in the buddha realms.*

In other words, the cause is the view, which is characterized by understanding; the condition is the meditation, which is characterized by engaging; and the result of treading the path is the four vidyadhara levels. All the characteristics of the Guhyagarbha are condensed in these three and taught in this way.

The third way of teaching, like a sword held at the end, is explained in the second stanza of the last chapter of the *Guhyagarbha Tantra*. It says that the whole tantra can be taught by grouping everything into the four ways of appearing: the way the ground nature appears, the deluded way that wrong understanding appears, the way the path appears for those to be tamed, and the way the result appears for the buddhas. Also, the Zur way of teaching the *Guhyagarbha Tantra* emphasizes five similar points: the nature of the way things are, the deluded appearances for those who have not realized the true nature, the way that enlightened beings see reality, the way that great compassion arises in them, and the way they work for the benefit of beings.

The contemporary way of teaching this tantra follows the saying of Vimalamitra:

For the highest beings, the title is given,
For the medium level, a small amount of explanation is given,
For beings without much understanding, a word-by-word
*   explanation is given.*

As it says, the title alone is taught to those of the highest ability; a general understanding is imparted to those of medium ability; and a word-by-word explanation is given to those of lesser ability. To explain this in more detail, first, teaching only the title is described in three ways: according to the tantra, or Mahayoga; according to the oral transmission, or Anuyoga; and according to the pith instructions, or Atiyoga. The title could also be taught in two other ways: through the upper door, which is the way of method; and the lower door, which is the secret way.

Second, imparting a general understanding for beings of medium ability is done in two ways: by explaining the various meanings, and by explaining a general understanding of the words. The meaning can be explained in five ways: how the tantra first came into being; how the tantra was taught; the result, or the actual meaning of the tantra; how a true understanding of the tantra is conveyed to students; and how the teaching is established.

The third style of teaching is to go through each word or stanza by teaching its essence, definitions, and classifications.

This was an overview of how the Mahayoga tantras are taught. For the history of the Anuyoga and Atiyoga teachings and practices, please see the section in this book on the Nyingma practice lineages.

THE SARMA TEACHINGS OF THE MOTHER AND FATHER TANTRAS

In describing the Sarma, or New Translation, teaching lineages of the tantras, in the *Treasury of Knowledge*, Jamgön Kongtrul divides the tantras into the Father tantras and Mother tantras. Within the Father tantras, there are three classifications: the Desire class, the Anger class, and the Ignorance class, and we will examine the Anuttarayoga tantras in this order.

The Father Tantras

THE TEACHING LINEAGES OF THE *GUHYASAMAJA TANTRA*

First, the main tantra of the Desire class in the Father tantras is the *Guhyasamaja Tantra,* or the *Assembly of Secrets.* In India there were about twenty-four different teaching lineages connected with this tantra, such as those of Padmavajra, Anandavajra, Nagarjuna, Lalitavajra, Vajrahasa, Drinsum Wangpo, Madhuragoshapala, Buddhajnana, Shantipa, Anandagarbha, and others.

Six of these twenty-four traditions came to Tibet: the teaching lineages of Nagarjuna, Jnanapada, Shantipa, Padmavajra, Anandagarbha, and Vajrahasa. During the Early Translation period, the *Guhyasamaja Tantra* was translated into Tibetan by the translator Che Tashi, and it is included in the eighteen Nyingma tantras as the *Guhyasamaja Mind Tantra.* For the Nyingma lineage at that time, the main commentary and teaching lineage of Guhyasamaja was that of Vajrahasa.

From among the six teaching lineages that came to Tibet, the main ones were those of Nagarjuna and Buddhajnana. These two traditions contain all the empowerments, explanations, and pith instructions, and they still exist today. The other four teaching lineages did not exist as complete systems and are no longer extant.

First, the Guhyasamaja lineage of Nagarjuna, called the Arya tradition, or Phak Luk in Tibetan, came to Tibet at the beginning of the New Translation era. The great translator Rinchen Zangpo translated the *Guhyasamaja Tantra* and its commentary, the *Brilliant Lamp,* along with many long and short scriptures connected with this tantra. Rinchen Zangpo also received the teaching lineage and all the empowerments, and he spread them in Tibet. Many other translators during this time also studied the *Guhyasamaja Tantra* and they translated, taught, and spread these teachings in various ways. Until now the strongest and most popular lineages are the two lineages coming from Marpa Chökyi Lodrö and Gö Khugpa Lhatse, which began in the eleventh century. I will tell a little about these two traditions.

Marpa of Lodrak, the great translator Chökyi Lodrö, received the teachings of Guhyasamaja from Acharya Naropa, Jnanagarbha, and others, and he later transmitted them to his own students in Tibet. Marpa's foremost students were known as the Four Great Pillars, and from among them, Tölgyi Tsurtön Wang-nge was the one to whom Marpa gave the complete teachings of Guhyasamaja and entrusted the teaching lineage. Tsurtön later gave these teachings to Khampa Ronyam Dorje. It so happened that Ronyam Dorje was going to India in order to study the *Guhyasamaja Tantra,* and on the way he met two Indians who were coming to Tibet to receive the Guhyasamaja teachings from Marpa. This inspired Ronyam Dorje to return to Tibet to study with Marpa. However, Marpa had passed away by then, so Ronyam Dorje received these teachings from Tsurtön. This tradition was gradually passed down as the Mar Luk, or the teaching lineage of Marpa.

Second, the teaching lineage of Gö was begun by the great translator Gö Khugpa Lhatse, who received the empowerments, explanations of the commentaries, and pith instructions for the *Guhyasamaja Tantra* from about seventy different Indian pandits, including Atisha Dipankara, Devakarachandra, and Viryabhadra, as well as from two dakinis. In Tibet he corrected the earlier translations of this tantra, along with its commentaries and subcommentaries. He spread this tantra to his own students, and it is said that among them, four were like the four pillars of the tantra, eight were like the beams of the tantra, and countless students were like small joists upholding the tantra. Among them were six supreme students, including Marpa Senge Gyaltsen. It is from these students that the Gö Luk, or Gö teaching lineage, spread.

There are several other Guhyasamaja lineages. The Jo Luk teaching lineage was passed from Jowo Je Atisha to Nagtso Lotsawa, and from Nagtso Lotsawa to Rongpa Chagsorwa. The Chak Luk teaching lineage came from Pandita Revendra to Chak Chöje Pal, and from Chak Chöje Pal to Uyuk Kungrap Lama Pal, and it continued from there. Another lineage, called the Panchen Luk, came from Kache Panchen to Sakya Pandita and Chal Chökyi Zangpo and others. Sakya Pandita's lineage split into two branches, one called Sa Luk and the other called Chak Luk. It is generally said that there are six teaching lineages of Guhyasamaja, but it seems there are a few more that are slightly different.

For example, the lineage of Acharya Jnanapada, called the Shap Luk, first came to Tibet through Lochen Rinchen Zangpo, and from him to Kyangpo Chökyi Lodrö, and then to others. The pandita Mritijnana gave these teachings in Kham, and from there the Kham Luk, or Khampa teaching lineage, spread. Another lineage came from Pandita Sunaya Shri to Nyen Lotsawa and continued from him to the Sakyapas, and that is known as the Sa Luk, or Sakya teaching lineage. Another one came from Pandita Punya Shri and others to Ra Chörap, and that is called the Ra Luk. Nyö Jungpo received the Guhyasamaja teachings from Baling Acharya, and his lineage came to be known as Nyö Luk. In the two teaching systems of Nagarjuna and Jnanapada, a large number of works were written in Tibet on the Guhyasamaja commentaries, empowerments, instructions, and oral traditions.

According to Kongtrul, the main two teaching lineages of the *Guhyasamaja Tantra* that continued in Tibet were those of Marpa and Gö. Marpa's lineage put more emphasis on practice, and Gö's lineage put more emphasis on teaching the tantra. Marpa's teaching lineage went to Khampa Ronyam Dorje, and from him to Khön Gepakirti and others. Gradually, his lineage teaching became more like pith instructions emphasizing the practice. These days the Mar Luk lineage has the empowerments and pith instructions, but the teaching lineage exists only for the lung, or reading transmission. Marpa's real teaching lineage for Guhyasamaja, called the Seven Teaching Lineages of Marpa, does not seem to exist anymore.

The teaching lineage of Gö was transmitted by his students called the Four Pillars, and then to a lama called Kunkhyen Chöku Özer, who was able to memorize and retain all the commentaries after reading them only once. From him this teaching lineage went to Phagpa Ö, and from him to Butön Rinpoche, who became a great master of this tantra. He wrote many texts on this topic, including a commentary on the *Brilliant Lamp,* which is the great commentary on the *Guhyasamaja Tantra.* Butön's student, Jang Lhepa Shönu Sönam, gave these teachings to the great master Tsongkhapa, who is also known as Lozang Dragpa. Tsongkhapa spread the precious teachings of the Guhyasamaja all over Tibet.

In general, the practices, empowerments, reading transmissions, and instructions for the two main Tibetan lineages of the Guhyasamaja remain in all the schools of Tibetan Buddhism. It is said that the oral instructions on the five stages of Guhyasamaja practice were kept by the lineage holders of Shalu Monastery. The real teaching lineage still exists today due to the dissemination of Tsongkhapa's excellent commentary on the root tantra and on the great commentary the *Brilliant Lamp.*

Tsongkhapa's commentary is called the *Combination of the Four Commentaries*. His teaching lineage is kept mainly by the Geluk school, and when Jamyang Khyentse Wangpo and Kongtrul Yönten Gyatso received this teaching, they made great efforts to bring it to other schools of Tibetan Buddhism as well.

Gö Lotsawa based his teaching system on the five great treatises of Nagarjuna. He studied Nagarjuna's writings with many teachers, relying mainly on the teaching traditions of three great scholars: Abhijna of Bengal, Devikara of Sahor, and especially Krishna Samayavajra of Bodhgaya.

The essential meaning of the *Guhyasamaja Tantra,* or the *Assembly of Secrets,* is quoted as follows:

> *The three aspects of enlightened body, speech, and mind*
> *Are called the "secrets."*
> *They are called "assembly" since they are together.*
> *This is how all the buddhas are presented.*

It is said that this tantra has the name "secret" or *guhya* because it is to be kept secret from the shravakas and pratyekabuddhas, and even the mahayanists, unless they are very suitable for these teachings. "Secrets" also refer to the ultimate body, speech, and mind of the buddhas.

As for *samaja,* the union or assembly of all the buddhas, it is called "Vajradhara" or "all the buddhas." *Samaja* does not refer to an assembly of many buddhas who manifest to train beings; it refers to the ultimate topic to be understood, so the Guhyasamaya is said to be the highest of the tantras.

It is taught that the *Kalachakra Tantra* and its commentaries explain the real meaning of the Guhyasamaja; that the *Hevajra Tantra* leads to understanding of the Guhyasamaja; and that the *Chakrasamvara Tantra* clarifies the essence of the Guhyasamaja.

THE *YAMANTAKA TANTRA*

The second class of the Father tantras is the Anger class, with its teachings on Yamantaka, or the Slayer of the Lord of Death. It is said that the *Yamantaka Tantra* spread not long after the Third Council of Shakyamuni Buddha's followers. In India, the Yamantaka teachings were classified into five periods of time according to the spiritual accomplishments attained. According to the time divisions of ordinary people, the teachings were spread at first by Acharya Lalitavajra, in the middle by Buddhajnana, and at the end by Brahmana Acharya Shridhara. These three masters were called the First, Middle, and Final Holders of the Yamantaka practice, and the Vajra Masters of the Great Mandala. In particular, the great master Shridhara received all the teachings on the three forms of Yamantaka—Red, Black, and Vajrabhairava, and it was through him that the Yamantaka teachings gradually spread to Tibet.

It is said that in the seventh century, the dharma king Songtsen Gampo composed a sadhana of Yamantaka, which would make it the earliest tantra practiced in Tibet. Around the time the first Tibetans became monks, the *All-Victorious Yamantaka Tantra* was translated into Tibetan, and its empowerments, teachings, pith instructions, and practices were received. Nupchen Sangye Yeshe was very influential in spreading the teachings of Yamantaka, and many accomplished practitioners came from his lineage. So, Yamantaka can be considered one of the first tantric practices in Tibet.

During the later spread of Buddhism in Tibet, Chogdru Lotsawa Sherap Lama translated the *Black Yamantaka Tantra*, the *Seven Conceptions of Vajrabhairava*, and the *Sadhana of the Forty-Nine Vajrabhairavas*. He also spread the teachings and empowerments of the three Yamantaka practices of the Red-Faced, Six-Faced, and Vajrabhairava Yamantaka. Another great translator, Nagtso Lotsawa, received these teachings from Atisha, Samayavajra, and others. He translated commentaries on the *Yamantaka Tantra* and spread these teachings by giving many lectures and empowerments.

The great Nyingma master Rongzom Chökyi Zangpo received the teachings of Black Yamantaka and Vajrabhairava from Upaya Shri Mitra. He then translated these teachings into Tibetan and taught them. Yö Lotsawa, Ra Lotsawa, Shu-ke Lotsawa, and many others translated the tantras, scriptures, and pith instructions of the Red, Black, and Vajrabhairava Yamantakas, and revised many of the existing translations.

There are eight accomplished masters of Yamantaka who established their own lineages in Tibet: Chalo, Sakya Pandita, Chak, Lo, Ra Lotsawa, Cho, Shang, and Nyö. To mention each of them in turn, Chalo

Chöpal Zangpo received teachings on the Black and Red Yamantakas from Nishkalangka and then spread them in Tibet. Sakya Pandita began a teaching system based on the Yamantaka teachings of Danashila, and Chak Lotsawa translated the writings of Virupa and established another system. Lo Lotsawa received these teachings from Darpan Acharya and others, and spread them. This first group of four lineages transmitted in Tibet the empowerments, explanations, and pith instructions, particularly in connection with Red Yamantaka.

For the second group of four lineages, first, the Ra Luk, or teaching lineage of Ra, came from Ra Lotsawa Dorje Drak. He went to Nepal to study with Baro Chak Duma and Metsa Lingpa, and received from them all the empowerments, tantras, and pith instructions on Vajrabhairava. In particular, from Balpo Thugje Chenpo he received the complete teachings on the three Yamantakas—Black-Faced, Six-Faced, and Vajrabhairava Yamantakas. Ra Lotsawa established a large cycle of Yamantaka teachings in Tibet. It is said that he gave these teachings to only two thousand of his many students. His main students in this lineage were Ra Chörap and others—there are too many to record here.

The Cho Luk came from Lama Cho, who received all the Vajrabhairava teachings from Amoghavajra, and he spread those in Tibet. The Shang Luk came from Chogdru Lotsawa, who received the Black and Vajrabhairava Yamantaka teachings from Devakarachandra. His way of teaching these tantras was gradually established in Tibet.

Lastly, the Nyö Luk came from Nyö Lotsawa, who received the three cycles of Black Yamantaka from Baling Acharya and others. Among all these different systems, the most powerful has been the system of the great master Ra Lotsawa, in both its teaching and practice lineages. The Ra Luk began in the eleventh century, spread into all the schools of Tibetan Buddhism, and remains vibrant today.

THE *MANJUSHRI TANTRA*

The third class among the Father tantras is the Ignorance class, and its primary text is the tantra of the *Manjushri Namasamgiti,* or *Chanting the Names of Manjushri.* This text is the "Net of Meditations" chapter from the large tantra, the *Manjushri Net of Magical Display in Sixteen Thousand Stanzas.* This tantra is explained in different ways. For example, the bodhisattva kings of Shambhala explain it according to the *Kalachakra Tantra,*

Lalitavajra explains it as a Father tantra of Anuttarayoga, and the bodhisattvas Manjushrikirti and Manjushrimitra explain it according to Yoga Tantra. In Tibet it is sometimes explained according to Atiyoga, and in India it is sometimes explained according to Madhyamaka.

Around the year 1000, Lochen Rinchen Zangpo translated *Chanting the Names of Manjushri* into Tibetan. Later on, several translators revised the translation. Panchen Smritijnana gave the complete teaching of this tantra, including the empowerment, tantra, and pith instructions, to Kyi Jema Lungpa, who transmitted it to Ngogtön Chöku Dorje. This teaching lineage accords with the Yoga Tantra. Marpa Chökyi Lodrö received this teaching according to the Anuttarayoga Tantra from Maitripa. Marpa's lineage of the empowerment and reading transmission still exists today, as does the teaching lineage that began with Panchen Smritijnana.

There are many different translations of *Chanting the Names of Manjushri,* but there are not many different meanings. The only difference is the wording, "the empty essence—one hundred letters" according to the Yoga Tantra, and "the empty essence—six letters" according to the Anuttarayoga Tantra.

It is said that if one gains confidence in this king of tantras, then one will gain confidence in all the Anuttarayoga tantras. And if one does not understand the meaning of this tantra, then one does not understand the meaning of Anuttarayoga altogether. It says in the *Stainless Light*:

> In order to free all beings from doubt, the Tathagata collected
> *Chanting the Names of Manjushri* from all the Mantrayana
> teachings and taught it to Vajrapani. Whoever does not know
> *Chanting the Names of Manjushri* does not know the wisdom
> body of Vajradhara. Whoever does not know the wisdom body
> of Vajradhara does not understand the Mantrayana. Whoever
> does not understand the Mantrayana remains in samsara, sep
> arated from the path of the conqueror Vajradhara.

The Mother Tantras

The Mother tantras are sometimes categorized in six classes and sometimes as three classes. Here, in accordance with the views of Jamgön

Kongtrul, the Mother tantras will be explained in three classes: the Heruka class, the Permanence class, and the Vajrasasttva class.

THE HERUKA CLASS

The *Chakrasamvara Tantra*

First, within the Heruka class, the *Chakrasamvara Tantra* is said to be the quintessence of the Mother tantras. There were about twenty-seven Chakrasamvara lineages in India, and most of the empowerments, reading transmissions, and teaching lineages of the root tantra and commentaries came to Tibet. The reason there were so many different lineages was that many of the great siddhas in India attained realization by doing Chakrasamvara as their main practice. Even so, the main sources of this teaching were Luipa, Nagpopa, and Drilpupa, who is also known as Vajraghantapada. These three are compared to the sun and moon in terms of their importance.

The teachings of the three lineages of Luipa, Drilpupa, and Nagpopa were translated into Tibetan. Commentaries on the root tantra by other Indian masters were also translated into Tibetan, particularly those written by Darikapa, Demgipa, the lesser Indrabhuti, Jinabhadra of Langka, Durjayachandra, Lavapa of the eastern direction, Shunyatasamadhi, Bhavabhadra, the Brahman Ratnavajra, and an unknown author who followed the first part of the *Vajrapani Tantra* commentary. These commentaries are still available in the Tibetan language.

At least six mandalas of the explanatory tantra of Chakrasamvara came to Tibet. At the beginning of the second spreading of Buddhism in Tibet, Lochen Rinchen Zangpo, Gö Lotsawa, and other masters translated the tantra, the sadhanas, and many of the commentaries connected with the *Chakrasamvara Tantra*. Another translator, Lokya Sherap Tsek, received different Chakrasamvara teachings from the Pamthingpa brothers of Nepal, and he gave these teaching to Mal Lotsawa Lodrö Drak and others. Mal Lotsawa also went to Nepal and received these teachings from the Pamthingpa brothers, and he became a great master of Chakrasamvara. The great Sakya forefather, Sachen Kunga Nyingpo, received these teachings from Mal Lotsawa, and they were transmitted and spread extensively through the Sakya family lineage.

Marpa Lotsawa received the definitive, secret, supreme teachings of

Chakrasamvara from Naropa, and he later conveyed these to his students in Tibet. Marpa's lineage contains several special pith instructions on Chakrasamvara. In particular, one of Marpa's spiritual heirs, Marpa Dopa Chökyi Wangchuk, went to Manaka Shri, a student of Naropa, and to many other lamas from whom he received the empowerments, explanations of the tantras, and pith instructions according to the tradition of Naropa. Marpa Dopa Chökyi Wangchuk gave these instructions to numerous students in Tibet, and he also translated many of the Chakrasamvara teachings.

Other Tibetan lineages came from the three Pamthingpa brothers in Nepal to Purong Lochungwa, Nyö Lotsawa, and others. The teaching lineage of Purong Lochungwa was said to be a particularly good system, and it lasted for a long time.

Atisha gave teachings on Chakrasamvara to Lochen Rinchen Zangpo, Rongpa Gar-ge, and others. Later, Rongpa Gar-ge gave these teachings to Yagde Semarwa, and a teaching system arose from them. Atisha also gave the Chakrasamvara teachings to Nagtso Lotsawa, and another teaching system came from there, which is called the lineage of Balpang Nawa. In addition, Sumpa Lotsawa, whose personal name was Dharma Yönten, received from Pandita Jayasena the *Ocean of Dakinis of Chakrasamvara,* including the root text, commentary, and auxiliary texts, all of which he translated into Tibetan.

All these lineages of empowerments and explanations spread in Tibet. The lineage of Marpa Dopa was propagated by his own students, particularly a great scholar from Tsang called Gyanam Dosewa Loden. His students preserved these teachings so well that both the teaching and practice lineages of Chakrasamvara entered all four schools of Tibetan Buddhism. These lineages were passed on to Butön Rinpoche, who wrote commentaries on the root *Chakrasamvara Tantra* and the *Explanation of Conduct.* Butön's teaching tradition of Chakrasamvara has been preserved in the Gelugpa school to the present time.

There are more than twenty different systems of the Chakrasamvara empowerment and practice instructions that came from Luipa, Drilpupa, and Nagpopa. These traditions of the creation and completion practices of the Mother tantras remain unbroken in all four Tibetan Buddhist schools.

The *Hevajra Tantra*

The ultimate Mother tantra is the *Hevajra Tantra*, which is also part of the Heruka class. In India, there were many Hevajra lineages; foremost among them were those of Acharya Saroruha, Krishna Samayavajra, Durjayachandra, Ratnakara, Naropa, Maitripa, and Khache Yashobhadra. Some people say that Yashobhadra is another name for Naropa. These seven systems were complete with the empowerments, explanations, and pith instructions. There were about twelve major commentaries in India, such as the *Vajra Essence Commentary* and the *Commentary on the Difficult Points, called Padma.* Among these seven lineages, those of Saroruha, Krishna Samayavajra, and Durjayachandra were distinct lineages, while the other Hevajra lineages were composed of the best parts of those systems.

As for how the Hevajra lineages came to Tibet, in the eleventh century Drogmi Shakya Yeshe received the teaching system of Virupa from Pandita Gayadhara and others. Drogmi received all the empowerments, pith instructions, and explanations of the *Hevajra Tantra*, and through him Virupa's lineage went to the Sakya family and the Sakya school. The lineages of Saroruha and Shantipa went to Gö Khugpa Lhatse, who received these teachings from Krishna Samayavajra, and then spread them in Tibet.

There are many other lineages as well. For instance, the translations and teachings of Gyijo Dawe Özer and the system of teaching from Panchen Naropa were received by Marpa Chökyi Lodrö, who passed these on to his students, particularly Me and Ngok. Also, Chal Lotsawa Sönam Gyaltsen received Naropa's teaching lineage from Pamthingpa, and spread that. A student of Ngok named Ram spread another lineage, which is called the Ram Luk. Later on, there was a teaching lineage called the Hevajra Jnana Luk, which was strongly held by the Taglung school within the Kagyu lineage. The teachings received by Jetsun Taranatha and which he spread are called the system of the Peaceful Secret of Hevajra. All these teaching systems prevailed in Tibet.

The two main unbroken lineages of Hevajra empowerments, explanations, pith instructions, and practices were those of Marpa Lotsawa and Drogmi Lotsawa. In particular, three students of Marpa—Me, Ngok, and Tsur—passed on Marpa's teaching, and Sakyapa Kunga Nyingpo and his lineage holders passed on Drogmi's teaching. These two teaching and practice lineages are like victory banners upheld endlessly.

The earlier generations of Sakya family lineage, the followers of Drogmi, had what are called the Six Traditions of Hevajra. These include the tradition of the pith instructions of Virupa, the commentarial tradition of Dombupa, the tradition of Saroruha, the tradition of Krishna, and the tradition of Naropa. However, the traditions of Krishna and Naropa have not continued in the Sakya school, and later generations have what are called the Four Transmissions of Hevajra.

The Marpa Kagyu lineage, who are the followers of Naropa and Maitripa, have four empowerment traditions which include the root tantra, the explanatory tantra, and supporting texts. Previously, they had teaching systems for all three Hevajra Tantras: the root tantra, the *Vajra Tent Tantra,* and the *Sambhuti Tantra,* as well as the practice instructions on the Six Yogas of Naropa. However, these days the Marpa Kagyu no longer have the teaching systems for the *Vajra Tent* and the *Sambhuti Tantra.* Marpa's system of teaching the *Hevajra Tantra* continues through three lineages: the Ngok Luk, the Me Luk, and the Tsur Luk. They contain the Hevajra father-mother tantra, the root tantra, the explanatory tantra, and fifteen different kinds of empowerments. These teaching lineages and practice instructions continue to this day.

THE PERMANENCE CLASS

The Permanence class of the Mother tantras is connected with the *Four Vajra Seats Tantra.* In India there were two systems, one that came from Aryadeva, which was based on the root tantra, and one that came from Bhavabhadra, which was based on the condensed tantra. In Tibet they had Pandita Smritijnana's translation of his own commentary on the *Four Vajra Seats,* the translations and teaching lineages of Gayadhara and Drogmi, and the teaching lineage of Gö Khugpa Lhatse.

Marpa Lotsawa received the *Four Vajra Seats Tantra* from Niguma, who is also known as Dakima Mirukyi Gyenchen, "the dakini ornamented with human bones." He received all the empowerments, explanations, and pith instructions, and although Marpa's teaching lineage no longer exists, the tradition for giving the empowerment and practice instructions remains unbroken to this day.

THE VAJRASATTVA CLASS

The *Kalachakra Tantra*

For the Vajrasattva class of the Mother tantras, the main tantra is the *Kalachakra Tantra,* or the *Wheel of Time.* The *Kalachakra Tantra* was well-known in India, and the wording of the tantra and its commentary are very clear, so different schools did not evolve on the basis of the root tantra and commentary. These teachings were brought from the land of Shambhala by Manjuvajra, who is called the Kalachakrapada, or the Great Master of Kalachakra; as well as by Acharya Chilupa, who is called the Lesser Master of Kalachakra; and by Pito Acharya. Each of them brought the *Kalachakra Tantra* separately, but their versions are more or less the same; the only differences are in a couple of verses.

In Tibet, the root text and commentary were first translated by Pandita Shri Bhadrabodhi and Gyijo Lotsawa. They also brought the empowerments, explanations, and pith instructions to Tibet. The lineage called the Gyijo Luk came through Trom Lotsawa; and the lineage called the Tsami Luk came from Tsami Sangye Drak, who received it from the Kalachakrapada, Manjuvajra. Tsami translated the great commentary and taught it to Ga Lotsawa and others. Ra Chörap received these teachings in Nepal from Pandita Samanta Shri; he translated them and taught them to Ra Yeshe Senge and others. That system is known as the Ra Luk.

Dro Lotsawa received the empowerments, explanations, and pith instructions on Kalachakra from Pandita Dawa Gönpo of Kashmir. Dro translated the commentaries and the tantra, except for the *Supreme Unchanging Chapter,* and later, his teacher Dawa Gönpo himself translated the *Supreme Unchanging Chapter* into Tibetan. Penyul Drapgom also received these teachings from Dawa Gönpo, and he became very learned and accomplished in the Kalachakra. Penyul Drabgom taught it to Drotön, and from there it spread widely. Since this teaching lineage was based on the translation originally done by Dro Lotsawa, it is called the Dro Luk.

There are many other Tibetan teaching lineages of the Kalachakra. Kache Panchen Shakya Shri gave this teaching to Chak Drachom, Chal Chökyi Zangpo, and Sakya Pandita, and different lineages began with these three masters. The teachings from Tsami and the Indian master

Abhayakara were spread by the translators Rongling Lotsawa Dorje Wangchuk, Teng Lotsawa Tsultrim Jungne, Sheu Lotsawa, and Se Lotsawa Shönu Tsultrim. Each of them formed their own lineage. Rongling Lotsawa established the monastery called Rongling Soka. Chak Lotsawa Chöje Pal received the entire teaching of Kalachakra from Rahula Shribhadra and Jina Rakshita, and his system is called the Chak Luk.

Panchen Vibhutichandra gave these teachings to many great masters of Tibet, including the tantra, empowerments, explanations, and instructions. In particular, he gave these teachings, including the Six-Branched Practice of Vajra Yoga, which he had received directly from Shavaripa, to nine of his main students, such as Kodragpa and others. Several teaching lineages stemmed from Vibhutichandra's students.

It is said that there are about twenty-four different translations of the *Kalachakra Tantra*. From among the lineages just mentioned, those of Ra, Dro, Chak, Tsami, and Panchen Vibhutichandra have the entire teaching of Kalachakra, including the empowerments, explanations, and pith instructions.

The third Karmapa, Rangjung Dorje, received all of these systems from Nyedo Kunga Döndrup. Then, Rangjung Dorje wrote the *Compendium of Astrological Calculations* to explain the meaning of the Kalachakra chapter on cosmology. To explain the meaning of the inner chapter, he wrote the *Profound Inner Meaning*. To explain the meaning of the chapter on the empowerments and practices he wrote a text called *Empowerments and Practices,* and for the wisdom chapter he wrote the *Clear Essence of the Three Yogas.* He also taught these texts extensively. From there came a teaching lineage for the pointing-out instructions, the scriptural transmissions, and the completion stage Six-Branched Practice. Rangjung Dorje's lineage remains unbroken to this day, and it is considered to be the essential teaching lineage of the Kalachakra.

The Dro system mainly transmitted the practice lineage, while the Ra system mainly transmitted the teaching lineage. These two lineages seem to have come down to the Jonang tradition of Jonang Taranatha and the Shalu tradition of Butön Rinpoche. Jonang Kunkhyen, who is also called Dölpopa, spread the practice lineage and attempted to spread the teaching lineage. His fourteen students who were said to be like him did preserve the teaching system, but later the Jonang tradition had only the practice lineage; the teaching lineage did not continue.

The holder of the Shalu Monastery seat, Butön Rinchen Drup, who lived in the fourteenth century, received these teachings from the Ra lineage, and he taught the Kalachakra thirty-two times. Shalu was the name of Butön's monastery, but Shalu is also a name used for Butön himself. Butön was very independent in terms of his affiliation with the different traditions. The Sakya lineage, as well as others, like to claim Butön as part of their tradition because he was so learned and accomplished.

Butön made notes on the tantra, and Kyorpa Dönyö Pal expanded Butön's notes to write on various aspects of the Kalachakra. He wrote a text on the way to give the teachings, called the *Precious Valuable Key,* another text called *Hearing the True Meaning,* a commentary called the *Light Rays Illuminating the Essence of the Profound Meaning,* an outline called the *Ornament of Stainless Light,* and a treatise on astrology called *Skillfully Doing Whatever One Likes.* This tradition was carried on by the translator who was Butön's main student and by others, so that the Shalu teaching lineage of Kalachakra remains unbroken to this day.

It was Butön's student Kangsumpa Dechen Chökyi Palwa who gave the Kalachakra teachings to Je Rinpoche, the precious lord Tsongkhapa. Je Rinpoche himself gave these teachings only once, but many great masters assembled to hear him. In response to his teaching, at least three of those masters wrote great commentaries on Kalachakra. The commentary by Khedrup Je was finished by Shangshung Chöwang Dragpa, and a teaching system based on that commentary still exists today. In summary, the Kalachakra teaching lineages of the Jonangpa and the Shalupa, with all the empowerments, practices, and instructions, in both profound and elaborate versions, remain today as unbroken lineages.

THE THREE LOWER TANTRAS

Next is a brief description of how the teaching lineages of Kriya Tantra, Charya Tantra, and Yoga Tantra came to Tibet. In India, the teachings on Kriya and Charya Tantras had spread very widely. In particular, Buddhaguhya taught the Kriya Tantra, and Acharya Uttamabodhibhagavan taught the Charya Tantra. Jetari and others were also renowned for spreading these teachings.

In Tibet, during the earlier spreading of the dharma, King Trisong

Detsen sent We Manjushri and other translators to invite the great master Buddhaguhya to Tibet. Although Buddhaguhya could not come, he gave to the translators various teachings on the Kriya, Charya, and Yoga Tantras, including his own commentaries. The translators noted down his teachings and brought them back to Tibet, gave them to the king, and taught them so that the lower tantras spread from there.

The teachings brought from Buddhaguhya include the *Tantra Requested by Subahu,* the *General Secret Tantra,* the *Last Meditation Tantra,* and especially the *Enlightenment of Mahavairochana Tantra.* Buddhaguhya wrote a condensed, essence commentary on the latter tantra. The commentary on the *Vajrapani Empowerment Tantra* also came to Tibet at that time, and all these were translated into Tibetan.

During the later spreading of the Buddhist teachings, Bari Lotsawa Rinchen Drak brought many empowerments and permission-blessings that he spread in Tibet. Many other masters brought various teachings and practices connected with the lower tantras, but no fully established teaching lineage was brought from India. Ngorchen Dorje Chang Kunga Zangpo, the founder of the Ngor subschool of the Sakya lineage, did a strict three-year retreat in the gateway library of Sakya Monastery, and during that time he studied the tantras and their Indian commentaries. Ngorchen Dorje Chang wrote a general commentary on the Kriya and Charya Tantras, and energetically spread them.

What remain these days are the reading transmissions, practice lineages, empowerments, and initiations. For the three general kinds of Kriya Tantra, these include the Two Stainless Ones, the Establishment of the Three Samayas, the Forty-Seven Medicine Buddhas, Numerous Deities of the Ultimate Lasso, the Nine Deities of Akshobya, the Eleven-Faced One, and Vajrapani. For Charya Tantra there are the empowerments of the Hundred Deities of Fully Enlightened Vairochana, the Twenty-Two with the Two Attributes, the Five Deities of A RA PA TSA Manjughosha, and so on. Even though there are lineages of empowerments and practices, no teaching lineage has continued unbroken.

Yoga Tantra

For the Yoga Tantra in particular, there were three renowned systems in India: those of Shakyamitra, who was learned in the words; Buddhaguhya, who was learned in the meaning; and Anandagarbha, who was learned in both the words and the meaning. Buddhaguhya's lineage came to Tibet during the first dissemination of Buddhism, but it did not continue. During the later dissemination of Buddhism, only the lineage of Anandagarbha spread.

When the great translator Rinchen Zangpo went to Kashmir, he contacted many lamas from whom he received the tantras and pith instructions. He became very learned in the tantras in general, and especially in the Yoga Tantras. Most of the Yoga Tantras were already translated into Tibetan, but after comparing the earlier translations with the commentaries, he retranslated many of them. He translated many commentaries, such as the *Light of Suchness,* which is a commentary on the *Gathering of Suchness.* He taught Yoga Tantra, and established its actual practice as well as a teaching lineage. Rinchen Zangpo transmitted this lineage to his main students, including his four heart sons—Lochung Legpe Sherap, Gungshing Tsöndru Gyaltsen, Drapa Shönu Sherap, and Kyinor Jnana. Many of his students were able to hold both the teaching lineage and the practice lineage.

Podrang Shiwa Ö was another great teacher of Yoga Tantra. He is renowned for inviting Pandita Kalasha to Tibet, for doing many translations, and for teaching his students the *Vajra Pinnacle,* which is the explanatory tantra of Yoga Tantra.

Atisha gave the empowerment and oral instructions for the *Purification Tantra* to Gomi Gomchen, who in turn gave it to Kyinor Jnana and Nyalpa Nyima Sherap and others, and gradually this teaching spread widely. Zangkar Lotsawa was another translator who did a great deal of study of Yoga Tantra, and he translated the entire three sections of the *Latter Commentary.* Zangkar gave these teachings to Nyalpa Nyima Sherap, Marpa Dorje Yeshe, Nyentön Tsultrim Bar, and Chang Tsangpa Senge Gyaltsen, who were called the Four Sons of Zangkar, and from there these teachings spread extensively. Later, Tsakyawa Tönshak, Nyalpa's student Nur Nyima Özer, and Dzimpa Lochen were the three principal holders of this teaching lineage of Yoga Tantra.

In addition, Balpo Revendra taught it to Mal Lotsawa, and Vibhutichandra taught it to Yagde Semarwa, and these masters started separate lineages. Later on, when the teaching lineage of Yoga Tantra had become weak and almost broken, a master appeared with a strong karmic link to the Yoga Tantra, and he fully revived it. This was Butön Rinchen Drup, who composed sadhanas and made mandalas for many of the Yoga Tantra teachings. He wrote a great deal on it; in particular, he wrote a great commentary called the *Great Explanation of the Condensed Meaning of Yoga Tantra*.

These days there are about thirteen large and small empowerments and practices of Yoga Tantra, such as the Condensed Family of the Glorious Supreme One, the Condensed Family of the Vajra Peak, and the Vajra Space. Although the Twelve Mandalas of Purification and other empowerments and reading transmissions remain today, the teaching lineages seem to no longer exist.

4

THE HISTORY OF THE
EIGHT PRACTICE LINEAGES

I N TIBET, the land encircled by fans of snow mountains, there
have been several greater and lesser traditions of Buddhist practice lineages. The practice lineages are broadly categorized and usually
known as the Eight Great Chariots. These eight are the Ngagyur
Nyingma; the Kadam; the Lamdre, or Path with Its Result; the Marpa
Kagyu; the Shangpa Kagyu; Shije and Chod, or Pacification and Cutting; the Jordruk, or Six-Branched Practice of Vajra Yoga; and the Dorje
Sum Gyi Nyendrup, or Approach and Accomplishment of the Three
Vajras. To explain how each of these lineages developed, we will begin
with a detailed explanation of the spreading of the Nyingma, or Early
Translation school, and then give shorter accounts of the other seven
lineages, called the New Translation schools.

The Teachings of the Nyingma Lineage

The Ngagyur Nyingma, or Early Translation school, is said to come
from three lineages: the Mind Transmission of the Enlightened Beings,
the Symbolic Transmission of the Vidyadharas, and the Hearing Transmission of the Individuals.

THE MIND TRANSMISSION LINEAGE

The first is the Mind Transmission of the Enlightened Beings. The wisdom appearance of the primordial buddha Samantabhadra manifests in
the sambhogakaya as Vajradhara. In the nirmanakaya, the kaya of compassionate appearance for others, Samantabhadra manifests as the five

dhyani buddhas. The five dhyani buddhas show the highest Vajrayana teachings to the bodhisattvas on the tenth bhumi. These Vajrayana teachings are called the Yanas of the Skillful Means of Mastery, which form the yanas of Mahayoga, Anuyoga, and Atiyoga. In the heavenly realm of Akanishtha, Samantabhadra manifests in a simulated sambhogakaya form and teaches both the Sutrayana and the lower tantra teachings. The Sutrayana is composed of the Shravakayana, Pratyekabuddhayana, and Bodhisattvayana, which are called the Yanas That Lead to Renunciation. The lower tantras, composed of Kriya, Upa, and Yoga, are called the Yanas of Vedic Austerities.

The Atiyoga, or Dzogchen teachings, were collected by Vajrasattva; the Anuyoga teachings were collected by Rigdzin Kunjara; and the Mahayoga teachings were collected by Dharmevajra. These teachings were entrusted to the three great bodhisattvas who are the Lords of the Three Families—Manjushri, Avalokiteshvara, and Vajrapani, and to the dakini Lekyi Wangmo. Through these teachings, the teachers and their followers had the same level of realization. Although there was no showing of the dharma and no dharma to be shown, the teachings appeared spontaneously through the radiance of wisdom. This is why it is called the Mind Transmission of the Enlightened Beings.

THE SYMBOLIC TRANSMISSION LINEAGE

For the second lineage, the Symbolic Transmission of the Vidyadharas, the Atiyoga teachings were transmitted to the divine child Semlhagchen, then to Garap Dorje, Manjushrimitra, Shri Singha, Vimalamitra, and so on. The Anuyoga and Mahayoga teachings came from the Lords of the Three Families, who merely showed signs to the Five Excellent Beings, who immediately understood them.

THE HEARING TRANSMISSION LINEAGE

For the third lineage, the Hearing Transmission of the Individuals, which is passed from mouth to ear, the texts of the eighteen tantras dropped onto the roof of King Ja's palace through the blessings of Vajrapani. Similarly, the Anuyoga volumes dropped down into the forest of Singhala, or Sri Lanka. King Ja encountered Vajrapani face-to-face, and received teachings and empowerments from him. From there, the teachings gradually passed to Kukuraja, Indrabodhi, Simharaja, and other human vidyadharas. This is how the lineage of the Hearing Transmission arose.

This is an outline of how the three extremely profound lineages of Atiyoga and Anuyoga arose. These lineages were kept secret in India and only transmitted to certain individuals. The kings and masters together made a commitment that these teachings would not be openly transmitted. It is said that all these texts were buried in Bodhgaya and other places.

THE SIX TRANSMISSION LINEAGES

In terms of the way the inner tantra teachings came to Tibet, the great master Rongzompa categorized seven transmissions of the secret Vajrayana teachings.[1] These seven transmissions are the oral tradition or kama, the earth terma, the rediscovered terma, the mind terma, the hearing lineage, the pure vision lineage, and teachings recollected from a former life.

However, Jamgön Kongtrul Rinpoche defined six, rather than seven, lineages of transmission of the inner tantras.[2] These six are the lineages of (1) Padmasambhava, (2) Vairochana, (3) Vimalamitra, (4) Nup Sangye Yeshe, (5) Ma and Nyak, and (6) Terma. We will use Jamgön Kongtrul's presentation to briefly discuss the transmission of the Nyingma practices. According to Kongtrul, the Ngagyur Nyingma is divided into two main traditions: the kama, or oral tradition; and the terma, or hidden treasure tradition. The first five transmission lineages are kama, and the sixth lineage is terma.

The Lineage of Padmasambhava

The first transmission lineage came from Guru Padmasambhava, who was invited to Tibet by the great dharma king Trisong Detsen in the eighth century. Padmasambhava was chief among all the realized masters, and he is known by various names, such as Padmakara and Guru Rinpoche. When he came to Tibet, the only text he taught to the general public at Samye was the *Garland of Views*. However, to the extraordinary and fortunate students, including the five known as the King, Subjects, and Companion, he gave numerous teachings in many different places, such as the five great practice caves of body, speech, mind, quality, and action. There he taught the Eight Sadhana Teachings, various sadhanas of the peaceful and wrathful deities, along with their associated activities, and countless other practices.

In particular, he gave immeasurable empowerments, explanations, and pith instructions on the Clear Light Great Perfection, or Dzogchen, which is the heart essence of all dharma practices, as well as the practices of the peaceful and wrathful lama. It was not the right time for most of these instructions to be spread, so for the benefit of future beings, he buried one million named treasures and countless unnamed treasures in the five main treasure spots in the four directions and the center, and he sealed them with seven different kinds of seals.

Guru Rinpoche established retreat centers in Chimphu, Yerpa, and Chuwori, and he traveled all over Tibet with his miraculous powers, including the areas of U, Tsang, and Kham. People say that there is no place as big as a horse's hoof that he missed. He blessed all the mountains and caves as practice places. Through his instructions, countless fortunate students attained realization, including the twenty-five great siddhas of Chimphu, the fifty-five realized beings of Yang Dzong, the 108 who attained the rainbow body in Yerpa and the 108 who attained it in Chuwori, the thirty lay mantra practitioners of Sheldrak, and the twenty-five dakinis who attained the rainbow body. Guru Padmasambhava's lineage was carried on by Nyang, Pang, Khön, Nup, Ma, Rongzom, and others, and through his teachings, realized vidyadharas have continued to appear without interruption.

The Lineage of Vairochana

The second transmission lineage came from Vairochana. The great translator Vairochana of Tibet was sent by King Trisong Detsen to India, where he met the great vidyadhara Shri Singha, who is known in Tibetan as Palgyi Senge, at the top of the ninth cave in the sandalwood forest of Dhanakosha. Vairochana asked for teachings on the effortless practices, and Shri Singha brought forth the essence of his heart. These heart instructions on Dzogchen were the eighteen sections of the

Semde, or the Mind Section, with all the empowerments and instructions on the sixty tantras, as well as the White, Black, and Variegated teachings of Longde, or the Space Section. In order to evade punishment by the local king for spreading secret Dzogchen teachings, during the day Vairochana studied the Sutrayana, and at night Shri Singha taught him the Vajrayana teachings using various skillful means to prevent discovery.

Vairochana went through great difficulties and adventures to receive these teachings, to the point of risking his life fifty times. He met twenty-one great masters in India, and he emptied their heart treasures. He met Garap Dorje in the great charnel ground called the Smoky Place. From Garap Dorje he received the essential lineage of the 6,400,000 Dzogchen teachings, and in one moment he attained the siddhi of experiencing realization and liberation together. He also accomplished the ordinary siddhi of fast walking, and then returned to Tibet.

When Vairochana returned from India, he secretly gave the teachings to King Trisong Detsen and made the first Tibetan translations of the Semde teachings. There are eighteen Semde teachings, and at this point he translated the first five, which are called the Five Earlier Translations of Semde. Due to having been slandered, Vairochana was exiled to Gyalmo Tsawa Rong, an area near the border of China. Over time, five main Dzogchen lineages emanated from Vairochana: one through Yudra Nyingpo, whom Vairochana met at the monastery of Dragla Gönpo in Gyalrong; one through Sangtong Yeshe Lama, whom he met at the castle of Taktse in Tsarong; another through Pangen Sangye Gönpo, also known as Mipham Gönpo, the old man whom he met in the Dragmar Göndzong of Tong Khung Rong; one through Nyak Jnanakumara in Central Tibet; and one through the queen Liza Sherap Drönma.

For many generations, all the practitioners in Mipham Gönpo's lineage attained the rainbow body, mainly from their practice of the Dzogchen Longde teaching called the *Vajra Bridge*. Vairochana's teachings on Semde continued in two lineages, which are known as the Nyang Luk and the Aro Luk. The first of these, the Semde Nyang Luk, came from Vairochana to Nyak Yeshe Shönu, and gradually to Nyang Yeshe Jungne and the Zur family, particularly to Zurpoche and Zurchungpa, and the transmission continued from there. The second Semde lineage of Vairochana, the Aro Luk or Aro tradition, came through a great tulku from Kham named Aro Yeshe Jungne. He went to India and China and received teachings from seven great masters.

The great translator Vairochana was not only a master of the Dzogchen Semde and Longde teachings, but he translated many sutras, tantras, and texts of the other branches of knowledge. He made an immeasurable contribution to the establishment of Buddhism in Tibet.

The Lineage of Vimalamitra

The third transmission lineage stemmed from Vimalamitra. The great Indian pandita Vimalamitra came to Tibet and gave the Dzogchen teachings of Mengagde, the Pith Instruction Section, particularly to Nyang Ben Tingdzin Zangpo, the Nyang family monk who later attained the rainbow body. Vimalamitra translated the thirteen Semde teachings that Vairochana had not translated, and he did this with Yudra Nyingpo acting as the Tibetan translator. These are called the Thirteen Later Translations of Semde. His student Nyang passed on all these instructions to Lodrö Wangchuk of Ba. These instructions were concealed as treasure teachings and were later discovered by Dangma Lhungyal, who also received the oral tradition of these teachings. This lineage passed to Chetsun Senge Wangchuk, who attained the rainbow body. From there, Gyalwa Shangtön and others formed the lineage of the *Heart Essence of Vima,* or the *Vima Nyingtik.*

There are several other Nyingtik lineages besides that of Vimalamitra. Padma Ledrel Tsal discovered the terma of Padmasambhava called the *Khandro Nyingtik,* the *Heart Essence of the Dakinis.* Padma Ledrel Tsal gave these teachings to the third Karmapa, Rangjung Dorje, who established a new tradition called the *Karma Nyingtik,* or *Heart Essence of Karmapa.* Padma Ledrel Tsal also gave the *Khandro Nyingtik* teachings to Gyalse Legpa of Sho, who is more widely known as Kumaraja. Rangjung Dorje became a student of Kumaraja, as did Longchen Rabjam Tri-me Özer, or Longchenpa. Longchenpa received the *Khandro Nyingtik* from Kumaraja, and he also received the teachings on the *Vima Nyingtik.*

Part of Longchenpa's mind terma is his commentaries on the *Khandro Nyingtik* and the *Vima Nyingtik* teachings: the *Lama Yangtik* or the *Quintessence of the Lama,* the *Zabmo Yangtik* or *Profound Quintessence,* and the *Khandro Yangtik* or *Quintessence of the Dakinis.* Put together with the Nyingtik teachings he received, these are called the *Nyingtik Yabshi,* the *Four Branches of the Heart Essence,* and he taught these widely. His mind terma also include the texts grouped as his *Seven Treasuries* and his *Trilogy on Natural Ease.* Longchenpa wrote many root texts as well as commentaries, and he produced many great students who could hold the lineage. Longchen Rabjam extensively spread the Nyingtik secret teachings, and for the Nyingtik lineage he is like a second Buddha.

In general, Vairochana made the greatest contribution in establishing the Mind Section and Space Section teachings of Dzogchen in Tibet, and Vimalamitra and Padmasambhava were seminal is establishing the Pith Instruction Section of Dzogchen.

The Lineage of Nup Sangye Yeshe

The fourth transmission lineage of the three inner tantras came from Nup Sangye Yeshe. The primary teachings transmitted in this lineage are the four main scriptures of Anuyoga. These include the *Scripture of the Embodiment of the Realization of All Buddhas,* together with its empowerments, explanations, and pith instructions, and the stages of the path of Anuyoga. Nup also transmitted extensive instructions on Yamantaka, principally the form called Yamantaka Abhibhavamudra. Nup Sangye Yeshe was an accomplished master known to be on the third bhumi. He received teachings from many great teachers like the Indians Krishna Samayavajra and Virupa, Vasubhasha of Nepal, and Lotsawa Chetsen Kye of Brusha. Nup then transmitted these teachings in Tibet, and taught them especially to his four heart sons, such as So Yeshe Wangchuk, and in particular to his biological son, Yönten Gyatso, through whom Nup's lineage spread. Most of the wrathful mantra practices of Nup Sangye Yeshe were hidden as terma.

The Lineage of Ma and Nyak

The fifth transmission lineage came from Ma Rinchen Chok and Nyak Jnanakumara, and is related to the tantras and practices of Guhyagarbha, Samyak Heruka, and Vajrakilaya. Mathok Rinchen Chok was the main translator of the *Guhyagarbha Tantra,* and through his teaching of this tantra many learned and realized masters studied, practiced, established, and spread the Guhyagarbha in Tibet.

It is commonly said that the Vajrayana teachings first went to Nyak, then to Nup, and then to Zur. First, the master Nyak Jnanakumara embodied the four great rivers of teachings from Guru Padmasambhava, Vimalamitra, Vairochana, and Yudra Nyingpo. The first of these is the river of scriptural explanations, which has commentaries and discussions of difficult points. The second is the river of oral instructions, which has the pith points and the experiential, practical instructions. The third is the river of blessings and empowerments, which has the instructions on how to give the empowerments and tranmissions. The fourth is the river of ritual activities, which includes the dharmapalas and wrathful mantras.

Nyak's five main disciples had the name Pal within their full name. Among them, it was Sogpo Palgyi Yeshe who gave all of Nyak's instructions to Nup Sangye Yeshe.

Another lineage stems from the time when Namkhe Nyingpo went to India and received all the teachings on Samyak Heruka from the master Humkara. Through the practice of Samyak Heruka, Namkhe Nyingpo attained the nondual wisdom body. Namkhe Nyingpo gave the Samyak Heruka teachings to So Yeshe Jungne, who started the So lineage, and these instructions have been passed down until the present time.

There are several other lineages connected with the teachings on Samyak Heruka. Khön Lui Wangpo received the teachings on the deities Samyak Heruka and Vajrakilaya from Guru Padmasambhava, and these instructions remain in the Sakya lineage to this day. Other lineages developed from the great Lang family, including those of Khampa Kocha, the later Palgyi Senge, Odren Palgyi Wangchuk, Kharchen Palgyi Wangchuk, Drogmi Palgyi Yeshe, Nyen Palyang, and Nanam Dorje Dujom. These great masters spread their own traditions, and great holders of their lineages have continued to appear. Most of the great translators and masters of the Sarma tradition descended from these great teachers.

The Lineage of Terma

The sixth transmission lineage is the short lineage of terma. Before discussing it, I would like to say more about the long lineage of kama and the way it has been handed down.

KAMA: THE ORAL TRADITION

Kama, the undistorted long lineage, is mainly connected with the teachings of the three inner tantras of Mahayoga, Anuyoga, and Atiyoga. In Tibetan these are referred to as Do-Gyu-Sem-Sum. *Do* is short for the *Do Gongpa Dupa*, the *Scripture of the Embodiment of the Realization of All Buddhas*, which is the main Anuyoga scripture. *Gyu* is short for the Tibetan *Gyutrul Drawa*, the English *Net of Magical Display*, or the Sanskrit *Mayajala Tantra*, which is another name for the *Guhyagarbha Tantra* of Mahayoga. *Sem* stands for Semde, Longde, and Mengagde, the three sections of Atiyoga teaching; and *Sum* means "the three parts." The common lineage of the Do-Gyu-Sem-Sum is what we call "kama."

It is said that in the Land of Snow, the Vajrayana teachings of the Early Translation tradition went first to Nyak, then to Nup, and then to Zur. These are three important stages in the kama lineage transmission.

Nyak Jnanakumara

The first of these, Nyak Jnanakumara, was born in the ninth century in the area of Yarlung Chö. His father was named Nyak Tagdra Lhanang, and his mother was named Suza Drönkyi. He had the sign of moles on his neck in the shape of a crossed vajra, and he was given the name Gyalwe Lodrö. He took monastic ordination with Khenpo Shantarakshita, and he translated many sutra and tantra teachings. He received the four great rivers of teachings from four great masters: Padmasambhava, Panchen Vimalamitra, the great translator Vairochana, and Yudra Nyingpo of Gyalmorong.

Nyak Jnanakumara was ripened by Guru Padmasambhava in the mandala of the deity Guna Amrita, and as a sign of realization he was able to bring water from a rock at Sheldrak. Renowned as a holder of the lineage of the Do-Gyu-Sem-Sum, he was also very accomplished in Vajrakilaya practice, through which he was able to subdue his enemies. He attained realization through practicing the teachings of the *Hearing Lineage Vajra Bridge* and the Pith Instruction Section of Atiyoga. At the end of his life he displayed his realization by dissolving into the rainbow body. Nyak greatly benefited the Nyingma teachings and produced many exceptional students, especially the five sons named Pal. Through Sogpo Palgyi Yeshe, Nyak's lineage was transmitted to Nupchen Sangye Yeshe.

Nup Sangye Yeshe

In the middle, between Nyak and Zur, it fell upon Nup to further the transmission of the Early Translation teachings. The great Nup, Sangye Yeshe Rinpoche, lived from 832 to 962, according to the biographical history by Khetsun Zangpo. Sangye Yeshe's father was Nup Salwe Wangchuk, and his mother was Tashi Tso from the Chim family. The boy was called Dorje Tritsuk, and during his first seven years he studied reading and writing with Odren Palgyi Shönu. He was ordained as a monk by Khenchen Bodhisattva Shantarakshita. Nup Sangye Yeshe met the Nepalese master Vasudhara at Samye and received instructions from him. He received the empowerments of the Eight Sadhana Teachings from Guru Padmasambhava, and he opened the secret treasures of the four learned masters of India, Nepal, and Brusha, who were mentioned above as part of Nup's transmission lineage.

Nup Sangye Yeshe took as his teachers Nyak Jnanakumara, Nyak's eight students named Pal, especially Sogpo Palgyi Yeshe, and Shang Gyalwe Yönten, who was the chief student of both Ma and Nyak. He took to heart the teachings of the Sutrayana and Mantrayana, the outer and inner tantras, and the pith instructions of his teachers. Nup wrote many books, such as the *Armor against Darkness*, which is a commentary on the *Embodiment of the Realization of All Buddhas,* and the *Weapon of Speech That Cuts through Difficult Points,* which is a commentary on the eighty visualizations of the *Mayajala Tantra.* He also wrote renowned pith instructions on meditation and Dzogchen.

Nupchen Sangye Yeshe visited India seven times, and he brought back many teachings on Yamantaka from India and Nepal. It is widely accepted that when King Langdarma was trying to destroy Buddhism in Tibet, it was due to the activity of Nup Sangye Yeshe that the Vajrayana teachings remained intact. He spread the teachings of the three inner tantras to large numbers of students and kept the teachings from declining. According to Dudjom Rinpoche's history, Nup lived to be 113 years old, and his life ended when he attained the rainbow body through the path of the Natural Great Perfection. This master was born during the time of King Trisong Detsen and lived until the time of King Palkhor Tsen. Among his students he had one special noble son and four heart sons.

The First Zur

The way that Nup's lineage passed to Zur was that Nup's one special son, Khulungwa Yönten Gyatso, had a student named Nyang Sherap Chok, who was the student of both Khulungwa Yönten Gyatso and So Yeshe Wangchuk. Nyang Sherap Chok taught Nyang Yeshe Jungne, who taught the great Zur, or Zurpoche. This Zur is the third lineage holder in the group of Nyak, Nup, and Zur. Zurpoche also received teachings from Tongtsap Phagpa Rinpoche, who was one of the four heart sons of Nup, so it can be said that there was only one lama between the great Nup and the great Zur.

There is a Tibetan saying that finally, it came down to Zur to carry on the transmission of the Early Translation teachings. It is also said that the root of the later spreading of the Nyingma teachings was firmly planted by Lhaje Ugja Lungpa. Lhaje Ugja Lungpa is one of Zurpoche's names, and means "the venerable one from Owl Valley," which is a place where he meditated.

There were three generations of the Zur family who were famous lineage teachers. The first Zur, Zurpoche Shakya Jungne or Lhaje Ugja Lungpa, was considered to be the root, and the second Zur, Deshek Gyawopa, nurtured the growth of the branches. Then, the third Zur, Sangdak Drophugpa, made the leaves and fruit appear.

Lhaje Ugja Lungpa's father was Zur Sherap Jungne, who is said to have descended from the gods, and his mother was Dewa Cham, who was his father's patroness. Zurpoche was born in Do Kham, in a place called Yardzong or Yarmo. According to Khetsun Zangpo's history, he was born in the tenth century.

Zurpoche studied reading, writing, and the Guhyagarbha practice with his father. He was ordained by Lachen Gongpa Rabsal, one of the early holders of the Lower Vinaya lineage. With his grandfather, Zur Rinchen Gyatso, he studied the three pitakas and the outer and inner Vajrayana practices. Zurpoche went to central Tibet, and when practicing in Yarlung he awakened to the real experience of the unexcelled Mahayana. As predicted in his dreams, he received the teachings on Guhyagarbha and Semde from Nyang Yeshe Jungne of Chölung. There were many other learned and accomplished lamas with whom he studied the three inner tantras, and whom he pleased with his pure dedication and offerings. In particular, he studied with Che Shakya Chok, Thogar Namkha De, Dre Trochung of Nyangtö, Shutön Sönam Shakya, Tongtsap Phagpa Jangchup, Gyatön Lodrö, Kadö Yeshe Nyingpo, Nyenak Wangdrak, and Che Shakya Gyal.

The great Zur became very learned in the Tripitaka, the tantras, and the tenets of the various Buddhist schools, and his learning deepened into experience and realization. Then, he made the teachings available to others by joining the root tantras and their explanatory tantras, the root texts and their commentaries, the tantras and their practice manuals, and the practice manuals and the rituals.

Zurpoche practiced on Samyak Heruka in the deep forest of Nagsalchen, and he developed confidence from mastering the visualization, mantra recitation, and completion stage practices. The knot in the channel of his throat chakra was released and his intelligence became boundless. He received the empowerments and instructions of sixty-four mandalas from Rok Shakya Jungne of Chimphu. As predicted by the dakinis, he went to Tanak and practiced in a cave that faced east and had a nest of owls in it. There he had a vision of the nine deities of Samyak. After that he was called Lama Ugpa Lungpa, the Lama of the Owl Valley.

Zurpoche's main students were called the Four Peaks and the Ultra Peak, which made five main students. Among his many students there were 108 who were great meditators and attained realization. The Four Peaks were Zurchungpa, or the Lesser Zur, also named Sherap Dragpa, who was the peak in relation to the view; Menyak Khyungdrak, who was the peak in terms of teaching the *Guhyagarbha Tantra*; Shang Göchung, the peak of wisdom and compassion; and Zangom Sherap

Gyalpo, the peak in terms of meditation practice. The Ultra Peak was Tsak Lama, who was the peak of manly courage as well as the peak of the dharma.

In the area of Ugpa Lung, Zurpoche miraculously constructed an image of Shri Heruka. In Drophuk he established a monastery and extensive dharma activities. When Zurpoche got a hundred pieces of gold from nonhuman beings, he gave them to Drogmi Lotsawa to offer to the panditas in India. When he was sixty-one years old, he entrusted his teaching responsibilities to Zurchungpa, and then he dissolved into the heart of the image of Shri Heruka.

The Second Zur

The second Zur was Zurchungpa Sherap Dragpa. Among the students called the Four Peaks, he was like the leader of the elephants. His father was Zur Thagpa Gomchen, who was the son of Atsara. Atsara was the son of the elder brother of Zurpoche's father, Zur Sherap Jungne. Zurchungpa's mother was named Sherap Kyi. Zurchungpa was born amid wondrous signs in the Wood Tiger year, 1014 in the Western calendar. When he was seven years old he could read and write, and when he was nine he could do the practices of the peaceful and wrathful deities. When he was thirteen years old he had a wife who often fought with him. This aroused his revulsion for samsara, and he ran away to study with Zurpoche. When Zurpoche asked his family name, Zurchungpa thought it might sound presumptuous to say he was a close relative of his lama, so he said, "I am a very small Zur," or Zur-chung-chung in Tibetan. So, after that he was called Zurchungpa, the Lesser Zur.

At first he was very poor and he used to eat the thrown-out tormas. His teacher saw this and told him to come eat in his kitchen. But Zurchungpa decided that he would not presume to eat the lama's food, and he continued to endure that hardship. He exerted himself in study, reflection, and meditation, and soon the expanse of his wisdom burst forth. Limitless experiences, realizations, and qualities arose in him. According to the command of his teacher, he began living with a wealthy female practitioner and her daughter. This woman contributed to his support, so he was able to obtain all the empowerments and oral instructions.

Zurchungpa wrote down the teachings in their entirety. Sometimes when he was circumambulating a stupa, he was seen walking a foot above the ground; and when he was staying on the mountaintops, the nonhumans gave him food. He effortlessly accomplished whatever he had in mind. When he was explaining the *Scripture of the Embodiment of the Realization of All Buddhas,* at one point there were about three hundred people studying together. Since Zurchungpa did whatever Zurpoche asked him to do, he accomplished the service of his teacher.

After receiving three subsequent predictions to do so, Zurchungpa gave his shedras, or monastic colleges, to his three students known as the Three Incompetent Ones. Then he went to Drak Gyawo Gudu, the Group of Nine Dark Rocks, and took his practice to heart. After that he was called Deshek Gyawopa, the Enlightened One of the Dark Place. He practiced there for fourteen years. Appearances, conceptual mind, and suchness merged in One Taste, and he gained complete realization. He was able to pass unobstructed through rocks, earth, and mountains. He could fly in the sky like a bird, and he could control the five elements. Intellectuals came to debate with him, but he subdued them with his miraculous powers, and they became his students.

It is said that Zurchungpa was so radiant and dignified that all the Vajrayana practitioners in Tibet would prostrate to him, and they would not consider taking a higher seat. There is a story about a feast where the practitioners of the Early and New schools came together. Gö Lotsawa Khugpa Lhatse told the other followers of the Sarma tradition, "That kind of respect is okay for the Nyingmapas, but we Sarmapas need not prostrate to him or sit below him." However, right before the feast began, Gö himself prostrated to Zurchungpa. After the feast his fellow monks asked Gö why he did that, since he was the one who had told them not to do so. Gö said, "It is because when I went near Zurchungpa, I felt he was the bhagavan Shri Heruka in person. I did not perceive him as an ordinary human being."

Zurchungpa looked after three institutes for practice and study: Ugpa Lung, Drophuk, and Drak Gyawo. In this way he illuminated the Vajrayana teachings of the Early Translation tradition. His students were known as the Four Pillars, the Eight Beams, the Sixteen Ledges, the Thirty-Two Cornices, the Two Great Meditators, the Man Who Grumbled a Lot about Being Unappreciated, the Two Ordinary Ones, the Two Young Steeds, the Three Incompetent Ones, and there were many more.

The Four Pillars were Gungbu Kyotön Shakya Yeshe, the pillar of the Semde teachings of Atiyoga; Yangkhye Lama of Kyong Lung, the pillar of the Anuyoga teachings; Len Shakya Zangpo of Chubar, the pillar of the Mahayoga teachings; and Datik Joshak of Nagmo Ri, the pillar of activities and practice. The Eight Beams were Mathogpa, Kyotön Chöseng, Len Shakya Jangchup, Shakring of Tsak, Nuptön Bagma, Upa Kathor, Shutön Dadrak, and Tsetön Changbar.

With his first wife, Zurchungpa had two children, a boy named Shakya Dorje Bar and a girl named Shakya Cham, who carried on his family line. Before he passed away he had another son, Zur Shakya Senge, or Sangdak Drophugpa, who became renowned as the Third Zur.

After accomplishing his life work, Zurchungpa passed away in Drak Gyawo, in the Wood Male Tiger year of 1074, at the age of sixty-one. His parinirvana was accompanied by lights, sounds, and earthquakes, and he went to the City of the Vajra Array in the pure realm of Akanishtha.

The Third Zur

The Third Zur, Sangdak Drophugpa, was like the source of the river of teachings of the Guhyagarbha in Tibet. He was the son of Zurchungpa and Damo Tsugtor Cham. His mother was the sister of Datik Joshak, one of Zurchungpa's Four Pillars. He was born in the Wood Tiger year, 1074, and lived until 1134. At the time of his birth, all the Four Pillars had wonderful dreams. Zurchungpa predicted that his son would have very positive energy and greatly benefit beings, and he gave him the name Shakya Senge.

His father died when Sangdak Drophugpa was eight months old, so he was raised by his mother and his uncle. He stayed in Daphur for fifteen years. He studied with all the Four Pillars in succession and received all of his father's teachings, including the main texts of the three inner tantras. When he was nineteen he was enthroned and from then on his activities flourished. The Third Zur invited learned and realized lamas to his area, and he completed his studies with them. He practiced for a long time in Drophuk and perfected the four binding forces in the creation and completion stage practices, becoming inseparable from the body, speech, and mind of Shri Heruka.

From an early age, the Third Zur was very brilliant and could over-power everybody. He received teachings from Pha Dampa Sangye of India, who encouraged him and predicted that Sangdak Drophugpa would be very influential in the spread of Buddhism. One time, when Sangdak Drophugpa was giving instructions to the artists on painting a thangka of Vajrapani, he told them, "Draw it like this," and mani-fested himself as Vajrapani. Another time, when he was sitting on a throne without a back rest and all his students were sitting around him, all of them could see his face. These are just a couple of examples of his miraculous powers.

Among his students were more than a thousand great geshes who could hold the dharma and were the heads of their own monasteries. During his dharma teachings in summer and winter, there were about five hundred people in each line of students, and in fall and spring there were about three hundred per line. His teaching assemblies usu-ally had about ten thousand students; they say that people would pay a gold coin to get a good seat. He had abundant qualities of wisdom, compassion, and power. He mainly taught the *Guhyagarbha Tantra*, and by encouraging the study and practice of it, he made the Vajrayana teachings of the Nyingma lineage arise like the sun in the sky.

At the end of his life, when it was time to display his final activity, the Third Zur went to the top of the Lharidong Mountain near Dro-phuk. He went with his students known as the Four Teachers and they made a large feast offering. Sangdak Drophugpa gave them many instructions and told them, "Please don't grieve when I am no longer here. This time I am not giving up my body, but I am taking it to the realm of the vidyadharas. This will be very auspicious for you, causing both my bodily lineage and teaching lineage to prosper." Then, he sang a vajra song and ascended into the sky, going higher and higher until he disappeared. The Four Teachers felt like their hearts were being ripped out, and they cried, rolled on the earth, and called out his name. Then, Sangdak Drophugpa came back down like a bird descending to earth. He said to his students, "I asked you not to do that and I already gave you plenty of instructions. You didn't listen to me. Now my line-age will experience some inauspicious consequences." He remained until the next year, when he passed away in the Wood Tiger year, at the age of sixty-one.

The Third Zur had twelve main students. Four were called the Four Black Ones because of the word *Nak* in their names: Chetön Gyanak, Zurnak Khorlo, Ngang-nak Dowo, and Danak Tsugtor. Similarly, four with the Tibetan word *Tön* in their names were called the Four Teachers: Nyitön Chöseng, Japtön Dorgön, Shangtön, and Gyatön. The last four of the twelve were called the Four Grandfathers: Tsangpa Jitön, Yutön Horpo, Pangtön Chagkyu, and Upa Chöseng.

Through the activities of these three generations of the Zur family, the kama teachings spread to a large number of students, who in turn spread the Vajrayana kama teachings among countless people in all directions. However, as the times degenerated, the Nyingma tradition declined. Then, the time came when the aspirations of the great translator Vairochana and his heart son ripened. This was when Minling Terchen Gyurme Dorje and his brother, Lochen Dharma Shri, compiled the Nyingma lineage instructions, particularly the Do-Gyu-Sem-Sum, from all directions. Once again the victory banner of these teachings was raised aloft and did not decline for a long time.

Minling Terchen Gyurme Dorje

To tell a little about Minling Terchen Gyurme Dorje, who is also known as Terdak Lingpa, his father was Sangdak Thrinle Lhundrup from the Nyö clan and his mother was Lhadzin Yangchen Drölma. He was born at Minling amid auspicious signs on the tenth day of the second month of the Fire Dog year, 1646, and he lived until 1714. From the time he was young there were clear signs that he was a bodhisattva. When he was four years old he received the empowerment of the Eight Sadhana Teachings Secret Perfection from his father. He realized the mandala in every appearance and activity, and he saw the lama and the main deity as inseparable. When he was ten years old he received the empowerment of the *Eight Sadhana Teachings, the Assembly of the Sugatas*. At that time, in an experience of clear light, he saw Guru Padmasambhava giving him the empowerment. By the power of these blessings he was able to see all appearing objects as illusions. From that time onward, he acted as his father's representative and performed his father's activities.

When he was eleven years old, Minling Terchen Gyurme Dorje was

ordained by the fifth Dalai Lama. He received profound empowerments and instructions from the fifth Dalai Lama, his father, and sixteen great holders of the teachings. He also received various profound
teachings from thirty-five great teachers. Included in his record of
received teachings are the Tripitaka, the four orders of tantra, and the
conventional sciences in general; and in particular, the Do-Gyu-Sem-
Sum; the *Samayoga Tantra;* Samyak and Vajrakilaya combined; the
Yamantanka cycle of teachings; the kama lineage up to that time; the
termas on Guru Yoga, Dzogchen, and Avalokiteshvara; the most
renowned teachings of the tantras, both general and specific; most of
the Vajrayana empowerments and instructions of the Nyingma and
Sarma traditions; and the scriptures of the entire Kangyur, which are
the root of all of the Buddhist teachings.

In particular, Minling Terchen Gyurme Dorje studied intensively
the teachings of Longchen Rabjam, through which he attained unobstructed intelligence and cut through all misunderstandings about phenomena. Dagtön Chögyal Tendzin and Dodrak Rigdzin Chogi Tulku
gave him all the empowerments and instructions, as well as his secret
name, Gyurme Dorje.

Minling Terchen Gyurme Dorje discovered many terma teachings.
When he was eighteen years old, he revealed the terma of the *Heart
Drop of the Vidyadharas.* When he was twenty-two years old, he discovered the terma of *Yamantaka Who Conquers the Arrogant Ones.* When he
was thirty-one, he revealed the teachings on Guru Dragpo, or wrathful
Guru Rinpoche, as well as teachings on Vajrasattva and Atiyoga. When
he was thirty-five years old, he discovered the Avalokiteshvara terma
called the *Great Compassionate One Who Embodies All the Buddhas.* These
are just a few of his treasure findings.

At various times in his life Minling Terchen Gyurme Dorje did
retreats in solitary places. Altogether he practiced about thirty-five different mandalas of the Sarma and Nyingma traditions. His main
emphasis in practice was on the quick path of the creation stage, completion stage, and Dzogchen. He stabilized the creation stage practice
so that all his activities proceeded without obstruction. Through his
completion stage practice, the movements of his channels, wind energy,
and essence element were purified in the central channel so that the
wisdom of great bliss blazed in a hundred directions. In his practice of

Dzogchen, he had the realization of naturally occurring nonduality, so that he was free from the characteristics of perceiver and perceived. His fixation on the reality of samsara and nirvana collapsed. He gained mastery of the clear light all the time, so there was no difference between meditation and postmeditation. All appearances and activities arose as the play of primordial wisdom.

Minling Terchen Gyurme Dorje gave empowerments of many teachings of kama and terma, including his own termas, and he freely gave instructions on the profound path to everyone. When he was thirty-one years old he traveled to many places and sowed the seeds of liberation and realization in countless beings. From the age of thirty-two, he continued to give deep and extensive teachings. After turning thirty-eight, he gave his students the most essential teachings and did whatever he could to ripen them. The main way he did this was by forcefully making his students experience their self-arising primordial wisdom. You can find details about this in his outer, inner, and secret biographies.

To make the dharma teachings last a long time, Minling Terchen Gyurme Dorje compiled the profound teachings of the three inner tantras. He did a great deal of writing—he collected teachings that had been scattered, he straightened out those that were convoluted, he revealed hidden ones, and he wrote out the empowerments, practices, rituals, and instruction manuals of both the kama and terma of the Nyingma tradition. Minling Terchen Gyurme Dorje also arranged to have block-prints made of all his writings. There is a list of all his writings that was compiled by his son Padma Gyurme Gyatso.

Minling Terchen Gyurme Dorje used all the offerings he received to support the sangha of Mindroling Monastery, to construct sacred images, and to propagate the teachings. In this way, he upheld the teachings of the Early Translation school and spread them for a long time. When he was sixty-nine years old, in the first month of the Wood Horse year, 1714, he showed signs of ill health. Omens began to appear, such as the pleasing sound of gyaling horns from the western direction, and a sweet fragrance in his room. On the second day of the following month, when the sun had fully risen, he took seven steps in the eastern direction, sat in the vajra posture, and spontaneously spoke this verse as a final instruction:

Appearances are deities, sounds are mantras, and awareness is the
*   dharmakaya.*
These are the pervasive kayas and wisdom displays of the buddhas.
May practitioners of the profound and secret Great Perfection
Remain inseparable from the innermost, one-taste awareness of
*   wisdom mind.*

Then, Minling Terchen Gyurme Dorje said, "Now the dakinis have come to receive me," and he made a gesture of playing the hand drum and bell. He adjusted his eyes into a particular gaze, and in an instant he passed away into a pure realm. At his cremation, his skull came out intact, along with relic pills, buddha images, and other marvelous signs of his attainment.

Lochen Dharma Shri

The younger brother of the Minling Terchen Gyurme Dorje, Lochen Dharma Shri, also reached a very high level of scholarship and realization. He thoroughly studied the sutras and tantras and all branches of knowledge, and he practiced all the teachings of Sarma and Nyingma, and kama and terma, especially the teachings of the three inner tantras. He repeatedly taught all the teachings he had received, and he wrote many important texts. Lochen Dharma Shri is especially renowned for causing the Vinaya vows to spread further than before. He was a learned and accomplished being who brought immense benefit to the Vajrayana teachings of the Nyingma tradition.

The two Terchen brothers had a large number of great students. These included the fifth Dalai Lama and Desi Sangye Gyatso, who were their main patrons. Other important students were Sakya Dagchen, Chabdo Phagpa Lha and his retinue, Drigung Könchok Thrinle Zangpo, Taglung Tendzin Sizhi Namgyal, Druk Thamche Khyenpa, Gompo Chogtrul and his family lineage, Tsurphu Gyaltsap, Treho, and Lhodrak Sungtrul with his heart son and family lineage. There were many tulkus, such as Öchok Tulku, Thangdrok Tulku, Bönlung Tulku, Yöndo Tulku, Khampa Tulku, Drepa Tulku, Palri Tulku, and Zanglakhar Tulku. Also notable were Dalai Huthoktu Ngawang Shedrup Gyatso,

Rongpa Dzogchenpa, Khampa Dzogchen Padma Rigdzin, Kathok Gyalse, Kongpo Bakha Kukye, Lhatsun Gangshar Rangdröl, Nawo Dungyu, and Merak Lama.

There were also many people of very high rank, many who were learned in the scriptures and reasoning, many experienced and accomplished practitioners, and many great chiefs and lesser chiefs. Besides countless well-known people there were many nomads and farmers, both rich and poor, who studied with the two Terchen brothers. Many of the learned ones became lineage holders, and the students of these great students spread all over Tibet. Particularly noteworthy as a holder of this tradition is the great siddha Dzogchen Padma Rigdzin, who established his seat at Rudam Chöling and founded Dzogchen Monastery, and from there the Minling teachings spread throughout Kham.

From the Minling Terchen brothers, the Minling Terchen family lineage passed to the father and son, Gyalse Rinchen Namgyal and Khenchen Orgyen Tendzin Dorje, who spread the Minling tradition to the large monasteries in Kham, including Kathok, Palyul, Shechen, and Dzogchen. There were also many streams of this lineage which extended from the area of Gyalmorong in the east to the areas of Amdo and Golok in the north. From Khenchen Orgyen Tendzin Dorje came the Minling throne-holders Gyurme Thrinle Namgyal and his son Gyurme Padma Wangyal. Then, the lineage passed to his sister Jetsunma Thrinle Chödrön, to the throne-holder Gyurme Sangye Kunga, and to Jetsunma Tendzin Paldrön. These last three masters gave many teachings to Jamgön Kongtrul and Jamyang Khyentse Wangpo, so they were especially helpful in continuing the teachings. In addition to these, there are countless other lineages that stemmed from the Minling Terchen brothers.

Terma: The Hidden Treasures

Next is an overview of the history of the terma teachings. The terma tradition began with Buddha Shakyamuni, who mentioned treasure findings in several sutras. For example, he said in the Mahayana sutra, the *Sutra of the Samadhi That Gathers All Merit:*

Bodhisattva Vimalatejas, for the sake of the great bodhisattvas who desire the dharma, there are treasures of teachings kept in the mountains, in the ridges, and in the trees. Dharanis and countless entrances to the dharma will be made into books and come into their hands.

He also mentioned terma in the *Sutra of the Play of the River:*

Hide the dharma scriptures I taught
As treasures from one mind to another,
Or put them in the womb of the earth.
Why? Because the heretics are strong
And the meaning could be distorted. Beware!
Do not stop the flow of the river.

There are many other similar quotations.

The Types of Terma: Earth Terma

There are three types of terma: earth terma, mind terma, and pure vision teachings. The first of these is the earth terma. Guru Rinpoche, who was very skillful in training beings according to their needs, gave, in addition to the general teachings, countless teachings related to the three yogas of Mahayoga, Anuyoga, and Atiyoga, including their practice manuals and sadhanas. The dakini Yeshe Tsogyal collected all these teachings and held them in her memory with perfect recall. She set them down in the dakini script on five types of yellow paper, and put them in different types of treasure containers and sealed them so that they would not be destroyed by the five elements. Along with Guru Rinpoche or his direct students, she concealed the treasure teachings in specific terma places and entrusted them to the terma guardians for protection. Especially after Guru Rinpoche left Tibet, Yeshe Tsogyal buried innumerable treasures all over the land of Tibet.

In addition, terma was hidden by other students of Padmasambhava, such as Panchen Vimalamitra, King Trisong Detsen and his sons, the great translator Vairochana, Nup Sangye Yeshe, Namkhe Nyingpo,

Nyak Jnanakumara, Nanam Dorje Dujom, and Nyangben Tingdzin Zangpo. Guru Padmasambhava predicted that fortunate beings would be able to discover these teachings in the future. He focused his mind on fortunate sons and daughters, made aspirations, and gave them the mind-mandate transmission to find the terma. In later times, their emanations have appeared as sublime vidyadharas, their powerful aspiration prayers have ripened, and their karmic connections have been awakened. When the protectors of the terma have urged them, the vidyadharas have revealed those treasures of the dharma, as well as treasures of wealth and medicine, in vajra rocks, in lakes, in containers, and other places.

The Types of Terma: Mind Terma

The second type of terma is mind terma. The Buddha said in a sutra:

> Manjushri, the four elements come from the treasure-house of space. In the same way, all the teachings come from the treasure-house of the mind of the buddhas. Therefore, learn how to enjoy the meaning of the treasure findings.

In accordance with what was just said, noble beings who are beyond samsara can have the treasures of the dharma come forth from the space of their minds. Another sutra says:

> If you find confidence in the ultimate meaning, then a hundred thousand treasures of the dharma will issue forth from your mind.

Throughout the regions of India, Nepal, and Tibet, there have been immeasurable instructions that arose from profound mind terma.

Pure Vision Teachings

The third type of terma is the Pure Vision teachings. The Buddha said in the *Sutra of the Samadhi That Gathers All Positive Deeds:*

For great bodhisattvas who desire the dharma, who are respectful and have excellent intentions, the buddhas show their faces to them and cause them to hear the dharma, even if they live in other worlds.

In the perception of noble beings there is no negativity; everything is pure. They can discuss the dharma with an infinite number of deities, and countless profound instructions arise from that. Those who are worthy of spreading those instructions to fortunate students do so through their pure vision. Many Pure Vision teachings are described in the life stories of the Indian panditas and siddhas, in the biographies of great Tibetan masters of the Nyingma and Sarma traditions without partiality, and among other Tibetan tertöns and siddhas.

The Tertöns

The first tertön, or treasure revealer, in Tibet was Sangye Lama. He was a contemporary of the great translator Rinchen Zangpo, who lived from 957 to 1055. There are a large number of tertöns, including those known as "the hundred major tertöns." Chief among them are Nyangral Nyima Özer and Guru Chökyi Wangchuk, who are called the Two Chief Tertöns, and their terma teachings are known as the Upper and Lower Treasures. Of the main tertöns with the name of Lingpa, there are eight in particular—Sangye Lingpa, Dorje Lingpa, Rinchen Lingpa, Padma Lingpa, Ratna Lingpa, Kunkyong Lingpa, Dongak Lingpa, and Tenyi Lingpa. There are the tertöns who discovered the Northern Terma, such as Rigdzin Gökyi Demtruchen, and the twenty-one tertöns called Nuden, principally Dudul Nuden Dorje. In recent times, since Khyentse Wangpo, Jamgön Kongtrul, and Chogyur Lingpa discovered their terma in the nineteenth century, genuine tertöns have continued to appear in Tibet, in accordance with Guru Rinpoche's predictions, such as this one:

In the age of degeneration, as the Buddhadharma ends, it will be nurtured by the terma teachings.

The predictions seem to say that the terma teachings will continue to benefit beings and will not end until the teachings of Maitreya Buddha appear.

In this way countless terma teachings have come down to the present degenerate age, when people are obsessed with materialism. Fearing that these teachings would be lost, Jamgön Kongtrul made the collection called the *Treasury of Precious Terma*. Because of this collection we still have the opportunity to enjoy the terma teachings of the great tertöns and lesser tertöns, even after the extensive destruction of the Buddhist teachings in Tibet. It is important to realize that this is due to the great kindness of the two Jamgön gurus, Kongtrul and Khyentse.

The History of the Kadampa Tradition

Jowo Je Atisha

The great learned and realized master and founder of the Kadampa school Jowo Je Atisha, also called Dipankara Shri Jnana, was invited to Tibet, with great difficulty, by the king Lha Lama and his nephew. Atisha lived from 982 to 1054, and he came to Tibet in 1042. At that time, Langdarma, the king with mistaken views, had decimated the Buddhadharma that had been established by the three previous generations of dharma kings in Tibet. The teachings of the Vinaya and Sutrayana had deteriorated, and even the Vajrayana was practiced in a distorted way. In order to stop the mistaken practices and illuminate the stainless dharma again, Jowo Je Atisha wrote the treatise called the *Lamp of the Path of Awakening*. This book describes the stages of the path for the three types of individuals, based on teachings such as the *Ornament of the Mahayana Sutras* and the *Bodhisattva Stages*. In Atisha's text, the view is Madhyamaka, the practice is Vinaya, and the instructions are mainly on bodhichitta. All the *ka*, or Buddha's teachings, are *dam,* or instructions, for helping an individual to become enlightened. This is how the name *Kadam* shows the style of teaching that Atisha established in Tibet.

It is said that the holders of the Kadampa lineage have their bodies adorned with the four deities, their speech adorned with the three pitakas, and their minds adorned with the three trainings. The four deities refer to Shakyamuni as the founder of the teachings, Avalokiteshvara as the deity of compassion, Tara as the deity for protection from outer fears, and Achala as the deity to dispel inner obstacles. These are the four deities practiced by the Kadampas. The three pitakas of Vinaya, Sutra, and Abhidharma correspond with the three trainings of discipline, meditation, and wisdom, so there are said to be Seven Divine Dharmas practiced in the Kadampa tradition.

ATISHA'S MAIN STUDENTS

Chief among the Tibetan students of Jowo Je Atisha were Khu, Ngok, and Drom, who were renowned as emanations of the three main bodhisattvas—Avalokiteshvara, Manjushri, and Vajrapani. The first of these was the teacher from the Khu family, Khutön Tsöndru Yungdrung. Khutön was famous for reviving the monastery of Yarlung Sölnak Thangpoche. This monastery had been established by the master Drumer, who lived during the time of the great Vinaya teacher Lu-me, at the beginning of the later spreading of the dharma in Tibet. Khu made this monastery his center and nurtured the teachings there.

The second of Atisha's main students was Ngok Legpe Sherap. In the Iron Pig year, 1071, Ngok established the dharma center of Sangphu Neuthok and cultivated the teachings there. Later on, this institute was developed further by his nephew, the great translator Ngok Loden Sherap, and it became the source of all the Tibetan shedras, or centers for advanced study.

Atisha's third main student was the teacher from Drom named Dromtön Gyalwe Jungne. He established Radreng Monastery in the north, and he nurtured the dharma there. He had countless students, but the main ones were the great spiritual masters Putowa, Chengawa, and Phuchungwa, who were called the Three Kadampa Brothers.

The first of these, Puto Rinchen Sal, received the transmission and responsibility to hold the teaching lineage of the six Kadampa treatises. These six treatises are the *Jatakamala* and *Udanavarga*—the stories and sayings of Shakyamuni Buddha, which are the treatises which generate devotion; the *Compendium of All Practices* and the *Way of the Bodhisattva* by Shantideva, which are the treatises on conduct; and the *Stages of the*

Bodhisattva Path by Asanga and the *Ornament of the Mahayana Sutras* by Maitreya, which are the treatises on meditation. Putowa gathered many students, including his main students Langthangpa and Sharawa, who were like the sun and moon together. From among Sharawa's students, Tumtön Lodrö Drak established Narthang Monastery, where the first edition of the Buddhist canon was published in Tibet. The masters of Narthang Monastery took these teachings as their main focus, so they were known as the Scriptural Kadampas.

The second of Dromtön's main students, Chengawa Tsultrim Bar, received the transmission and responsibility for the oral tradition of instruction, which was primarily the instruction on the four noble truths. His students, such as Jayulwa, inherited a special practice lineage called Chenga Kagyu. These days that lineage has also been incorporated into the Dagpo Kagyu lineage.[3]

The third, Phuchungwa Shönu Gyaltsen, received the transmission and responsibility for the pith instructions of the sixteen circles of the Kadampa. As supports he received the empowerments, instructions, and secret teachings for Atisha's *Lamp of the Path of Awakening*. This is the main text of the Kadampas, and they called it the "precious book." He passed on these instructions to Tapkawa Rinchen Gyaltsen. The teachings were passed down in a single transmission, to one student in each generation, until the time of Narthangpa Shönu Lodrö, when the secrecy was lifted and the teachings spread. Pal Tsuglak Trengwa received these from Nyugpa Panchen, and from him these teachings entered the Karma Kamtsang lineage of the Kagyupas. These particular teachings also went from Lochen Thugje Palwa to the first Dalai Lama, Gyalwa Gendun Drup, so they were also incorporated by the Gelugpa lineage.

Another important student of Atisha was Nagtso Lotsawa Tsultrim Gyalwa, who brought Jowo Je Atisha to Tibet, and then served him for nineteen years while receiving many instructions. Nagtso Lotsawa also received teachings from Jnana Akara and others, and his main lineage is called the Nagtso Kagyu.

Rongpa Chagsorwa, who was a student of Dromtön and several other teachers, also received many Vajrayana instructions from Nagtso Lotsawa. According to a prediction, Rongpa Chagsorwa built a monastery in Rong Lagsor. From there Jadulwa and the students called the Four Sons of Rongpa spread the lineage teachings of Nagtso throughout Kham and central Tibet.

In general, the Kadam tradition has been continually upheld by all four of the great schools of Buddhism in Tibet.

The Gelugpa Tradition

TSONGKHAPA LOZANG DRAGPA

The Gelugpa or Gedenpa tradition, which is also sometimes called the New Kadampa, was begun by Tsongkhapa Lozang Dragpe Pal, who was an emanation of Manjushri. Tsongkhapa is renowned for his unassailable wisdom and compassion, and he was like a second Buddha coming to this world. By the fourteenth century, the number of practitioners who held only the Kadampa tradition had declined, and Tsongkhapa revived those teachings. Although he mainly taught the scriptural tradition of the Kadampas, his instructions incorporated the profundity of all three aspects of the Kadampa teachings. His book, the *Great Exposition on the Stages of the Path to Enlightenment,* was taken by his followers as his heart teaching.

To tell a little about his life, Jamgön Lozang Dragpa was born in Amdo, in a place called Tsongkha, in the Female Fire Rat year of 1357, on the first day of the tenth month in the Tibetan calendar. His birth was accompanied by many wondrous signs. As soon as he was born, the realized master Chöje Döndrup Rinchen predicted that Tsongkhapa was an emanation of Vajrabhairava, or wrathful Manjushri. When Lozang Dragpa was three years old, he received the full upasaka vows from the fourth Karmapa, Rölpe Dorje, who named him Kunga Nyingpo. When he was seven years old, he was ordained as a monk by Chöje Döndrup Rinchen and given the name Lozang Dragpa. Tsongkhapa went on to study extensively with Chöje Döndrup Rinchen.

When he was seventeen years old, he went to central Tibet and studied various topics for many years. He studied medicine at Tsal Gungthang, and Sanskrit with Lotsawa Rinchen Namgyal and Sazang Mati Panchen. Tsongkhapa studied poetry and other outer sciences with Lotsawa Namkha Zangpo, and he also received a vast number of teachings on the inner sciences. From Rendawa Shönu Lodrö he received teachings on Madhyamaka, Pramana, Prajnaparamita, the *Treasury of Abhidharma,* and the *Compendium of Abhidharma.* In Kyormolung he received the Vinaya teachings, and from Lodrak Namkha Gyaltsen he received the graded path of the Kadampa tradition. He received Drilpupa's instructions on Chakrasamvara from Lama Dampa, and teachings on Kalachakra from Gongsumpa Dechen Chökyi Palwa. He received the four tantras, such as Guhyasamaja, from Khyungpo Lhapa Shönu Sönam.

He reflected deeply on all these topics and became a great scholar. Not leaving it at that, when he was thirty-six years old, he and his eight pure followers went off to live as hermits. He made supplications to the lama and Manjushri as inseparable, and he reflected on the great Buddhist treatises and practiced them one-pointedly. He was held closely by the compassion of his lama and his special deity, and he was especially blessed by Nagarjuna and his spiritual son Aryadeva. When Tsongkhapa looked at the *Buddhapalita,* the commentary on the eighth chapter of Nagarjuna's *Wisdom, a Root Text of the Middle Way,* he demonstrated that he completely understood the meaning of emptiness. In this way, Tsongkhapa completely mastered all the qualities of study and realization.

In order to bring others to the path, he devised a system based on precise practice of the Vinaya teachings, supported by the instructions and vows of the Bodhisattvayana and the Vajrayana. These became the ground for his students' practice. In the place called Mönkhar Tashi Dong, he taught unerringly every day on fifteen different great treatises. Then, he went to Sangphu, Sakya, and Tsedong and debated on the five great treatises.[4] He became famous throughout the land for his victories in debate.

Tsongkhapa wrote about eighteen volumes in all. Due to the blessings he received from Atisha Dipankara and his students, as well as from many panditas and siddhas of India, he wrote the *Great Exposition of the Stages of the Path to Enlightenment,* as well as a smaller version called the *Short Exposition of the Stages of the Path to Enlightenment,* the *Great Exposition on the Stages of the Tantras,* and many commentaries on the shastras.

When he was fifty-three years old, in the year of the Ox, he established the Great Prayer Festival in Lhasa, at which he offered services to ten thousand monks. That spring, according to the predictions of the deities and lamas, he established Ganden Monastery, which caused his three spheres of practice, teaching, and activity to flourish even further. When he was sixty-three years old, on the twenty-fifth day of the tenth month of the Earth Pig year of 1419, his emanated manifestation passed away.

Gölo Shönupal, who wrote the *Blue Annals,* said that the whole land of Tibet was covered at this time by one large white umbrella, which was Tsongkhapa. And his words are true—Tsongkhapa's activities of teaching, debate, and composition were extremely influential. Tsongkhapa's activity was like a second Buddha in spreading the dharma in Tibet.

TSONGKHAPA'S STUDENTS AND LINEAGE HOLDERS

Tsongkhapa's accomplishments in teaching, debate, and composition affected a large number of disciples. Particularly well-known are those called the Four Teachers from Whom He Received Instructions, the Four Earlier Students, the Eight Pure Followers, the Three Special Sons, the Four Great Sons of Limitless Activities, the Ten Lamps of the Dharma in U and Tsang, the Ten Bodhisattvas Who Spontaneously Benefit Beings, the Two Imperial Preceptors, his Two Nephews Who Received Extensive Teachings, the Greater and Lesser Chok Who Were Holders of the Qualities of Experience, and the Six Great Prayer Flags Who Brought the Dharma to Faraway Places. In summary, most of the lineage holders of the Sakya, Ngok, Kadam, and Mahamudra lineages showed great respect for him.

Tsongkhapa's main students were Togden Jampal Gyatso, Gyaltsap Je, Khedrup Je, Jamyang Chöje, Jamchenpa Sherap Senge, Gyalwa Gendun Drup, and the two called She and Sang. After Tsongkhapa, the precious teachings of the incomparable Riwo Gedenpa lineage were held by Gyaltsap Darma Rinchen and Khedrup Gelek Pal. From then on, this lineage has been held by the Ganden Tripas, the throne-holders of Ganden Monastery. The current throne-holder is Khensur Lungri Namgyal Rinpoche, the 101st Ganden Tripa, who nurtures the dharma like the rising sun.

In discussing the history of the Gelugpa lineage, we should mention the founding of their great monasteries, which began in 1416. Drepung Monastery was established in the Fire Monkey year by one of Tsongkhapa's close students, Jamyang Chöje Tashi Palden. In the Earth Ox year, Jamchen Chöje Shakya Yeshe established Sera Thegchen

Chöling, or Sera Monastery. Gyalwa Gendun Drup, the first Dalai Lama, established Tashi Lhunpo Monastery in the area of Tsang during the Fire Rabbit year. Amdo Jamyang Shepa Ngawang Tsöndru founded Tashi Khyil Monastery in Amdo. As well, Kumbum and Jambaling and other large and small monasteries of this lineage were built in Amdo and throughout Tibet. The monastery of Ganden Sichagling was built in Peking, and throughout China and Mongolia other Gelugpa monasteries were established, which still remain today.

In addition to the great beings who were already mentioned as lineage holders of the Yellow Hat lineage, there were many great teachers and writers such as the successive reincarnations of Gyalwa Rinpoche, who is more commonly known as the Dalai Lama, and the successions of Panchen Rinpoche, the Upper and Lower Changkya Dorje Chang, Ngachen Könchok Gyaltsen, Kyishö Tulku Tendzin Thrinle, the earlier and later reincarnations of Jamyang Shepa, Phurchok Jampa Rinpoche, Jamyang Dewe Dorje, Takphu Rinpoche, Khachen Yeshe Gyaltsen, Shizang Phagpa Gelek Gyaltsen, Thukan Rinpoche, Longdöl Drubchen Ngawang Lozang, Kungthang Jampeyang, and others—countless great beings who have furthered the sutra and tantra traditions. Their activities of teaching, debate, and composition resound like the lion's roar, and even in this degenerate age their teachings continue to spread.

The History of the Lamdre Practice Lineage

VIRUPA AND DROGMI

The tradition of Lamdre, or the Path with Its Result, began with the lord of yogins, Palden Chökyong, who is more commonly known by his Sanskrit name Virupa, which the Tibetans pronounce as Birwapa. He was empowered within a mandala miraculously created by the dakini Dorje Dagmema, who was the same as Vajrayogini. Virupa had the realization of a sixth bhumi bodhisattva, and was known as a great siddha. He wrote a treatise called the *Vajra Verses,* which is a brief text of pith instructions on the *Hevajra Tantra,* and he gave this teaching, along with extensive oral instructions on the practice, to Krishna Samayavajra of east India.

Krishna Samayavajra gave these teachings to Damarupa, who taught them to Avadhutipa, who gave them to Gayadhara. Gayadhara came to Tibet three times, and on his first visit he taught the complete pith instructions on the *Hevajra Tantra* to Drogmi Lotsawa. Today we call these instructions the Lamdre, or the Path with Its Result. There are eight other instructions on Lamdre, which are called the Eight Later Lamdre Teachings, and Drogmi received these as well, from Gayadhara, Vairavajra, and others. So, these nine Lamdre instructions entered the Sakya lineage through Drogmi.

Virupa also gave an elaborate explanation of the *Hevajra Tantra* with pithy oral instructions to Dombipa. Dombipa passed these to Alalavajra, who transmitted them to Vanaprastha, who taught them to Garbharipa, who taught them to Jayashri. From Jayashri they went to Durjayachandra, and from him to Vairavajra. In India, Drogmi received these teachings from Vairavajra. These teachings are called the Lamdre without the Root Text or the Lamdre Commentary tradition. Before Drogmi returned to Tibet, he also received teachings from each of the six great masters called the Six Great Gatekeepers of Nalanda. These teachings are called the Integration of Sutra and Tantra, the Outer Negative Spirits, the Imbalances of the Elements in the Body, the Three Instructions Which Clear Away the Mental Obstacles to Samadhi, the Mahamudra Which Eliminates the Three Types of Suffering, and another Mahamudra teaching called the Clear Mindfulness of the Natural State. By receiving these teachings, Drogmi became the source of an ocean of instructions.

In general, it is said that Marpa Lotsawa, Gö Lotsawa, and Drogmi Lotsawa were the main sources of the Vajrayana teachings during the later spread of Buddhism in Tibet. Since Marpa and Gö initially received teachings from Drogmi, Drogmi is actually the primary source.

The famous students of Drogmi included those known as the Seven Siddhas, of whom three were male and four were female; the Seven Who Were Accomplished in the Scriptures, such as Khön Könchok Gyalpo and Gyijong Ukar; and the Four Who Were Accomplished in the Pith Instructions, such as Sekhar Chungwa, Jo-se, and Indra. Drogmi had eighteen main students, and from them came the eighteen lineages of Lamdre.

Drogmi's lineage also passed through his physical son and his spiritual son. Drogmi's student, Sekhar Chungwa, had two male lineages through his student and his son, called the Shama male lineages. Sekhar also had three female lineages and four mixed gender lineages, which together make seven lineages. Drogmi's students Manglam and Shingphuk formed two lineages, Gyijo had a single lineage, and Khön Könchok Gyalpo engendered four lineages. Eventually, there were eighteen in all. From these lineages the Sakya tradition spread widely and became very active, and it remains so to the present day.

The name Sakyapa is associated with an ancient family called Ösal Khön. That family contained a succession of vidyadharas of the Nyingma teachings who attained realization through their practice of the yidams Samyak Heruka and Vajrakilaya. Khön Könchok Gyalpo, who was just mentioned as a lineage holder of Drogmi Lotsawa, was born into this family as the son of Khön Shakya Lodrö. Khön Könchok Gyalpo was an exceptionally learned and accomplished master. Due to his previous prayers and karmic connections, his activities connected him with the Sarma tradition rather than the Nyingma tradition, and in 1073 he established Sakya Monastery. *Sakya* means "white earth," and refers to the color of the ground where the monastery was founded. Since that time the name Khön Sakyapa has been famous.

SACHEN KUNGA NYINGPO

Khön Könchok Gyalpo's son, Kunga Nyingpo, was a person of such great kindness that he was considered to be Avalokiteshvara in person. Kunga Nyingpo is also known as Sakyapa or as Sachen, which means "the great Sakya." He lived from the Water Monkey year of 1092 to the Earth Tiger year of 1158. His noble qualities awakened at an early age. From the age of eleven, he was closely looked after by the bodhisattva Manjushri, and he instantly saw all the key points of the path of the Prajnaparamita. Sachen Kunga Nyingpo received the Sutrayana teachings from Drangti Darma Nyingpo and others. He received the general Vajrayana teachings from his father Khön Könchok Gyalpo, Lama Bari Lotsawa, Mal Lotsawa, and others. He received the nectar of the precious Lamdre teachings from Shangtön Chöbar, who had received these teachings from Drogmi Lotsawa himself. Through all these instructions, the flower of his realization bloomed again.

Sachen Kunga Nyingpo received transmission of the tantric oral instructions from four great translators. He received the three tantras of Hevajra from Drogmi and teachings on Chakrasamvara from Mal Lotsawa. From Rinchen Zangpo he received teachings on yoga and Mahakala, and from Bari Lotsawa he received the hundred sadhanas that Bari Lotsawa had collected. Especially, when Sachen was forty-seven years old, Virupa came in person with four followers to Sachen's cave, and stayed with him for a month to give teachings. These teachings included those called the Four Profound Teachings Which Should Not Go beyond the Boundaries, as well as the empowerments, explanations, and instructions on seventy-two different tantras. Virupa also bestowed the direct, short lineage of the hidden Lamdre teachings.

As his lama predicted to him, Sachen Kunga Nyingpo had three students who attained siddhi, seven students who attained stability in the unborn nature, and eighty students who were realized beings. Sachen had four sons. His eldest, Kunga Bar, died in India, but Sachen gave all the instructions to two other sons, Sönam Tsemo and Dragpa Gyaltsen.

Sönam Tsemo was so famous for his learning that he was renowned as far away as the Ganges River in India. Above the doorway of the stupa at Bodhgaya, the wisdom dakinis wrote a proclamation praising him, saying that Sönam Tsemo was a great pandita well versed in the five sciences and an incarnation of the Indian master Durjayachandra. His activities of teaching and practice were immeasurable, and he attained the rainbow body.

Sachen Kunga Nyingpo's son, Dragpa Gyaltsen, was another master who was closely looked after by the bodhisattva Manjushri. Dragpa Gyaltsen's understanding of sutra and tantra came forth like the opening of a treasure-house. His father gave him the short lineage transmission of Lamdre within the clear light, and Dragpa Gyaltsen attained a very high level of realization. His character was so learned, disciplined, and accomplished that Khache Panchen Shakya Shri called him the Vajra Holder of Guhyasamaja. Through his Vajrayana practice and the instructions of Khache Panchen Shakya Shri, Dragpa Gyaltsen definitely became the crown ornament among the Vajrayana practitioners of Tibet and India. Dragpa Gyaltsen was blessed with a long life, and the Tibetans say that he caused the profound and vast teachings to shine brighter than the sun.

SAKYA PANDITA AND CHÖGYAL PHAGPA

The youngest son of Sachen Kunga Nyingpo was the realized vidya-dhara Palchen Öpo, who had two sons, Jamyang Sakya Pandita and Zangtsa Sonam Gyaltsen. The master we know as Sakya Pandita was named Kunga Gyaltsen Pal Zangpo, and he lived from the Water Male Tiger year of 1182 until the Iron Female Pig year of 1251. He could comprehend any teaching on the outer and inner sciences after hearing it only once, or twice at the most. Especially due to the blessings of his Guru Yoga practice, Sakya Pandita saw Jetsun Dragpa Gyaltsen and Manjushri as inseparable. Through this, all the outer, inner, and secret auspicious conditions coincided, and his learning, realization, and power to benefit others burst forth. He was very learned in all branches of knowledge and his fame spread from India to China. For example, Jamyang Sakya Pandita was able to subdue six great Hindu masters who had attained realization in their own tradition. By means of his teaching and debate, and the miraculous powers he attained through a close connection with his meditation deity, he was able to establish them in the Buddhadharma. Near the end of his life Sakya Pandita was invited to China by the emperor, and in the temple of Trulpa De in Peking he passed away amid many miraculous signs.

Sakya Pandita's brother, Zangtsa Sönam Gyaltsen, had three famous sons: Drogön Chögyal Phagpa Lodrö Gyaltsen, Druppe Wangchuk Drogön Chagna, and Loppön Yeshe Jungne. The eldest, Chögyal Phagpa, lived from the Wood Male Sheep year of 1235 to the Iron Male Dragon year of 1280. Right from the beginning, Chögyal Phagpa was a very special person, an emanation of a great bodhisattva on the bhumis who consciously took the form of a human being. His bodhisattva qualities, activities, and kindness were very apparent, so he was called Phagpa, the word for a noble being on the bhumis.

Once his inexhaustible understanding and liberation came forth, Chögyal Phagpa displayed many miraculous powers. For instance, he took off his five fingers and showed the five dhyani buddhas residing there. Chögyal Phagpa's actions of body, speech, and mind were so perfect that even Kublai Khan, the fierce emperor of Mongolia and China, developed strong devotion to him and took empowerments from him three times. The emperor declared that Chögyal Phagpa should rule the three regions of Tibet as far as the Li Province of China, so Chögyal Phagpa took on the combined roles of being a monk and a king. He promoted the happiness of Tibet by nurturing the various philosophical tenets without prejudice, and he caused the explanations and practices of all the teachings to become as clear as day.

Phagpa's brother, Drogön Chagna, had a son named Chökyong Sungwa who became the Sakya throne-holder for several years. The third son of Zangtsa was Loppön Yeshe Jungne, and Yeshe Jungne's son was Dagchen Zangpo Pal, who also became a Sakya throne-holder. Dagchen Zangpo Pal had seven wives and fifteen children. The oldest brother, Tishri Kunga Lodrö, divided his family into four labrangs, or households. These labrangs were called Shithok Labrang, Labrang Rinchen Gangpa, Lhakhang Labrang, and Duchö Labrang.

OTHER SAKYA LINEAGE HOLDERS

From the sixteenth through the eighteenth centuries, the Sakya throne-holders came from the Duchö Labrang. In the early nineteenth century, the throne-holders began to alternate between the labrangs of Phuntsok Phodrang and Dölma Phodrang. Presently, the forty-first throne-holder, whose full name is Ngagwang Kunga Thegchen Palbar Thrinle Samphel Wangi Gyalpo, comes from the Dölma Phodrang.

In all of these labrangs there were many learned and realized beings. In particular, Palden Lama Dampa Sönam Gyaltsen was part of the Labrang Rinchen Gangpa. Lama Dampa lived from the Water Male Mouse year of 1312 to the Wood Female Rabbit year of 1375, and he became a great chakravartin of learning and realization. He received the transmission of an ocean of oral instructions and teachings from most of the great Tibetan masters of his time. He maintained the two oral traditions of the Lamdre teachings, known as the Teaching for the Assembly and the Teaching for the Individual. The fact that both these traditions continue to the present day is attributed to the activity of Lama Dampa.

He had countless students, and among them, his heart students were known as the Two Great Regents of the Vajrayana, the Eight Who Held the Secret of His Teachings, and the Eleven Renowned Scholars. Lama Dampa's student Yarlungpa Senge Gyaltsen had a cousin, Sönam Gyal-chok, who had eight great heart sons who held the Lamdre teachings. From them the Lamdre teachings spread to the Ngor, Dzong, Bodong, Geluk, and other lineages.

To give a little detail on these Sakya lineages, starting with the Ngorpa tradition, the first master of this lineage was Ngorchen Dorje Chang Kunga Zangpo, who received the Lamdre Teaching for the Assembly from Drupchen Buddha Shri. In 1430, when Ngorchen Kunga Zangpo was forty-eight years old, he established the Ngor Evam Monastery. He had countless students, and it was mainly through Muchen Sempa Chenpo Könchok Gyaltsen and Kunkhyen Sönam Senge that the Ngor lineage spread. Within the Ngor tradition there is a special Khenpo lineage, and their practice and beneficial activities continue to this day.

The Dzong tradition of the Lamdre Teaching for the Assembly stemmed from Ngagchang Sungi Palwa. The great master Butön Kunga Namgyal received this tradition from Dragthogpa Sönam Zangpo. Butön established the large monastery of Gangkar Dorje Den. He combined the teachings of the Dzong Luk of the Sakya lineage with his own tradition, called the Bu Luk, and this became a separate, special system called Gangkarwa.

The Tsarpa lineage began when the second Lamdre oral tradition, the Teaching for the Individual, came from Dagchen Lodrö Gyaltsen to his student, Doring Kunpongwa Chenpo, and from him to Tsarchen Dorje Chang Losal Gyatso. This tradition is called the Tsar Luk Teaching for the Individual. Tsarchen Losal Gyatso had two heart students: the one resembling the sun was Jamyang Khyentse Wangchuk, and the one resembling the moon was Mangthö Lodrö Gyatso. The Tsar tradition also continues to flourish.

In summary, because of the spreading of the teachings by the Sakya lineage, the creation and completion stage practices of the *Hevajra Tantra* expand like a summer lake, even in these modern times, and the Sakya lineage teachings have spread all over the world.

The History of the Marpa Kagyu Lineage

The fourth of the eight practice lineages is the Kagyu lineage that came from Marpa Lotsawa. The original source of these teachings is the glorious Tilopa, who transmitted both a long lineage and the short lineage. In relation to the long lineage, Tilopa said: "My lamas for the four transmissions were Nagarjuna, Charyapa, Lavapa, and Sukhasiddhi." He received the transmissions on Inner Heat from Charyapa; Illusory Body and Clear Light from Nagarjuna; Dream Yoga from Lavapa; and the Intermediate State and Transference of Consciousness from Sukhasiddhi, who is also known as the dakini Kalpa Zangmo. In addition, from the middle Indrabhuti he received teachings on the Transcendent Wisdom of Another's Body, and from Matangi he received instructions on Transference of Consciousness to Another Body.

In relation to the transmission of the short lineage, Tilopa said: "I, Tilopa, do not have any human lamas. My lama is the Omniscient One." He received the four tantras with their instructions directly from Buddha Vajradhara, and he received the teachings called the Three Precious Oral Instructions directly from Vajrayogini. This is how he received the essence of all the instructions.

In the presence of Tilopa, the pandita Naropa underwent twelve great difficulties, and eventually, through words and signs, he attained realization of the entire meaning of the secret Mantrayana.

Marpa Lotsawa

After Naropa, the next in succession was Lodrak Marpa Chökyi Lodrö, who lived from the Water Male Horse year of 1012 to the Water Male Bird year of 1097. Marpa went to India three times and he studied with Panchen Naropa for sixteen years and seven months. Through integrating his study, contemplation, and meditation, he reached a high level of realization. In particular, the last time Marpa went to India, Naropa had already left to engage in yogic conduct. With great difficulties, Marpa searched for him and supplicated him, and finally met him face-to-face in the northern hermitage of Pushpahari, which is also called Phullahari. Marpa stayed with him for six months, and he received the complete instructions on the practice of Chakrasamvara and Consort in Union.

Marpa also studied with many learned and accomplished masters, such as Maitripa, who was a close student of the glorious siddha Shavaripa; Yeshe Nyingpo, the learned one of Lakshetra in the west; the siddha Shiwa Zangpo, who lived on an island in the poison lake in the south; and the dakini Niguma. Through studying with them he gained a thorough understanding of all the sutras, tantras, and oral instructions. In particular, he was empowered by Naropa and Maitripa as their regent to teach in the snowy land north of India. Je Lodragpa, which is another name for Marpa, manifested inconceivable secrets and helped innumerable beings in Tibet.

Marpa had many students who were holders of his instructions, especially the Four Heart Students and the Ten Head Teachers. Chief among his students were the Four Pillars. He primarily transmitted his teaching lineage to three of them: Ngogtön Chödor of Shung, Tsurtön Wange of Döl, and Metön Chenpo of Tsangrong, and his practice lineage went primarily to Jetsun Mila Shepa Dorje. Ngogtön passed away to the celestial realm without leaving his body behind. Ngogtön's activity was particularly far-reaching, since both his family lineage and his student lineage were full of renowned great masters.

MILAREPA

Jetsun Mila Shepa Dorje, or Milarepa, who lived from 1040 to 1123, is the most famous yogi of Tibet. He extracted the heart essence of the great translator Marpa, and pleased his master through undergoing great austerities. After practicing for a long time in mountain caves, even without human food, he became just like the great siddhas of India. In one lifetime he attained the state of union, the ultimate state of Vajradhara, and he subdued countless beings, both human and non-human.

Among his most renowned students were the Three Excellent Ones Who Tame Beings, the Three Male and Four Female Students Who Went to the Celestial Realm, and the Eight Great Repas, or cotton-clad yogis. Gampopa and Rechungpa were his greatest students, who were said to be like the sun and moon in holding his oral instructions.

RECHUNGPA AND HIS LINEAGE

Milarepa's moonlike heart son, Rechung Dorje Dragpa, lived from 1084 to 1161. After assimilating the oceanlike teachings of Lord Mila,

Rechungpa was sent to India in accordance with predictions from Marpa. In India, Rechungpa received the essential instructions of Machik Druppe Gyalmo, Tephuwa Tri-me Shenyen, and others, and he brought back to Tibet the heart treasures of these spiritual masters, which are called the Later Teachings of the Formless Dakinis. When he passed away, Rechungpa went to Atakavati, the pure land of Vajrapani, without leaving his body, and with his wisdom body he continued to look after Palden Drugpa and many other fortunate students. He gave his real instructions to about twelve heart students, primarily Gyalwa Khyungtsang, to whom he entrusted the treasure of his oral instructions. Gyalwa Khyungtsang passed these on to the female master Machik Ajo, and eventually to Drogön Tsangpa Gyare. From that time onward, Rechungpa's oral teachings were spread openly.

An important teaching coming from Rechungpa's lineage concerns the practice of Lokeshvara Jinasagara. Lama Sangri Repa gave this teaching to Drogön Rechen, and from there it spread throughout the Kamtsang Kagyu lineage. It is said that the great master Karma Pakshi attained siddhi mainly through this practice of Lokeshvara Jinasagara. Among Rechungpa's Eighteen Instructions with Appendices, the appended practice, Amitayus Who Benefits Beings, entered the Sakya, Kagyu, and Geluk lineages, so Rechungpa's profound dharma instructions were incorporated into many schools of Tibetan Buddhism.

GAMPOPA AND HIS LINEAGE

Lord Mila's sunlike heart son was Dagpo Lhaje, the doctor from Dagpo named Daö Shönu, who is more commonly known as Gampopa. His father was Nyipa Gyalpo and his mother was Checham of the Shoma family. Gampopa lived from 1079 to 1153. He was very learned in medicine, and after his wife died, he felt an intense revulsion for samsara and became a monk. He then received many Sutrayana and Tantrayana teachings from several masters of the Kadampa tradition. Later, irreversible faith was born in him by merely hearing the name of Jetsun Milarepa. He went to Milarepa and listened to his oral instructions, and by practicing them he actualized the result. He became Milarepa's best student. In foreseeing the growth of his lineage, Milarepa predicted that his students would be better than he had been, and his students' students would be even better.

In accordance with the command of his teacher, Gampopa established his main center at the Gampo Mountain in Dagpo. Gampopa taught the stages of the path from the Kadampa tradition and the meditation of Sutra Mahamudra to his general students. To his special students he taught the Vajrayana path of skillful means that he had learned from his lama Milarepa, emphasizing the special meditation of Tantra Mahamudra. By turning the wheel of dharma in that way, he ripened and freed countless students, including five hundred fortunate beings who were like arhats. Gampopa was such a great being that he resembled the Buddha coming to the earth. He was able to mature and liberate all those who saw, heard, touched, or remembered him, so his pure activity was inconceivable. His students included eight hundred great meditators; the chief among them were called the Three Men from Kham.

The leadership of Gampopa's main seat continued through three generations of his nephews: Öngom Tsultrim Nyingpo, Dagpo Duldzin, and Khedrup Tashi Namgyal. This was the root of the Dagpo Kagyu lineage, which branched into four main schools and eight subschools, which spread the teachings of the practice lineage like the sun. Next, I would like to briefly describe each of these, starting with the four greater lineages: the Tsalpa Kagyu, the Barom Kagyu, the Kamtsang Kagyu, and the Phagdru Kagyu.

THE TSALPA KAGYU AND BAROM KAGYU

The Tsalpa Kagyu lineage began in the twelfth century with Shang Tsalpa Tsöndru Dragpa, a student of Öngom Tsultrim Nyingpo. Early on, the Tsalpa Kagyu accomplished a great deal of dharmic and secular activity in the area of Tsal Gungthang.

The Barom Kagyu also began in the twelfth century. It arose from Baram Darma Wangchuk and his succession of students. Many great siddhas came from this lineage, notably Drogön Tishri Repa, who became a teacher of the Chinese emperors. In the early days, the Barom Kagyu lineage established eighteen monasteries in the Nangchen kingdom of Kham, with widespread religious and temporal activities.

THE KAMTSANG KAGYU AND THE KARMAPAS

The Kamtsang Kagyu lineage is renowned as the heart of all the practice lineages. It is headed by the succession of incarnations called the Karmapas, who are considered to be emanations of the bodhisattva Avalokiteshvara in human form. This lineage began with the first Karmapa, Dusum Khyenpa, who was born in Kham Treshö and lived from 1110 to 1193. Also named Khampa U-se, he was one of Gampopa's students called the Three Men from Kham. When Dusum Khyenpa went to central Tibet he studied and practiced with lamas such as Gampopa, and he reached a high level of realization. People with pure perception saw him wearing a black hat given to him by the wisdom dakinis, and he became widely known as the Holder of the Black Crown. He built three important monasteries: at the age of fifty-five he built the Kampo-ne Monastery in Kham; when he was seventy-seven he built Karma Gön, which is sometimes called Karma Riling; and at the age of eighty he established Tsurphu Monastery in the Tsur valley. He entrusted his lineage to Sangye Nyenpa Rechen, and at the age of eighty-four he passed away for a while.

The second Karmapa, Karma Pakshi, was born in Le Tsagtok in the Amdo region. He performed unlimited miracles and activities. He transmitted his lineage to the siddha Orgyenpa and then passed away at the age of seventy-four.

The third Karmapa was the all-knowing Rangjung Dorje. He was born in Mangyul Gungthang in the late thirteenth century. He remembered everything from his past lives without being obscured by birth, so he had an amazing and inconceivable life story. His heart son was the first Shamarpa, Dragpa Senge, and he passed on his lineage to Yungtön Dorje Pal.

The fourth Karmapa, the dharma lord Rölpe Dorje, was born in Alarong in Ngö. He was the preceptor who first ordained Je Tsongkhapa as a monk.

The fifth Karmapa was Deshin Shegpa, who was born in the area of Nyangpo Ösal. He was revered as a teacher by many great beings, including the Chinese emperor Ta Ming Yung Lo. He accomplished great benefit for beings and his compassion and activities were inconceivable.

The sixth Karmapa was Thongwa Dönden. He was born near Karma

Gön Monastery in a place called Ngom. Among his heart students was the first Gyaltsap Rinpoche, Go Shri Paljor Döndrup.

The seventh Karmapa was Chödrak Gyatso, who was born in Ngö. He became a great scholar, and the works produced from his teaching, debate, and composition are still in use today.

The eighth Karmapa was Mikyö Dorje, who was born in the sixteenth century in the region of Ngom. He became a great pandita who could teach brilliantly on all branches of the sciences, and he wrote many treatises.

The ninth Karmapa, Wangchuk Dorje, was born in Kham, in the lower part of Tre, in a place called Khawa Langri. He continued to foster the activities of the Karmapas.

The tenth Karmapa was Chöying Dorje. He was born in the lower part of Gulok, in a place called Töguda. During this time the Kagyu teachings were damaged a great deal. However, the tenth Karmapa went to Jangyul and other places, and rather than being defeated by these obstacles, he was able to bring new life to the Kagyu teachings.

The eleventh Karmapa was Yeshe Dorje, who was born in the area of Gulok near the end of the seventeenth century. He continued to carry out the activities of the Karmapas.

The twelfth Karmapa was Jangchup Dorje. He was born in Derge, in a place called Öntö Kyilo. He continued to carry the great responsibility of the lineage.

The thirteenth Karmapa was Dudul Dorje, who was born near the southern place of Geri. These Karmapas—the twelfth, thirteenth, and the fourteenth in particular—formed reciprocal teacher and student relationships with the Palpung Situ emanations.

The fourteenth Karmapa was Thegchok Dorje, who lived in the nineteenth century. He was born in the area of Riwoche, near Karma Gön. Jamgön Kongtrul taught Sanskrit and other subjects to this Karmapa.

The fifteenth Karmapa was Khakhyap Dorje. He was born in Tsang Nyangtö Shelkar Gyaltse. He received the real lineage, the introduction to the nature of mind, from Jamgön Kongtrul. He was the only one of the Karmapas who remained a ngagpa, or householder.

The sixteenth Karmapa, Rigpe Dorje, was born in the Denkhok in the area of Derge. He lit the torch of dharma throughout the world.

In this way the activities of the sixteen Karmapas have spread in every direction, not only in Tibet, India, and China, but throughout the world. They carried the load of the entire teaching of the Buddha. Through the three spheres of teaching, practice, and other activities, they actualize the benefit of beings in all parts of the world in lasting, extensive, and spontaneous ways.

The Karma Kamtsang has two separate traditions within it. The first of those is the Surmang Kagyu. One of the main students of the fifth Karmapa was Ma-se Lodrö Rinchen, also known as Trung Ma-se, who was a realized master of the *Khandro Nyingtik* teachings. Trung Ma-se was given the Chakrasamvara Dakini Hearing lineage called the Three Cycles of the Precious Jewel. He established Surmang Monastery, from which the Surmang Kagyu lineage developed.

The second tradition within the Karma Kamtsang is the Nedo Kagyu, which stems from the learned and accomplished master, Karma Chagme, who lived in the seventeenth century. He was a student of the sixth Sharmapa, Garwang Chökyi Wangchuk, who was the heart son of the ninth Karmapa. Karma Chagme perfected the practices of countless mandalas of both the Sarma and Nyingma traditions. He fully stabilized the creation and completion stage practices and became the lineage holder of many great tertöns. Because the place where he stayed was called Nedo, his lineage is called the Nedo Kagyu. This lineage incorporates both Kagyu and Nyingma traditions.

In addition, there are several successions of reincarnations who have fostered the dharma of the Karma Kamtsang. These include the Sharmapa reincarnations; the Gyaltsaps of Tsurphu; the Tai Situs with the names Chö and Padma, who were predicted by Guru Rinpoche as the Six with the Dharma Eye and the Six with the Lotus Tongue; as well as the reincarnations of Nenang Pawo, Treo, Kongtrul, and others.

THE PHAGDRU KAGYU LINEAGE

The fourth of the four greater Kagyu lineages is the Phagdru Kagyu. It was begun by another of the Three Men from Kham—Je Phagmo Drupa Khampa Dorje Gyalpo, who lived in the twelfth century. He first received teachings from Sachen Kunga Nyingpo. Although he became very learned, he was not confident about his understanding until he came into the presence of Gampopa, at which time he immediately realized the truth of suchness. Phagmo Drupa had eight hundred students, five hundred of whom were very high lamas. Several of his great students established their own monastic seats, and from them came the eight Kagyu subschools. His own seat was located at Phagmo Dru, which continued for a long time to produce many great meditators, as well as great secular rulers who are called the Desi.

The First Three of the Eight Kagyu Subschools

The lineages of the eight Kagyu subschools, which are sometimes called the four pairs or eight branches, came from eight of Phagmo Drupa's students, who lived in the twelfth century. These lineages are named in pairs: Drigung and Taklung, Trophu and Ling-re, Martsang and Yelpa, and Yangzang and Shugsep.

The first of these is the Drigung Kagyu. It was founded by Kyopa Jigten Sumgön, who was called the One Who Perfected Interdependence. He established Drigung Monastery, and he is renowned for having 180,000 students. Most famous of these are the three siddhas Nyö, Gar, and Chö, as well as Drigung Lingpa. There is a saying that all the Tibetan mountains are the mountains of Drigung and all the Tibetan plains are the plains of Drigung. In other words, their adherents covered the whole of Tibet. Later on, during the time of Chögyal Rinchen Phuntsok and his students, the Drigung Kagyu incorporated the treasure trove of both Nyingma and Sarma teachings into their study and practice.

The second of the eight subschools is the Taglung, which was begun by Taglung Thangpa Tashi Pal, who is known as the One Who Perfected Devotion. He established Taglung Monastery, while Sangye Ön established Taglung Marthang Monastery. This lineage produced many great beings, such as Chöku Orgyen Gönpo. Later on, they practiced the Nyingma Kama and terma teachings as well as their own Sarma tradition. The Taglung lineage continues to this day.

The third is the Trophu lineage, founded by Gyaltsa Kunden Repa, who established Trophu Monastery. His nephew, Trophu Lotsawa Jampa Pal, invited three great panditas from India to Tibet—Mitra Joki, Buddha Shri, and Khache Panchen Shakya Shri. Trophu Lotsawa constructed the great image of Maitreya Buddha called Thongdröl Chenpo, or Great

Liberation Through Seeing. About four or five generations after him, Butön Rinpoche came to Trophu Monastery. This monastery had kept the cup of Khache Panchen Shakya Shri, so Trophu Monastery was also called Shalu Densa, or the Monastic Seat of the Cup. Shalu is the name of Butön's monastery, but it is also a name used for Butön and his tradition.

THE DRUGPA KAGYU LINEAGE

The fourth of the eight subschools is the Drugpa Kagyu. It began with the Ling-re Kagyu lineage, which came from Lingje Repa, who was renowned at that time as the most realized being north of the Ganges River. He transmitted this lineage to his student, the great siddha Tsangpa Gyare, who established the Druk Ralung Monastery in 1193. From then on, this lineage was called the Drugpa Kagyu, and its fame spread like the wind.

The great siddha Tsangpa Gyare gathered countless students, and he assembled all of them on three occasions. There was a saying that the teachings of the glorious Drugpa have spread as far as a vulture can fly in eighteen days. As for the succession of his great students, from Je Göt-sangpa Gönpo Dorje came the Upper Drugpa lineage, whose members were as numerous as the stars in the sky. From Lo-re Darma Wangchuk came the Lower Drugpa lineage, whose members were said to be as numerous as the particles of dust on the earth. The Middle Drugpa lineage came from Tsangpa Gyare's own student lineage, which is known as the Nine Lions.

Another lineage began with Je Ngawang Namgyal, who became the King of Bhutan. By means of great miracles, he brought the four sections of the Mönpa people under his control. Je Ngawang Namgyal promoted both spiritual and secular teachings, and his lineage became known as the Southern Drugpa. A proverb arose that half of the people are Drugpas, half of the Drugpas are beggars, and half of the beggars are sid-dhas. In this way, the precious dharma was extensively and continuously preserved by the Drugpa Kagyu. Especially noteworthy in this lineage is the all-knowing Padma Karpo, who excelled in explaining the sutras and tantras, and was very influential in transmitting the teachings.

THE LAST FOUR KAGYU SUBSCHOOLS

The fifth of the eight subschools is the Martsang Kagyu, which came from Marpa Drubthop Sherap Senge. From his lineage came many great beings, such as Yangön Yeshe Gyaltsen, Rinchen Lingpa, Pang Khenchen Özer Lama and Drogön Shingo Repa. Later on, his teaching lineage went to the Tagphu lamas, and these days this stream of blessings is said to reside in the Palyul tradition.

The sixth is the Yelpa Kagyu lineage, which arose from Yelpa Drubthop Yeshe Tsegpa. He founded several monasteries, such as Lo Yelphu and Chang Tana. Yelpa Yeshe Tsegpa was taken as the teacher of the kings of Ling, whose predecessor was the great king, Gesar of Ling. The kings made offerings of the armor and weapons that had belonged to Gesar to the lamas, and these objects were kept in Chang Tana Monastery. The monasteries founded by Yelpa Yeshe Tsegpa maintained the Kamtsang Kagyu lineage teachings.

The seventh of the eight subschools is the Yangzang Kagyu. It came from the lineage of Zarawa Kalden Yeshe Senge. Many realized masters came from this lineage, as well as powerful temporal rulers called the Yazang Desi.

The eighth is the Shugsep Kagyu. Nyamme Gyergom Chenpo established the Nyiphu Shugsep Monastery and this lineage came from there. It accomplished many great activities, but these days one does not hear that this lineage is still active.

At this time, from among the four greater and eight subschools of the Kagyu, the Kamtsang Kagyu and Drugpa Kagyu are very widespread, and Drigung and Taglung are well-established and flourishing.

The History of the Shangpa Kagyu Lineage

The founder of the Shangpa Kagyu, Khyungpo Naljor, was predicted by the Buddha as the Shravaka with Great Miracles. Born in 1086, he initially studied Bön, which was his father's religion, and then he studied the Nyingma teachings and became very learned and accomplished in them. Due to the ripening of his bodhisattva aspirations, he was not content with only this much, so he went to India. He studied immeasurable teachings on the Sutrayana and Tantrayana at the feet of 150 realized masters, especially Amoghavajra and three other root gurus. In particular, he received teachings from the dakinis Sukhasiddhi and Niguma. Niguma was a wisdom dakini on the third bhumi who had received teachings directly from Vajradhara.

Khyungpo Naljor accomplished five of the tantras within his five bodily centers. These five tantras are Hevajra, which gives the ultimate teaching on Inner Heat; Chakrasamvara, which gives the ultimate teaching on Karmamudra; Guhyasamaja, which gives the ultimate teaching on Illusory Body and Clear Light; Mahamaya, which gives the ultimate teaching on Dream Yoga; and Vajrabhairava, which gives the ultimate teaching on enlightened activities. Through these practices he became a great lord of siddhas. He established his seat in a valley called Shang, in the place of Shang Shong in the Yeru area of Tsang, so he came to be known as Lama Shangpa, and his lineage is called the Shangpa Kagyu.

Khyungpo Naljor lived for 150 years, and during that time he matured and liberated countless beings. He had 180,000 students, including six main students. There were five earlier heart sons and one later heart son. The five earlier heart sons were Meu Tönpa, the Trunk of Stainless Wisdom; Yerpo Gyamoche, the Branch of Benevolent Mind; Ngultön Rinwang, the Leaves of Compassion; Latö Könchok Bar, the Flower of Loving-Kindness; and Shangom Chöseng, the Essence of Clear Light. The one later heart son was Mochogpa Rinchen Tsöndru, who was ripened to fruition in the practices of the Illusory Body and Dream Yoga. From among these six students, Mochogpa is the only one who received the transmission of the single lineage of the Secret Words of Vajradhara.

For a long time, this single lineage was passed to one student in each generation, going to Öntön Kyergangpa, Sangye Nyentön, Drogön Tönpa, and so on. In accordance with the prophesy of Vajradhara and the wisdom Dakini Niguma, the lineage holder called the Seventh Precious One, Chöje Tönpa, broke the vajra seal of secrecy and made public this single lineage. From then on, the followers of this lineage spread all over, and many became great siddhas.

Chöje Tönpa's main lineage holders were Tsangma Shangtön, Samdingpa Shönu Drup, and Jagchen Gyaltsen Bum, who were called the

Three Learned and Accomplished Ones. These three put Chöje Tönpa's oral instructions in writing. From Tsangma Shangtön's student, Khyungpo Tsulgön, came the students called the Seven Later Precious Ones. Samdingpa Shönu Drup and Jagchen Gyaltsen Bum established their own seats, which developed several separate lineages. Another of Chöje Tönpa's close disciples, Serlingpa Tashi Pal, established a lineage, as did Latö Könchog Khar, so there were many subschools of the Shangpa Kagyu which stemmed from Chöje Tönpa.

One particularly renowned master of the Shangpa Kagyu lineage was Thangtong Gyalpo, or Drupchen Tsöndru Zangpo—he had five different names. He was an incarnation of the all-knowing Dölpo Sangye. Thangtong Gyalpo received the oral instructions of the Upper lineage of Rigong from Jangsem Jinpa Zangpo, who traced his lineage back to Muchen Gyaltsen Palzang, one of Tsangma Shangtön's students. Through his practice of the oral instructions, Thangtong Gyalpo was looked after by the wisdom dakinis, and he experienced three short lineage transmissions from them. First, in Riwoche of Tsang, Niguma appeared in person and gave him teachings on the Six Yogas of Niguma, Mahamudra, Carrying Experiences onto the Path, Deathlessness, and the Inseparable Lama and Protector. The second short lineage transmission came at the foot of a pine tree in Amdo, where Thangtong Gyalpo received the empowerments of each of these practices again. The third instance was when he received the instructions on the Celestial Realm, called the Signs without Words. He passed on these three transmissions to Mangkhar Lodrö Gyaltsen, and to this day this oral tradition remains unbroken.

Another great holder of the Shangpa Kagyu was the great siddha Taranatha, Palden Kunga Drolchok, who lived in the sixteenth century. He received the long lineage teachings from Chöje Tönpa's students, Samdingpa Shönu Drup and Jagchen Gyaltsen Bum, as well as teachings from twenty-four other lineages, including Thangtong Gyalpo's. Like Thangtong Gyalpo, Taranatha received twice the short lineage transmission of special instructions from Niguma in person. Taranatha received instructions from those twenty-five lineages more than a hundred times, and in turn he gave instructions to his students more than a hundred times and established them in realization. In this way, he received the long lineage, the short lineage, and the very short lineage. The root teachings of the long oral lineage, the pure Golden Teachings of the Shangpa, were enhanced by the sharp oral instructions of the short lineage teachings called the Warm Breath of the Wisdom Dakinis. Taranatha's teachings on the Liberating Protector Vajrapani, which include the *Vast Display of the Deep Meaning,* are the special lineage teachings of Taranatha, and these days they are considered to be the highest type of instruction.

The Six-Armed Mahakala was Khyungpo Naljor's special protector, and the Shangpa Kagyu extensively spread this mahakala practice. In earlier times it spread extensively from the Rigong Upper lineage, and in later times from the Rigong Lower lineage. In particular, the Six-Armed Mahakala became the main protector of Tsongkhapa and his close students, and this practice spread throughout U, Tsang, Kham, and even into China.

Similarly, many other teachings from the Shangpa Kagyu lineage spread to all the schools of Tibetan Buddhism. They include the teachings on Avalokiteshvara by Kyergang, the Secret Practice of Hayagriva, and the Yogic Postures of Deathlessness by Nyentön.

Jamgön Kongtrul Rinpoche put the teachings of the Shangpa Kagyu into the *Treasury of Instructions,* and he established a retreat center for the practice of the Six Yogas of Niguma. Because of his work to teach and spread these teachings, they will continue for a long time.

The History of the Shije, or Pacification, Lineage

The Shije, or Pacification, lineage began with the great master known in Tibet and China as Pha Dampa Sangye. He was born in India, in the area of Beta called Tsata Senga, and in India he was known as Kamalashila. During his life he received all the profound instructions from fifty-four female and male siddhas. Through one-pointed practice, he attained the eight great siddhis, such as subsisting on extracted essences. He is reputed to have lived for 570 years. With his pure vision he saw the twelve buddhas, as well as the thirty-six lamas of the marvelous celestial realms. He attained the supreme siddhi, the wisdom of the path of seeing. This great learned and accomplished master condensed as his main practice the meaning of the *Prajnaparamita Sutra* in its long, medium, and short versions, along with the tantra of the *Great Stream of Ali Kali.*[5] He based his way of life on the three vows as the foundation, strong ascetic practice as the path, and activities to benefit others as the result. He caused as many beings as there are stars in the sky to cross over into buddhahood. In general, this teaching is considered to be the noble dharma that pacifies suffering, but in this case, the name Pacification, or Shije, is applied to Pha Dampa Sangye's specific lineage. The Pacification lineage has several different ways of teaching in accordance with the capacities of the practitioners.

Pha Dampa Sangye went to Tibet about five times, and three lineages of Shije practice developed. The first lineage began when he taught to Khache Jnanaguhya the three cycles of the *Torch of Pacification,* as well as the practices of Yamantaka. Ang Lotsawa received these teachings from both Pha Dampa Sangye and Khache Jnanaguhya. Pha Dampa Sangye also taught the *Torch of Pacification* to Khache Putra Lochung, and both Khache Jnanaguhya and Khache Putra Lochung transmitted it to Rok Sherap Ö.

Second, the middle lineage is named after the three lineage holders with the short names of Ma, So, and Kam. Pha Dampa Sangye gave the Mahamudra word lineage and meaning lineage transmissions to Ma Chökyi Sherap. He gave the transmission of the *Prajnaparamita Sutra* of the upper and lower lineages to Kam Yeshe Gyaltsen, and to So Gendun Bar he gave the word lineage and meaning lineage transmissions of the Oral Instructions on Seeing Naked Rigpa.

Also, there are three branch lineages coming from Pha Dampa Sangye. First, he taught Geshe Drapa the six or the nine cycles of the *Torch of Pacification.* Second, he taught Che Chandrakirti the instructions on the Union of Sutra and Tantra, and third, he gave the Prajnaparamita without Words to Jang Kadampa.

The middle lineage also contains what are called the scattered lineages. It is said that Pha Dampa Sangye gave to Drogom the instructions called the Golden Pointer of the Names of Manjushri. He gave the Karmamudra instructions to Bugom, and the Chöd teaching and fifteen various instructions to Machik Labdrön. Like the first lineage, the middle lineage teachings gradually went to Rok Sherap Ö, who lived around 1200.

The third lineage developed from Pha Dampa Sangye's fifth visit to Tibet. After a trip to China, he returned to India through Tibet. While he was staying in Dengri, he gathered many students, including the Twenty-Six Whose Delusions Were Destroyed, One Hundred Special Heart Sons, Twenty-Four Noble Female Practitioners, and the Twelve Who Could Step into His Place. From each of them came an immeasurable tradition of instructions, empowerments, and commentaries. However, the main students of his third lineage were called the Yogis of the Four Gates, who collected and wrote down his teachings. In the east Dampa Charchen collected Pha Dampa Sangye's instructions combined with the sutras; in the south Vajra Khrodha collected the combined jewels of meaningful instructions; in the west, Charchung collected the instructions in sets; and in the north, Jangchup Sempa Kunga collected various teachings.

The middle lineage of Pha Dampa Sangye is more related with the third-turning sutras of the Buddha, while the third lineage is more related with the Vajrayana practices.

The most special Pacification lineage came from Jangchup Sempa Kunga, whose realization was said to equal that of Pha Dampa Sangye. This lineage has a complete path of instructions, empowerments, commentaries, and all the different branches. Jangchup Sempa Kunga gave all his instructions to Khetsun Patsap Gompa, who passed them on to Gyalwa Te-ne, who transmitted them to Rok Deshek Chenpo Sherap Ö. So, it is clear that Rok Sherap Ö received the complete instructions of the Shije lineages. From him these teachings went to Rok Thamche Khyenpa and others, and then spread widely.

Later, in the seventeenth century, when the Pacification teachings had become weak, the karmic propensities of Rok Thamche Khyenpa awakened in Minling Lochen Dharma Shri, and he made a great effort to receive all the empowerments and instructions of this lineage. Lochen Dharma Shri also wrote texts on the Pacification lineage instructions, empowerments, and commentaries, and because he gave those teachings extensively, even today the Shije lineage remains unbroken.

THE CHÖD LINEAGE

Chöd, or Cutting, is a branch of the Shije Pacification practice, and it has two lineages, the male Chöd and female Chöd. The male Chöd lineage began when Pha Dampa Sangye gave his teachings to Kyo Shakya

Yeshe and Yarlung Mara Serpo. He gave them a form of Chöd called the Instructions Combined in Six Parts, which is based on the Sutrayana teachings of Aryadeva's *Fifty Stanzas*. Kyo gave this teaching to his nephew, Sönam Lama, who gave four of these six parts to Machik Labdrön. Mara Serpo gave these teachings to his attendant, Nyönpa Be-re, and from him they went to Rok Sherap Ö, Khedrup Shönu Drup, and others, and became the male Chöd lineage.

The Prajnaparamita incarnated in human form as the female siddha Machik Labkyi Drönma, who was born in 1062. Machik recited the *Prajnaparamita Sutra* many times, in its long, medium, and short forms, and thereby experienced the view of emptiness. Her being was liberated from hearing only one word of heart instruction from Pha Dampa Sangye, and she spontaneously became a dakini.

The path of Chöd practice was opened wide from her experience and realization of the main meaning of the Prajnaparamita. She formulated countless instructions, which are categorized into the four lineages of the skillful means of the father lineage, the wisdom of the mother lineage, the meaningful nondual lineage, and the experiential lineage of the dakinis. Her many students included 128 male and female siddhas who lived throughout central Tibet and Kham. There were several groups of students who were the most important among them. The Four Heart Sons were Önse Gyalwa Döndrup, Gyudzin Tongde Ngagi Wangchuk, Thugse Drölde Gyalwe Jungne, and Khugom Chökyi Senge. The Four Princesses were Drogtsa Gyen, Palden Gyen, Sönam Gyen, and Rinchen Gyen. The Eight Equal to Herself were Kye-me Gayen, Phonyön Senge, Nyönpa Rangnang, Dölpa Sangthal, Shigpo Hurthön, Kalden Senge, Gyagom Harthön, and Jetsun Silnön. Another group was called the Sixteen Great Sons Who Received the Transmission. All these students were very influential.

The main Chöd lineage came through Machik's own son, Langlungpa Gyalwa Döndrup, who held the sutra lineage of Chöd. The holder of the tantra lineage of Chöd, Thönyön Samdrup, became a well-known siddha, and his lineage came to be known as the Gangpa lineage, which was another special Chöd lineage.

The holder of the union lineage was Khugom Chökyi Senge. His accomplished students spread many lineages. For example, Namtsowa Mikyö Dorje transmitted the Ru-pe Chöd lineage to Karmapa Rangjung

Dorje. Later, the Surmang and Nedo Chöd lineages developed from the Ru-pe Chöd lineage. Jetsun Kyase Togden started the Kyapche Chöd lineage, and Treho Chökyi Wangpo formed the Treho Chöd lineage. Each of these lineages spread extensively.

In addition, the long lineage came from Machik's daughter Lacham. Later, Gyalthangpa Samten Özer received many different Chöd lineages, and in a vision he met Machik in person. His lineage is called the short lineage or the Gyalthang lineage. There were many other profound teachings that Machik did not give to her students but hid as terma. Later, Ladu Dorje Drönma, who was an incarnation of Machik, discovered these terma teachings. Another master who discovered Chöd terma was Kunpangpa Tsöndru Senge, who was a reincarnation of Khugom Chökyi Senge. All these profound and vast instructions are called the Gyatön Chöd lineage, which remains unbroken to this day.

The activities of the Chöd practice have profound skillful means, which make them truly wonderful. They spread all over Tibet and still are widely known. Up to this time the masters of all different lineages practice them, as they are very effective in overcoming outer and inner obstacles that are difficult to subdue.

Jordruk: The Lineage of the Six-Branched Practice of Vajra Yoga

Jordruk, or the Six-Branched Practice of Vajra Yoga, originated with Buddha Shakyamuni at the Dhanyakata stupa, where Buddha gave the Vajrayana teachings of Anuttarayoga Tantra to a great gathering of worldly and transcendent beings. On this occasion, in accordance with the request of the dharma king Suchandra, the Buddha gave the teachings of the root *Kalachakra Tantra* in twelve thousand verses. It was extensively practiced in the country of Shambhala during the time of the twelve subsequent kings. Then, Manjushrikirti, the first Kulika, or Rigden king, formulated a concise tantra of it, and the second Rigden king, Pundarika, composed a long commentary on it, called the *Stainless Light*. The subsequent Rigden kings spread these teachings further.

In previous times, pieces of the Kalachakra had been taught to the great siddhas of India, but the first person to reveal the *Kalachakra*

Tantra to ordinary practitioners was Chilupa Pandita in the tenth century. He went to Shambhala in search of the Guhyasamaja teachings, but on the way he was accepted by a master who was an emanation of the Rigden king. He attained realization through receiving the blessings of all the Kalachakra empowerments, commentaries, and pith instructions. His student, Pandita Acharya Pindopa, was later known as the great Kalachakrapada or as the Lesser Chilupa.

Pandita Acharya Pindopa gave these teachings to Acharya Manjuvajra. Because Manjuvajra carried the blessings of the emanated Rigden king, he attained realization and went to Kalapa, the capital of Shambhala, in his own body. There he received the complete empowerments, tantras, and instructions. Later the Kalachakra became his main teaching, and he had many students such as Naropa, Ratnakaragupta, and others. Avadhutipa, Shri Bhadrabodhi, and Nalendrapa were later known as the Three Lesser Kalachakrapadas, and they fostered the teachings of Kalachakra.

This teaching first came to Tibet when Gyijo Lotsawa Dawe Özer invited the Kalachakrapada Shri Bhadrabodhi to Tibet, and then Gyijo Lotsawa translated the *Kalachakra Tantra*, with its commentaries and instructions. Gyijo Lotsawa had four great spiritual sons, including Trom Lotsawa Padma Özer. The practice lineage that came through Trom Lotsawa is called the Gyijo Luk. Nalendrapa's student, Manjukirti, had a Nepalese student named Samanta Shri, who gave these teachings to Ra Lotsawa, whose lineage is called the Ra Luk. Also, Nalendrapa's student, Khache Dawa Gönpo, taught this to Drolo Sherap Drak, who taught it to Gompa Könchok Sung, and this lineage is called the Dro Luk.

From Nalendrapa this teaching also went to Tsami Sangye Drak, and this became the Tsami Luk. Tsami Lotsawa's student, Se Lotsawa Shönu Tsultrim, passed this on to Nyö Darma Ö, and his lineage is called the Nyö Luk. Nalendrapa also taught this to Abayakara, who taught Nishkalangka, who taught the Nepalese pandita Revendra. Revendra taught this to Chak Lotsawa Chöje Pal, and his lineage is called the Chaklo Luk. Another lineage came from Abaya through Vikhyata Deva to the great Kashmiri scholar, Khache Panchen Shakya Shri. Then, it went to Chal Chökyi Zangpo in Tibet. This lineage is sometimes called the Panchen Luk and sometimes called the Chal Luk.

There are many more Kalachakra practice lineages that could be mentioned. A lineage passed from Ra Chörap to Yeshe Senge to Bum-seng and then to Rongpa Galo Namgyal Dorje, and this is called the Rong Luk. Another one went from Tsami Lotsawa to Khampa Galo Shönu Pal to Shang Tsalpa, and this is called the Tsal Luk. From Galo it also went directly to Sakyapa Kunga Nyingpo, and this is called the Sa Luk. From the great master Shawari Wangchuk, the Kalachakra teachings directly went to Panchen Vibhutichandra, who gave them to Kodragpa Sönam Gyaltsen, and this is the Kodrak Luk.

Gö Lotsawa received the Kalachakra teachings from both Nyen Lo-tsawa and Ga Lotsawa, and his lineage is called the Gö Luk. Another lineage passed from Chak Chöje Pal to Kolungpa Do-de Pal, and from him to Khedrup Orgyenpa, then to Nyedowa Kunga Döndrup, then to Karmapa Rangjung Dorje. This is mainly the lineage of Tsami, but it is sometimes called the Kar Luk. In addition, there is a lineage coming from Sang Pang Lotsawa called the Bodong Luk. There are also the Kok Trangwa Luk, the Latö Wangyal Luk, and many others.

Later on, the Kalachakra teachings spread in Tibet mainly through the Jonang and Shalu traditions. Both of these traditions were first held by the Ra lineage and later by the Dro lineage, so the Kalachakra teachings we have now came through the lineages of Ra Lotsawa and Drolo Sherap Drak. The teaching lineage descended from Butön, and it is called the Bu Luk. The evolution of Butön's teaching lineage is discussed in the chapter on the teaching lineages.

There were many great Jonangpa masters who were known to be ema-nations of the Rigden kings. From among them, the great master Kun-pong Thugje Tsöndru, the founder of Jonang Monastery, received all the Kalachakra teachings that were translated into Tibetan. His main stu-dents were known as the Four Sons of Kunpongpa. Another great Jonangpa master, the great Dölpopa, spread the Six-Branched Practice. He had fourteen great students who were equal to him, and each of them spread their own instructions and developed extensive, ongoing practice lineages. In particular, Kunkhyen Drölwe Gönpo, or Taranatha, opened up the practice of Kalachakra very widely.

Thus, the teaching and practice of the Six-Branched Practice of the Kalachakra spread to all the tantric lineages of the New Translation schools. Both Jamgön Kongtrul and Jamyang Khyentse received these teachings, and Mipham Jamyang Gyatso wrote a commentary on

Kalachakra, so that this practice spread throughout the Nyingma lineage as well.

The History of the Approach and Accomplishment of the Three Vajras

The great scholar and siddha Orgyen Pal, who lived from 1230 to 1309, perfected the study of the sutras and tantras, and was particularly renowned for his knowledge of the *Kalachakra Tantra*. He experienced the ultimate realization of the Path of Seeing through the teachings of Gyalwa Götsangpa, who praised him as his heart son with the same realization as himself. Orgyen Pal went to many places, such as Jalendara, in order to perfect his yogic discipline. Many obstacles and apparitions occurred when he traveled to Uddiyana in the west, but through his confidence in the view and his yogic practice, he overcame them all.

In Dhumatala in Uddiyana, Orgyen Pal was blessed by the dakinis of the four directions. In accordance with the prediction of the Emanated Beautiful Lady, in the town of Kaboka, Vajrayogini herself appeared to him in the form of a prostitute. She gave him food and drink and the pleasure of touching, and through this she loosened the knots in his channels. With miraculous signs, such as loud sounds and earthquakes, she showed herself as the Vajra Queen in person and gave him the complete instructions. The four dakinis mentioned before, as well the Lion-faced Dakini, Senge Dongpachen, also gave him one instruction each, and he attained all the ultimate and common siddhis.

After Orgyen Pal returned to Tibet, he put the *Vajra Verses* in writing, in accordance with the request of his predicted student Kharchu Rinpoche. Kharchuwa was the nephew of Zazangwa Nup Duldzin, and he wrote brief notes on these stanzas of instruction. The instructor Dasa Senge also put instructions on the *Vajra Verses* into book form. Then, Golungpa Shönu Pal wrote down the answers that were given to his questions, and Zurphugpa Rinchen Pal wrote a large commentary. Khepa Sangtön and Nyedo Kunga Döndrup also wrote commentaries on the *Vajra Verses*. These last four commentaries are called the Four Great Commentaries.

From Butrawa Sönam Özer these teachings went to Chöje Kangpa and from there to Palden Lama Sönam Gyaltsen. The Nyedowa brothers also spread these teachings, so there are many lineages. In particular, Karmapa Rangjung Dorje received all the teachings from Orgyen Pal himself. He unraveled the meaning of the *Vajra Verses* and composed many special instructions not included in other traditions. Those instructions were spread widely by his next incarnation, Karmapa Rölpe Dorje, and his lineage students. Later on, the teachings on the *Vajra Verses* were included in the *Treasury of Instructions* compiled by the two Jamgöns, Kongtrul and Khyentse, which caused these teachings to remain for a long time.

5

THE ESSENTIAL TEACHINGS OF THE EIGHT PRACTICE LINEAGES

Ngagyur Nyingma: The Early Translation Tradition

THE TEACHINGS of the Early Translation tradition of the Nyingma are usually categorized in nine yanas. The first six are the common yanas, while those special to the Nyingma lineage are the last three, the inner tantras of skillful means. They are also known as the three yogas: Mahayoga, Anuyoga, and Atiyoga. From among them, the ultimate one, the pinnacle of the nine yanas, is Atiyoga, the Great Perfection, or Dzogpa Chenpo in Tibetan.

DZOGCHEN

The Sanskrit term for Dzogpa Chenpo is *Mahasandhi*. This word can be translated as "great samadhi," "great meditation," and "great mind of great equality." Mahasandhi is also taught as the great completion stage practice. As it says in the *Oral Instructions of Manjushri*:

> *Dzogpa Chenpo is explained as the general embodiment of wisdom. Dzogpa Chenpo is the second of the two stages, the completion stage practice.*

This means that the eight conceptual yanas are transcended, and within the sphere of the natural state, all phenomena of samsara and nirvana spontaneously arise as primordial wisdom. This wisdom is called Dzogpa Chenpo.

Atiyoga is categorized in three sections. The *Great Display of Ati* states:

Semde is for those with conceptual minds,
Longde is for those with spacious minds,
Mengagde is for those beyond effort or gradual progress.

In practicing the naturally occurring primordial wisdom, the three sections of Dzogchen represent different degrees of profundity. In the outer Semde, or Mind Section, one realizes that all phenomena are just the display of the nature of mind, and one is liberated by realizing there is nothing to give up, since the nature of mind is beyond causes and conditions, effort and accomplishment.

In the inner Longde, or Space Section, which is free from activity, all the perceiving consciousnesses do not come or go within the sphere of Samantabhadri, the true nature. The three kayas are always imminent and unchanging, and by understanding this, one is free from applying antidotes.

In the secret, very deep Mengagde, or Pith Instruction Section, all phenomena of the ground, path, and result are the union of primordial purity and spontaneous presence. Through knowing one's nature fully, one is completely free, with nothing to give up and no antidotes to apply.

The primordial wisdom, the Dzogpa Chenpo, transcends the eight consciousnesses with all their thoughts and expressions, causes and results. That wisdom is the great simplicity free from extremes, the space in which the mind and mental factors are fully pacified. The rigpa awareness, the naturally occurring dharmata, is free from something to be done, it is free from all mental activity, and it is the primordial nature. Simply leaving it as it is, letting it remain in its own way—other than that, there is nothing to do or create. When you let it be, then the temporary defilements, which are actually the manifestation of the radiance of rigpa, spontaneously dissolve in the natural state. Therefore, the Great Perfection of Dzogchen is especially elevated above the lower Buddhist schools.

Also, it says in the *Great Self-Arising Awareness Tantra:*

E MA! As for Dzogchen Ati,
It does not fall into any side;
It partakes of natural wisdom.
Like the lion who naturally subdues
The other wild animals,

> *The Dzogchen teaching, with its own expression, naturally*
>   *overpowers the lower yanas.*
> *Dzogchen, with its own expression, abides in its own actuality.*

In that and other texts, the definitive secrets of the extraordinary view and meditation are fully explained. For instance, the *Great Display of Ati* states:

> *Therefore, this definitive secret essence*
> *Is like a lamp compared to darkness,*
> *An elephant compared to cows,*
> *A lion compared to wild animals,*
> *Or cavalry compared to foot soldiers.*
> *It is especially elevated over all the others.*

There are many other quotations which elaborate on this.

As for the main points of this path, Dzogchen has unsurpassed instructions through the four liberations: liberation through seeing, hearing, touching, and tasting. Especially, it has the special empowerment of the secret section of Mengagde, which introduces the student to her own rigpa. Then, if the student's devotion does not degenerate and her samaya is not transgressed, and if she is somewhat familiar with the daytime or nighttime yogas, she can reach the level of primordial liberation in one lifetime. Even if the student does not reach liberation in this life, because of the blessings of the vidyadhara lineage and by the power of the truth of dharmata, when the nets of the body dissolve at death, as soon as she thinks of the nirmanakaya pure realms, she will see the nirmanakaya realms of the ten directions and be led to the eleventh bhumi.

The way this happens is described in the *Great Display of Ati:*

> *At the end of the five-hundred-year degenerate age,*
> *This teaching of the secret essence will appear in the human realm.*
> *The fortunate beings who follow this teaching,*
> *Those who see this essence,*
> *Will pass into the indestructible bhumi.*
> *Since in this degenerate time people have short life spans and many*
>   *diseases,*

Even if one does not have the full experience of the ultimate essence,
Merely through seeing this, one will feel tremendous relief
And be miraculously born, free from the cage of the womb,
In the nirmanakaya realm of the eleventh bhumi.

In this way, the Ngagyur Nyingma system specializes in the three inner tantras and their branch teachings. Within the Nyingma, there are three main lineages of teaching: the long lineage of kama, the short lineage of terma, and the profound lineage of Pure Vision.

KAMA

The central teachings of the Nyingma Kama are the three inner tantras, based on what are abbreviated in Tibetan as the Do-Gyu-Sem-Sum. As previously mentioned, *do* is short for the *Do Gongpa Dupa*, the *Scripture of the Embodiment of the Realization of All Buddhas*, which is the main Anuyoga scripture. *Gyu* is short for the *Gyutrul Drawa*, the *Net of Magical Display*, which is another title for the *Guhyagarbha Tantra* of Mahayoga. *Sem* stands for Semde, Longde, and Mengagde, the three sections of Atiyoga teaching; and *Sum* means "the three parts."

The actual sequence of the three inner tantras is like this: first, the creation Mahayoga has the tantra of the *Net of Magical Display, Peaceful and Wrathful*, and the practices of the Eight Sadhana Teachings. Then, for the precept Anuyoga, the main teaching is the *Scripture of the Embodiment of the Realization of All Buddhas*. Then, the pith instruction Atiyoga, or Dzogchen, has eighteen Semde teachings, nine Longde teachings, and seventeen Mengagde teachings.

The kama lineage of the Ngagyur Nyingma has four main streams of transmission: the empowerments, the explanations of the tantras, the creation stage practices, and the completion stage practices. The support for these four streams of transmission are the twenty-five volumes of the Collection of the Nyingma Tantras.

TERMA

The short lineage of terma has three main types: earth terma, mind terma, and the Pure Vision teachings. First, the earth terma have been revealed from the ground, rocks, mountains, and lakes by a hundred great tertöns and a thousand lesser tertöns. One way that great tertöns are distinguished from lesser tertöns is that the great ones reveal a full path of terma, enough teachings for an individual to become enlightened. The lesser tertöns are those who discover some sadhanas and practices, but not a complete path. Another way of categorizing the tertöns comes from Minling Terchen Gyurme Dorje, who said that the great tertöns are those who reveal teachings in the three areas of Guru Yoga, Dzogchen, and Avalokiteshvara.

These days, the most well-known terma teachings are categorized in two groups of three. The first group of three is called Ka-Gong-Phur-Sum in Tibetan. These refer to the Eight Sadhana Teachings, the *Embodiment of the Master's Realization,* and the Vajrakilaya teachings. The second group of three is called Lha-Dzok-Thuk-Sum, which refers to the cycles on Guru Yoga, Dzogchen, and Avalokiteshvara.

To go through these in more detail, in the first group of three, the most famous of the Eight Sadhana Teachings are Nyangral Nyima Özer's terma called the *Eight Sadhana Teachings, the Assembly of the Sugatas,* which has thirteen volumes; Guru Chöwang's *Quintessence of the Eight Sadhana Teachings,* in six volumes; and Rigdzin Gödem's Northern Terma called the *Self-Arising Eight Sadhana Teachings,* in four volumes. Second, there is Sangye Lingpa's terma in thirteen volumes, the *Lama Gongdu.* Third, there are a great number of Vajrakilaya teachings, particularly Guru Chöwang's terma called the *Razor Scriptures of Vajrakilaya* and Ratna Lingpa's terma, the *Unsurpassed Quintessence of Vajrakilaya.*

In the second group of three, which are the terma of Guru Yoga, Dzogchen, and Avalokiteshvara, the Guru Yoga texts are practices on the lama as the source of blessings, in both his peaceful and wrathful aspects. There are a great number of these terma, including Guru Chöwang's *Secret Embodiment of the Lama,* the Northern Terma Heart Practice, Padma Lingpa's *Ocean of Jewels of the Lama,* Ratna Lingpa's Heart Practice, Nyangral Nyima Özer's Wrathful Red Lama, and Ratna Lingpa's Wrathful Lama.

The second in the second group is the ultimate of all profound teachings, the Dzogpa Chenpo. There are a great many terma, such as the *Vima Nyingtik,* or *Heart Essence of Vimalamitra,* discovered by Dangma

Lhungyal. The essence of this text is explained in Longchen Rabjam's terma, the *Quintessence of the Lama*. Guru Rinpoche's terma, the *Khandro Nyingtik*, or *Heart Essence of the Dakinis*, was discovered by Ledrel Tsal, and explained in detail in Longchenpa's *Quintessence of the Dakinis*. Longchenpa also discovered the terma called the *Profound Quintessence*, which extracts the essential meaning of the *Vima Nyingtik* and the *Khandro Nyingtik*. These texts are part of the collection known as the *Nyingtik Yabshi*, or *Four Branches of the Heart Essence*. Other particularly important Dzogchen terma include the Heart Essence of the Northern Terma called the *Unimpeded Realization of the Great Perfection*, Padma Lingpa's *Embodiment of the Primordial State of Samantabhadra*, Ratna Lingpa's *Clear Expanse*, and there are many more.

The third in the second group is the terma on the practice of Avalokiteshvara, the Great Compassionate One, who is the special deity of Tibet. There is the terma that was discovered first by Drubthop Ngödrup and again by Nyangral Nyima Özer, called the *Collected Works of the King* or the *Collected Works on the Mani*. There are a great many other Avalokiteshvara terma, particularly Guru Chöwang's *Embodiment of the Quintessence* and Minling Terchen's *Embodiment of the Sugatas*.

There are also many earth terma of the dharma protectors and activity deities, whose practices were collected by Jamgön Kongtrul in the *Treasury of Precious Terma*.

Within the category of mind terma, the great tertön Longchen Rabjam had many profound and vast terma, including his *Seven Treasuries* and his Heart Essence teachings. Among the many other mind terma traditions that are practiced today are Mingyur Dorje's *Sky Teaching*, and Jigme Lingpa's *Heart Essence of Longchenpa*.

PURE VISION

For the profound Pure Vision teachings, some of the most famous are the Heart Essence teachings of the master of medicine, Yuthok Yönten Gönpo; Lhatsun Namkha Jigme's *Vitality Practice of the Knowledge Holders;* the twenty-five Pure Vision teachings of the fifth Dalai Lama, and many more. There are also a large number of writings related to these teachings by the Nyingma lineage holders, and most of these writings are still available.

REFUTATION OF CRITICISM OF THE NYINGMA TEACHINGS

Several great scholars, such as Gö Khugpa Lhatse and Drigung Paldzin, wrote critiques of the Nyingma lineage teachings. These are discussed in detail in chapter 7. These objections were refuted in the writings of many great masters, including Kunkhyen Longchenpa, Nyamme Samten Lingpa, Ngari Pandita Padma Wangyal, and Pawo Tsugla Trengwa. There was a critique falsely attributed to Karmapa Mikyö Dorje, and when he found that someone had used his name to criticize the Nyingma teachings, Mikyö Dorje wrote a refutation of that work. Lama Sodogpa wrote two defenses of the Nyingma, one in prose and one in poetry. Minling Rabjampa Orgyen Chödrak's refutation is called the *Vajra Laugh of Scripture and Reasoning*. Kunkhyen Jigme Lingpa wrote a rebuttal to eliminate this criticism from his history of the dharma and his collected writings. Kathok Situ Panchen also wrote refutations of the criticism, as did the Gelugpa lama Thukan Dharma Vajra.

The Main Teachings of the Kadampa

To explain the meaning of the word *kadam*, in the system of teaching of Jowo Je Atisha, all the teachings, or *ka*, of the Buddha are seen as instructions, or *dam*, through which an individual can become enlightened. As mentioned previously, the holders of this lineage have their bodies enhanced with the four deities, their speech enhanced by the three pitakas, and their minds enhanced by the three trainings. The four deities refer to Shakyamuni, the source of the teachings; Avalokiteshvara, the lord of love and compassion; Tara, who dispels outer obstacles; and Achala, who dispels inner obstacles.

The three pitakas are the literary medium of the teachings and the three trainings are the content of the teachings. Since the Vinaya goes with discipline, the sutras with meditation, and the Abhidharma with wisdom, the pitakas and trainings can be combined into three pairs. These three added to the four deities comprise what are called the Seven Divine Dharmas, which is another name for the Kadampa teachings.

SPECIFIC SCRIPTURES, INSTRUCTIONS, AND ORAL INSTRUCTIONS

The Kadampas have three systems of scriptures, instructions, and oral instructions related to the Seven Divine Dharmas. In terms of the scriptures, they study six texts in particular. There are two that generate faith: the *Jatakamala* and the *Udanavarga*, which are collections of stories and sayings of the Buddha. There are two that teach conduct: the *Compendium of All Practices* and the *Way of the Bodhisattva* by Shantideva; and there are two scriptures on meditation: the *Bodhisattva Stages* by Asanga and the *Ornament of the Mahayana Sutras* by Maitreya.

For their instructions, the Kadampas focus on the four noble truths of suffering, its cause, its cessation, and the path to cessation. They give graduated instructions that show the unmistaken path of what to engage in and what to refrain from.

Third, the oral instructions of the Kadampas are to simply practice the graded path as taught in the secret teaching found in their most precious book, the *Lamp of the Path of Awakening* by Atisha. In that book, the oral instructions of Atisha say:

> *Remember the refuge lama*
> *And that your body has the nature of a deity.*
> *Use your speech to remind yourself of the mantra.*
> *See all sentient beings as your parents,*
> *And examine emptiness as the nature of the mind.*
> *By giving rise to these five,*
> *All of your virtuous actions will be pure.*

By being mindful of these five—the lama, the deity, the mantra, compassion, and emptiness, then the relative and absolute oral instructions, which are known as the Sixteen Circles of the Kadampas, are made into the path.[1]

TEACHINGS FOR THE THREE TYPES OF INDIVIDUALS

Jowo Je Atisha wrote the *Lamp of the Path of Awakening* to teach the scriptures and instructions together. He laid out an all-inclusive, unmistaken path that leads one to accomplish liberation and omniscience. This is called the graded path of enlightenment or the graded path of the three types of individuals. The *Lamp of the Path of Awakening* states:

> *One must know the three types of individuals:*
> *The lesser, the medium, and the supreme.*

At the beginning, everyone is taught how to relate to a spiritual friend and the preciousness of a free and favorable human birth. These teachings are the basis of the path for all three types of individuals. As Arya Nagarjuna says:

> *First, there are teachings for actualizing the higher realms,*
> *And later, teachings for liberation from samsara.*
> *Once one has attained the higher realms,*
> *One can gradually attain liberation.*

To explain the three types of individuals: first, the lesser type of individual could be described as a decent human being. In order to have a comfortable existence in future lives, the lesser individual renounces attachment to this life and behaves appropriately in relation to karmic cause and effect. Second, the medium type is capable of renouncing all of samsara and practicing the three trainings to become fully liberated. In relation to the yanas, this level corresponds to the disciples of the Shravakayana and the Pratyekabuddhayana, who meditate on the four noble truths and interdependence. Their training results in the realization of the selflessness of the person on both coarse and subtle levels.

The third type of individual, the sublime one, sees the faults of dwelling in either extreme of samsara and nirvana, and is capable of carrying the burden of establishing all sentient beings in buddhahood. This approach includes the two views of Madhyamaka and Chittamatra, and the two yanas of Sutrayana and Tantrayana.

The specialty of the graded path begins with generating bodhichitta and goes on to training in the general and specific bodhisattva practices, including the methods and the resulting manifestations. In general, the terminology of the three types of individuals is found in many different teachings, such as Asanga's *Compendium of Established Teachings* and

Vasubandhu's *Autocommentary on the Treasury of Abhidharma*. The practices for these three types of people are taught in various texts, such as Maitreya's *Ornament of Clear Realization* and *Ornament of the Mahayana Sutras*, Asanga's *Bodhisattva Stages*, and so on. Giving an overview of the stages of the three types of individuals summarizes the Kadampa approach, and one could even say that all the teachings of the Buddha are found in these three stages of the path.

The Essence of the Teachings of the Gelugpa

The school that is called the Gelugpa, Gedenpa, or New Kadampa was established in the area of Drok Riwoche in the monastery named Gaden Nampar Gyalwe Ling. From the place name of Gaden, the practitioners and their tenets became known as the Gedenpa, which is easier to pronounce in Tibetan. This school is also called the Kadam Sarma, or the New Kadampa. One reason is that the founder of the Gelugpa lineage, Je Rinpoche Lozang Dragpa, commonly known as Tsongkhapa, is considered to be the incarnation of Atisha, the founder of the Kadampa lineage. For the Sutrayana practices, Je Rinpoche relied mainly on the Atisha's teachings on the graded path of enlightenment, and he rekindled the fire of those teachings. Also, this connection was predicted in the *Collected Kadam Teachings*:

> Eventually, the embers of the teachings
> Will be rekindled by one named Dragpa.

The Gelugpa also became known as the Yellow Hat school. In the tenth century, the monk Lachen Gongpa Rabsal, who was important for preserving the Vinaya tradition in eastern Tibet after the persecution by King Langdarma, gave a yellow hat to his student Lu-me Sherap Tsultrim, who was instrumental in taking the Vinaya lineage back to central Tibet. From then on, many great Vinaya masters wore yellow hats. To make an auspicious connection with revitalizing the Vinaya teachings, Je Rinpoche also wore a yellow hat and he allowed his followers to do the same.

THE THREE FOUNDATIONS OF PRACTICE

There is a praise of Tsongkhapa by the fifth Dalai Lama, which says:

> *By having the pure vows of an excellent way of life*
> *And the great courage of tremendous bodhisattva activity,*
> *And by practicing the yoga of the sublime two stages of bliss-*
>   *emptiness,*
> *May I meet the teachings of Lozang Gyalwa.*

This verse summarizes the three foundations of practice that characterize the essence of the Gelugpa school. First, one purifies one's mindstream through renunciation, and holds the precepts and samayas one has taken as the basis of the path. One's doubts are cleared by studying and reflecting on the teachings by the great charioteers of the Sutrayana and Vajrayana. By holding the vows and studying extensively, all the scriptures become instructions. Through the activities of teaching, debating, and writing, which resound like the roar of a lion, the dharma becomes as clear as day.

Then, through meditation one puts the teachings into practice and trains in genuine bodhichitta. One realizes the right view through relying on the profound instructions of Madhyamaka. One does deity practices such as Guhyasamaja, Chakrasamvara, and Vajrabhairava through deep meditation on the two stages of yogic practice, along with their branch activities. Through this, one will attain the great state of union either before or during the bardo. To sum up, with the support of both scholarship and realization, and both Sutrayana and Vajrayana, the view of Madhyamaka is joined with the wisdom of great bliss and taken as the essence of the path.

GROUND, PATH, AND RESULT

The way to hold this view is described in three ways: how to establish the ground, how to practice the path, and how to actualize the result. First, the ground is established by not dividing the two truths; one does not separate appearance and emptiness by regarding either of them as prominent or distant.

In relation to the ultimate truth, one should not get caught in an extreme negation, but know just how much to negate the object of refutation. When refuting mental fabrications, one should avoid falling into the subtle precipice of eternalism and nihilism. Also, one needs to differentiate between the provisional and definitive meanings of the Buddha's words, and study both levels with great respect. What is provisional and what is definitive are distinguished not only in relation to the scriptures, but also in relation to their meaning. Emptiness and interdependence are not contradictory, but mutually supportive.

As for the relative truth, it is defined and established according to the individual schools of Buddhist philosophy, and these should be understood without mixing them up. The Gelugpa school is firmly rooted in Chandrakirti's exposition of relative truth. In particular, the correct view of the relative truth is that an unmistaken cause leads to an unconfused result. Being certain about the way that works, one puts great emphasis on the karmic consequences of actions. This is a synopsis of the view.

Then, for the way to practice the path, all the crucial points of sutra and tantra are practiced in accordance with the three types of individuals, as characterized by Atisha and the Kadampas. When one practices according to the four bodhisattva practices, and the three knowledges associated with the Shravakayana, Pratyekabuddhayana, and Bodhisattvayana, the result is attainment of the dharmakaya.[2] Then, as the basis for Vajrayana practice, by receiving authentic empowerments that ripen one's mindstream, and by purely observing the samayas and precepts one has taken, one practices the two stages of creation and completion. This results in the attainment of the seven aspects of union of a sambhogakaya buddha.

The third aspect is how the result is actualized. Through establishing the ground of the two truths as inseparable, one is able to practice the path of sutra and tantra, and means and wisdom, as inseparable. This causes one to quickly attains the two kayas—the rupakaya and the dharmakaya—which are also inseparable.[3]

The Teachings of the Glorious Sakyapa

The word meaning of *Palden Sakyapa,* the "glorious Sakyapas," was explained by Jetsun Rinpoche Dragpa Gyaltsen in this way:

> *On white earth like the face of a lion,*
> *The Palden Sakya is the body of the lion.*
> *Fulfilling the wishes of the six realms of beings,*
> *It is the place where Vajradhara resides.*

Sakya Monastery is located in an area of dry, white limestone, which looks like the face of a lion. *Sa* means "earth" and *kya* means "white." This is how the name of the place became the name of its inhabitants.

The essential teachings of the Sakyapa lineage are based on the completion stage of the three Hevajra Tantras: the *Vajra Tent Tantra,* the *Two Segments Tantra,* and the *Sambhuti Tantra.* The *Vajra Tent Tantra* is the teaching tantra of Hevajra, and the *Two Segments* is a condensed version of the *Hevajra Tantra.* The great yogi Virupa took the completion stage practice of these tantras to heart and composed a treatise of pith instructions called the *Vajra Verses.* This is the root text for the teaching known as the Precious Speech Having Four Valid Hearing Lineages, or more commonly, the Path with Its Result, or *Lamdre* in Tibetan. The Lamdre is the essence of the Sakya teachings.

The Lamdre teachings say that there are four ways of bringing fortunate students to the path. These four ways emphasize the three aspects of valid cognition and the four hearing lineages. The great Sakyapa, Sachen Kunga Nyingpo, described this training according to the elaborate treatises:

> *With the three visions as the basis of the path,*
> *All the practices are understood through the three continua.*

THE THREE VISIONS

The basis of the path is the Bodhisattvayana and the three types of vision: the impure vision, the experiential vision, and the pure vision. Here the three continua, or tantras, refer to the general categories of the continuum of the cause, the continuum of the means, and the continuum of the result.

The three visions are three levels of perceiving reality. On the level of impure vision, students develop confidence by seeing the faults of samsara, the preciousness of human birth, and karmic cause and effect. By meditating on these they accomplish the path of the shravakas.

On the level of experiential vision, ordinary practitioners meditate on love, compassion, and bodhichitta, so that they accomplish the general Mahayana path. Also on the level of the experiential vision, extraordinary yogis practice the Vajrayana path. Many different experiences arise through Vajrayana practice, which can be categorized as fifteen types of experience. By cutting off conceptual elaboration, the experiences that arise are recognized and allowed to come and go, such that the practitioners remain undisturbed by them.

On the level of pure vision, one is encouraged by understanding and remembering the qualities of buddhahood, such as the inexhaustible mandalas of wisdom, which appear at fruition. One thinks, "I also could attain those qualities," and is further inspired to meditate and completely purify one's mindstream.

THE PRESENTATION OF THE PATH

In terms of the Sakya presentation of the extraordinary path of the Vajrayana, as the ground, the student receives the empowerments and maintains the samaya commitments. The real path comes from practicing the three continua: the continuum of the cause, the continuum of the means, and the continuum of the result. For the continuum of the cause, which is the fundamental ground, the main view of the Sakya lineage is the inseparability of samsara and nirvana. To actualize the view, one is introduced to the union of clarity and emptiness and then meditates on that.

For the continuum of the means, which is the path, there are four paths related with the four empowerments. The path associated with the vase empowerment is the creation stage practice, in its outer and inner aspects. One receives the empowerment of the path, and to understand that, one meditates on the profound path during four sessions every day.[4] The path associated with the secret empowerment is connected with practices of the vital energy and inner heat. The path of the wisdom empowerment is the practice of Karmamudra, the union with another body. The path of the fourth empowerment is called the Vajra Waves. It involves meditating on the three paths of the completion stage to integrate the example wisdom and the actual wisdom. By practicing these four paths, the worldly path arises as the four views, such as the three natures, and by the transcendent path one passes through the four stages. This leads one to actualize the five kayas, which are the continuum of the result.

In summary, the three visions establish the ground of the path, and the three continua form the actual practice. The four aspects of valid cognition and the four oral traditions eliminate one's doubts, and the five aspects of interdependence are used to categorize the path. Through these practices one understands the three levels of experiences. This allows one to become learned in the seven instructions of how to help others and clear away obstacles. By practicing all these, one passes through the views of the various stages, which is another way of saying that one attains the result. This is the way to lead a student on the elaborate path.

The medium path of training has five categories, and the short path of training has four categories. For all of these, even at the time of the path, the result is attainable. The Sakyapas teach that the ground, path, and result are inseparable, so their teaching is called Lamdre, the Path with Its Result.

There are several particular teachings that the Sakya tradition upholds through study and practice. They study six Sutrayana topics: Madhyamaka, Prajnaparamita, Abhidharma, Vinaya, Sakya Pandita's *Three Vows,* and Sakya Pandita's *Treasury of Logic on Valid Cognition.* They also study the traditional sciences of grammar, healing, and so forth, and on top of that, they study the tantras.

TANTRIC PRACTICE

In relation to their tantric practice, first, for Kriya Tantra, the Sakyapas practice the general and specific tantras of the three bodhisattvas: Manjushri, Vajrapani, and Avalokiteshvara. They also practice Medicine Buddha, Vimalaprabha, teachings on Manjushri, Five Protective Deities, Maruche, Grahamatrika, White Umbrella, Achala, Amitayus, White Tara and Green Tara, Akshobya, Vajra Vidarana, Bhurkumkuta, the gods of wealth, and many others. The Sakyapas are the main holders of the Kriya Yoga Tantras.

Second, for the Charya Yoga Tantra, the lord of the Tathagata family is Manjushri. The Sakyapas take the empowerments of the A RA PA TSA Five Deities of Manjushri and also the Single Manjushri.

Third, for Yoga Tantra, the tantras include the Twelve Purification Mandalas, Sarvavid Vairochana, Vajrapani Conqueror of Death, and so on.

The fourth section of tantra, the Anuttarayoga, has three categories: Father tantra, Mother tantra, and Nondual tantra. Among the Father tantras, the Sakyapas particularly practice Guhyasamaja, Akshobya, Vajra Manjushri, Avalokiteshvara, the Five Red Yamantaka Deities, the Thirteen Black Yamantaka Deities, the Sakya System of Bhairava, the Ra System of the Eight Walking Corpses, the Ra System of the Thirteen Yamantaka Deities, the Kyo System of Concentration on the Tip of the Horn, the Ra System of the Hearing Lineage of the Dakinis, the extensive practice of Mahamayura, the Single Bhairava, and the Four Families of Karma Yamantaka. For all these deities, the Sakyapas have the empowerments, reading transmission, practice instructions, and supporting practices.

For the Mother tantras, which have six entrances, the Sakyapas practice the tantras of the Heruka family, including the Ocean of Dakinis, which is Chakrasamvara according to the Kalachakra; and Chakrasamvara according to the final secret Yoga Tantra, as explained by the three great yogis Luipa, Drilpupa, and Nagpopa. Also, they have Chakrasamvara with a Donkey Face, the Chal System of Vajravarahi, White Varahi, the Five Deities of Kurukula, the Niguma System of Amitayus, the Tsombu System of Avalokiteshvara, the Family of Hayagriva, the Bhagavan Vajrakilaya, the Nye-be System of the Twenty-One Taras, and others.

Third, among the Nondual tantras, for Hevajra they practice the pith instruction system, the commentarial system, the Tsokye system, and the Nagpopa system. These are the four transmission lineages of body, speech, mind, and essence, which have seven kinds of empowerments.

They also have the Female Hevajra Practice with Fifteen Dakinis, the *Vajra Tent*, which is the teaching tantra of Hevajra, and the supporting tantras. There are also the empowerments for the *Two Segments Tantra,* the elaborate teachings on the Three Deities of the elaborate *Vajra Tent Tantra,* the Vajrapani Who Subdues Elemental Forces, White Prajnaparamita, and White Pratisara. For Kalachakra they have the empowerment of body, speech, and mind as a whole, and the empowerments and supporting teachings for the three deities of the Kalachakra called Vajravega, Shabala Vajragaruda, and Vishvamater.

THE GOLDEN TEACHINGS OF THE SAKYA

The previous teachings are held in common by the Sakyapas and other lineages. The teachings that are special to the Sakya lineage, which come from the hearing lineage, are called the Golden Teachings of the Sakya. The first of these is the precious teaching of the Lamdre, which is based on the *Hevajra Tantra* and taught through pith instructions. There are two types of Lamdre teachings: there is Teaching for the Assembly and Teaching for the Individual, and there is a special teaching for the primary lineage-holders. Textual study focuses on what are called the Yellow Volume, the Red Volume, the Black Volume, and the Blue Volume. They have commentaries by Tsarchen Losal Gyalpo, Khyentse Wangchuk and others, as well as many spiritual biographies of the lamas of the two teaching lineages—the Teaching for the Assembly and the Teaching for the Individual.

They also have the Thirteen Golden Teachings of the Hearing Lineage of the Sakya, which are not to go beyond their courtyard. The Sakyapas have two special dharma protectors: the Four-Faced Dharmapala and Gurgön. In particular, the Sakya family continues to uphold the teachings that came from Guru Rinpoche concerning Samyak Heruka and Vajrakilaya put together.

There are many collected writings of the lineage holders that function as a support for their teachings. The works of the five Sakya forefathers were assembled into fifteen volumes called the *Collected Works of the Sakya Lineage.* In addition, they have the collected works of their lineage lamas such as Gyalse Thogme, Ngorchen, Muchen, Gorampa, Shakya Chogden, Könchok Lhundrup, Palden Döndrup, Shuchen Pandita, Tsarchen and his heart son, Panchen Namkha Palsang, Ngagwang Chödrak, Sangye Phuntsok, Morchen Kunga Lodrö, and many others.

The Teachings of the Dagpo Kagyu

To explain the word meaning of the name *Kagyu*, first, Dagpo Rinpoche, or Gampopa, received the instructions of the Kadampa lineage of Atisha. Later on, he practiced the instructions of Mahamudra, which came from Marpa through Milarepa. He put together these instructions, or *ka*. Those who practice this lineage, or *gyu*, take their name from these instructions, and so are called Kagyu.[5] This is one way of explaining the name. Another interpretation is that since Tilopa received the four traditions of oral instructions, or *ka*, then this lineage, or *gyu*, is called the Kagyu.

The Kagyu tradition came from Jetsun Naropa and Maitripa in India to Marpa Lotsawa in Tibet. This lineage is mainly connected with the tantras of Anuttarayoga, which include such a vast number of instructions that not all of them can be mentioned here. However, the primary meditation instructions can be summarized in two parts: the Six Yogas of Naropa as the path of skillful means, and the practice of Mahamudra as the path of liberation.

GROUND, PATH, AND RESULT

Each of these instructions has three great features: the ground, the path, and the result. As it says in the *Clear Compendium of the Five Stages* and the *Latter Authoritative Texts:*

> The nature of things, the path,
> And the result arise in sequence.

The ground is the nature of reality, the path is how to proceed in stages, and the result is the way actualization manifests. The nature of reality has two parts: the nature of things and the nature of the mind. Both of these are described as having coarse, subtle, and very subtle levels. These are the ground to be purified.

As for the path, it has two parts: ripening and liberating. First the mindstream must be ripened by receiving empowerment, in accordance with the power of the teacher and the supreme, medium, or lesser capacity of the student. Then there are the stages of the creation and completion practices to bring liberation. Beginners do these one after the other, and once they are familiar with the two stages of practice, they do them together. The completion stage also has two parts: the path of skillful means and the path of liberation. Specific practice methods are related to what individual students need to purify.

Through practicing the path the result is attained. The result also has two categories: common and uncommon. The common results are the ten signs, the eight qualities, the four activities, and so on. The uncommon results are the supreme siddhis of the seven branches of union, the eight qualities of mastery, the four kayas, and the five wisdoms. According to how fortunate and diligent the students are, these results will be achieved in this lifetime or in the bardo.

THE SIX YOGAS OF NAROPA

The path of skillful means is the practice of the Six Yogas. It is the profound and quick path that actualizes the pristine wisdom of Mahamudra by means of methods such as generating bliss. These practices come from the tradition of Naropa, and they are done by very intelligent and diligent students. These practices are chiefly based on five specific tantras: Chakrasamvara, Hevajra, Mahamaya, Chatuhpita, and Guhyasamaja. The Six Yogas are the essence of these tantras put together with the *Kalachakra Tantra* in general. The Six Yogas are sometimes called the Path of Skillful Means Related with the Tantras.

An important text on the Six Yogas, the *Authentic Words,* lists eight yogic practices:

> *Inner Heat, Union with Another Body,*
> *Illusory Body, Dream Yoga, Clear Light,*
> *Intermediate State, Transference of Consciousness, and Transference*
>   *into Another Body.*

Of these practices, it is said that Inner Heat is the root of the path, Union with Another Body enhances the path, Illusory Body is the central pillar of the path, Dream Yoga measures progress on the path, Clear

Light is the essence of the path, the Intermediate State brings confidence on the path, Transference of Consciousness is the guide on the path, and Transference into Another Body mends what has broken on the path.

From among these, the Inner Heat, Illusory Body, Dream Yoga, and Clear Light are the four main practices. These comprise the profound path through which one can attain the state of union, or the stage of no more learning, in one lifetime. The instructions for the Intermediate State and the Transference of Consciousness are for those who are not fortunate enough to actualize this result in one lifetime. Union with Another Body and Transference into Another Body are branch practices to enhance and revitalize one's practice, so they are not counted among the Six Yogas of Naropa.

This is how the Six Yogas are taught by all the Kagyu followers of Gampopa. However, there are several other ways of categorizing them. Lord Marpa taught them as four points for attaining enlightenment. Marpa's student, Ngok Chöku, and his son, Shedang Dorje, classified the essence of the Six Yogas in two parts, integration and transference. Jetsun Milarepa gave the instruction of eight intermediate states, and Tephupa classified them as four pairs and eight single practices. Rechungpa taught them as three types of integration or nine types of integration and transference. There are many ways of elaborating on them or summarizing them, but they all lead to the same result.

SUTRA MAHAMUDRA

The second part of the completion stage, the path of liberation, is the practice of Mahamudra. In this tradition there are two aspects of Mahamudra: Sutra Mahamudra and Tantra Mahamudra. In Sutra Mahamudra, one receives instruction on not holding on to concepts and then settles into meditation on the uncontrived clear light. Tantra Mahamudra is distinguished as being bliss and emptiness together, with emphasis placed on the coemergent wisdom recognized from receiving empowerment and applied to the vajra body.

Sutra Mahamudra comes mainly from the instructions of Maitripa and has three aspects: nature, definition, and categories. Its nature has seven qualities, but all these can be summarized as nondual wisdom, which is profound and clear and pervades all of samsara and nirvana. As for its definition, it is called *mudra* because all phenomena of samsara, nirvana, and the path cannot go beyond it. It is called *maha* or "great," because there is no phenomenon that is superior to it. Then, for its categories, there are three: the ground, the path, and the result.

First, in Ground Mahamudra, being liberated or deluded depends upon whether one recognizes the ultimate nature or not. Since all the dharmas of samsara and nirvana are not beyond this nature, it is called *mudra*. There is no dharmakaya to be found other than that; therefore it is called *maha* or "great."

Second, according to Path Mahamudra, when one practices this, after being introduced to it through the instructions of the lama, one's perceptions and all the perceived phenomena are not outside of this nature, so it is called *mudra*. There is no primordial wisdom of buddhahood that can be found other than that, so it is called *maha*.

Third, for Result Mahamudra, after the temporary defilements are purified by the path, when the natural state of the ground becomes manifest, the displays of kayas and wisdoms do not go beyond this nature, so it is called *mudra*. The ultimate attainment is nothing more than that, so it is called *maha*.

TANTRA MAHAMUDRA

In Tantra Mahamudra, coemergent wisdom has two categories: the natural coemergence and the coemergence of melting in bliss. This is not the conceptual meditation where, after analyzing and finding nothing, one rests in that state. Instead, although appearances and awareness do not cease, there are no thoughts holding on to them, and one's direct experience is free of concepts. Taking this as the path brings one to the ultimate coemergent wisdom, or coemergent union. Lord Gampopa says:

> *Mind, thoughts, and dharmakaya*
> *Initially arise together.*
> *With instruction, these are joined as one.*
> *This is called coemergent union.*

In order to practice the path in this way, Tilopa says:

> *Kyeho! Amazing! This is self-awareness, primordial wisdom.*
> *It transcends speech and words; it is not an object of the mind.*
> *I, Tilo, have nothing to show.*
> *You will understand it by looking at your own awareness.*

Tilopa also says:

> *To recognize the true nature, the view of the ground of being,*
> *There are the instructions called the Six Dharmas of Tilopa:*
> *Do not consider, reflect, analyze,*
> *Meditate, or think, but leave it as it is.*

Practicing in this way has the same meaning as Maitripa's instruction to not focus the mind on anything.

In addition to this, Gampopa used the *Double Armor of Mahamudra* by Atisha and the Kadampa style of instruction as the basis for the ngöndro, or preliminary practices. The four ngöndro practices are designed to give rise to meditative experience that has not yet arisen. For those who have already generated some meditative experience, there are three ways of pointing out how to bring what has arisen onto the path. Then, there are the instructions for enhancing one's practice, and these generate further qualities. The same instructions are given to everyone without classifying their abilities as highly developed or not. When the training is completed, those of lesser ability are also transformed and self-liberated, so this instruction is unexcelled in its skillful means.

The followers of Phagmo Drupa and Drigung Jigten Sumgön emphasize the practice of Mahamudra called the Instruction Having Five Aspects. The Karmapas, especially the third Karmapa, are renowned for ripening and liberating students through the Mahamudra instructions called the Four Essential Points, the Wheel of Dharmata, and the Introduction to the Three Kayas. The Drugpa Kagyu has three different sets of lineage instructions: the Upper Drugpa has the Eight Great Instructions; the Lower Drugpa has the Five Powerful Instructions; and the Main Drugpa Kagyu uses all the instructions of the Six Cycles of Teaching. The four main schools and eight subschools of the Kagyu spread from there, and each of them has its own special teaching systems. In these ways, innumerable beings have been taught according to their individual needs and have become accomplished siddhas. Over the years this has become apparent.

In terms of the instructions coming from the Kagyu schools, in general, there are the sutras, the tantras, and the arts and sciences, which are presented through instructions in words, the transmission of the ultimate meaning, and the heart practices. Countless numbers of these instructions remain intact. In particular, there are two special qualities of the precious Kagyu: the practice of Mahamudra as the ultimate truth, and the profound path of the Six Yogas of Naropa.

SPECIAL TEACHINGS OF THE INDIVIDUAL KAGYU LINEAGES

In addition, the various Kagyu schools have their own special teachings and practices. To begin with, the Kamtsang Kagyu previously had a great number of special teachings, such as the Hundred Tantras of the Tsurphu tradition and the Forty-Two Mandalas of the Yangpachen tradition. The special teachings that they still have include the empowerments, teachings, and initiations of Amitayus, Akshobya, and other deities of Kriya Yoga, as well as Vairochana and other deities of Yoga Tantra.

For Anuttarayoga Tantra, the Karma Kamtsang lineage practices Vajrayogini, the Five Deities of Chakrasamvara, Jinasagara, and other yidams. These teachings include the empowerments, the transmissions of many Indian and Tibetan scriptures, and related pith instructions. They also practice the Very Wrathful Vajrapani, the Slightly Wrathful Vajrapani, and the Seven Mandalas coming from Lama Ngok. The seven mandalas of the main Kagyu tradition are: Hevajra Father, Hevajra Mother Dagmema, the Vajra Tent, Mahamaya, Chatuhpita Father, Chatuhpita Mother Jnanishvari, and Manjushri Holder of Secrets.

They also have the more general teachings of the *Vajra Mala Tantra* from the traditions of Khache Panchen Shakya Shri and Panchen Vanaratna. They use several large collections, including the Gyagyam Sadhanas, the Source of All Jewels, and the Hundred Mandalas, which was the main practice of Mitra Yogi of India. Also, they have the ninth Karmapa's collection of initiations and practices on the peaceful deities, wrathful deities, and dharmapalas. This collection is called Knowing One Liberates All, and its three sections are the Peaceful Garland, the Wrathful Garland, and the Dharmapalas Lightning Garland.

In particular, concerning the true meaning, the Kamtsang Kagyu lineage has a large number of experiential instructions on Mahamudra from both Indian and Tibetan sources. These experiential instructions cover the Six Yogas of Naropa, and the Six Yogas according to the tradition called the Castle of the Son, which came from Marpa. They also train according to Karmapa Rangjung Dorje's *Profound Inner Meaning* and his writings on the *Two Segments Tantra* and the *Sublime Continuum*. They have countless teachings from the Surmang hearing lineage related to empowerments, transmissions, and pith instructions, as well as the Surmang Chöd empowerments, transmissions, and experiential instructions. From the Jonang tradition they have the Kalachakra instructions, including the full empowerments with the higher empowerment and the self-empowerment. For Chakrasamvara they use the commentaries by Luipa, Drilpupa, and Nagpopa, and the Coemergent Self-Empowerment and the Infinite Chakrasamvara. They also have Hevajra according to the Sakya tradition and Mahamaya according to the Ngok tradition.

Many of their practices are shared by the other lineages. The Kagyupas practice Chatuhpita Father and Chatuhpita Mother, Tara Yogini, three types of Vajrayogini, the Vajrakilaya Tantra, Guhyasamaja according to Nagarjuna and his spiritual sons, the Five Deities of Red Yamantaka, the Shangpa tradition of Black Yamantaka, the Thirteen Black Yamantaka Deities, the Eight Walking Corpses, Infinite Yamantaka, Unsurpassable Achala, the five tantras of the Shangpa tradition, Sambhogakaya Akshobya, the abhisheka of the Nine Deities of Amitayus, experiential instructions for the Six-Branched Practice of Vajra Yoga and the Six Yogas of Niguma, and the Hundred Instructions of Jonang Kunga Drölchok. They have many teachings on the dharma protectors including Bernachen, Rangjungma, the Five Retinues of Mahakala and Mahakali, the Four-Armed Mahakala, Tseringma, and so on.

As supports for these practices, the Kamtsang Kagyu have the biographies and songs of Marpa and Milarepa, and the collected works of

Gampopa, Phagmo Drupa, and the succession of Karmapas beginning with Tusum Khyenpa. They also study the writings of Shamar Khachö Wangpo, Shamar Könchok Yenlak, Situ Chökyi Jungne, Karma Chagme, Dolpopa, Taranatha, and many others. After some time, the Kagyupas also practiced the Nyingma teachings. Many Kagyu lamas, such as the Karmapas and their students, did a great deal of work on preserving and spreading the terma teachings of the Nyingma lineage.

Another Kagyu lineage, the Drugpa Kagyu, holds most of the teachings just mentioned, such as the four tantras, but they also have their specialties. It is said that for the view, their primary teaching is the instruction on Mahamudra. For meditation, their primary teaching is instruction on the Six Yogas of Naropa. For conduct, their primary teaching is instruction on the Equal Taste of the Elements. For the result, their primary teaching is instruction on the Seven Points of Interdependence. They consider the Guru Yoga to be very important for all of these.

The Drugpa Kagyu have five particular sadhanas and transmissions: Chakrasamvara as the cycle of siddhis; Vajrayogini as the cycle of blessings; Inner Heat as the cycle of powerful energy; Coemergent Chakrasamvara as the cycle of the kusali yogins; and the Crow-Faced Mahakala as the cycle of the dharma protectors. They also have four practices that are immediately necessary: Vajrasattva as the dharma for cleansing faults and downfalls; Kamkani as the dharma for purifying the lower realms; Amitayus as the dharma for attaining deathlessness; and Avalokiteshvara as the dharma for blessing one's mindstream.

The Drugpa Kagyu also have both the older and newer parts of Rechungpa's oral tradition, the four great instruction manuals of the Upper Drugpa coming from Götsangpa, Orgyenpa's oral instructions on the Three Vajras, Yangönpa's three cycles of Mountain Dharma, the Lower Drugpa Kagyu lineage instructions that came from Lorepa on the Five Powers, the heart practices of the Seven Virtuous Deeds, and so on. They study many collected writings of their lineage holders, such as those by Lingrepa, Gyarepa, Nyamme Senge Gutsar, Gyalwang Je, Padma Karpo, and many others.

Similarly, the Taglung Kagyu lineage has a separate practice of the Six Yogas called the Six Yogas, the Wish-Fulfilling Jewel. They have the collected writings of the earlier and later reincarnations of Taglung

Thangpa, and their own special teachings on the Four-Armed Mahakala, called the *Golden Volume.*

Lastly, the Drigung Kagyu lineage has a unique teaching called the *Sole Intention of the Drigung,* as well as the *Essential Point of the Drigung,* five Mahamudra teachings, and many collected works and other teachings that continue to this day.

The Teachings of the Shangpa Kagyu

The essence of the tradition coming from the learned and accomplished Khungpo Naljor has the vajra seal of a single lineage, which means that it was communicated to only one person at a time. Known as the Five Golden Teachings of the Shangpa Kagyu, its root is the Six Yogas of Niguma, its trunk is the Mahamudra, its branches are the three ways of bringing experiences onto the path, its flowers are the white and red forms of Vajrayogini, and its result is unwavering deathlessness. These instructions are the vajra words of Vajradhara and the wisdom dakinis, and each line of the teaching is precisely numbered. The verses of visualization and supplication cannot be created or changed by individuals. The words are like melted gold, which cannot be mixed up and adulterated, so they are known as the Five Golden Teachings of the Shangpa Kagyu.

THE SIX YOGAS OF THE SHANGPA KAGYU

The first of the Five Golden Teachings is the Six Yogas of Niguma. One receives empowerments of either the five tantras or the mandala of glorious Chakrasamvara, and one is ripened by receiving blessings. An individual who is well-trained in the common ngöndro practices starts the Six Yogas by purifying his or her mindstream through the practice of the letter A as a means of training in emptiness.

Then, there is the path of skillful means, with the Inner Heat practice in which bliss and heat are self-blazing. There is the Illusory Body in which attachment and aversion are self-liberated, the Dream Yoga in which the compounding of delusion is self-purified, and the Clear Light in which ignorance is self-clarified. These four are taken as the root practices, and with them one eliminates the stains of delusion connected with the four occasions of waking, dreaming, sleeping, and meditating.

The other two practices, Transference of Consciousness, in which one can become enlightened without meditating, and the Intermediate State, which brings one to the sambhogakaya, are auxiliary practices related to the meditation stages of students with less ability and exertion. Doing these practices in accordance with one's capacity as supreme, medium, or lesser, one will be liberated during the three intermediate states—the bardo of this life, the bardo of the time of death, and the bardo of becoming.

MAHAMUDRA IN THE SHANGPA KAGYU TRADITION

Second, for the Mahamudra teachings of the Shangpa Kagyu lineage, the *Vajra Verses* give the ultimate instructions on the nonconceptual essence. Khedrup Khyungpo Naljor held the root verses very dearly, and put them into a Nepalese amulet in the shape of a heart, which he continuously wore around his neck. So these teachings are referred to as the Amulet Mahamudra. As the preliminary practice, one generates calm abiding and penetrating insight through the three ways of resting naturally. As the main practice, the lama introduces Mahamudra in a stealthy way to awaken vajra wisdom. The four faults become self-liberated and doubts are erased as the nature of mind is resolved. As the conclusion, one maintains the state of the naturally occurring three kayas.

The instructions of the *Vajra Verses* contain extraordinary methods for enhancement and the clearing of obstacles. It is the essence of the teachings of all the sutras and tantras, and the quintessence of all pith instructions. Through Mahamudra the four kayas are self-liberated, and all appearances, sounds, and thoughts are understood in their nature to be the lama, the yidam, and a magical display. In that way all phenomena are brought onto the path.

DESCRIPTIONS OF ACCOMPLISHMENT

It is said that within months or years, one's experiences of clarity, emptiness, and great bliss become the naturally occurring three kayas. The Bhagavati Vajra Queen is invoked by means of special prayers and visualizations, such as the practice of the Radiating Sun and Moon. The inner heat of Chandali blazes up within the four chakras, either through the method of passion giving rise to bliss, or the method of liberation giving rise to emptiness. In that very body one attains the celestial sphere of great union.

Through the thirty-two yoga postures of deathless accomplishment, one's body is put on the path of liberation. By knowing that the mind is primordially unborn, one's mind reaches the deathless state of self-liberation, and the aggregates of one's coarse, karmic body are freed from being the basis of birth and death.

Finally, the body is seen as an appearance of the mind, and the mind is known to be beyond birth and death. When one has confidence in that, one's physical appearance is resolved as the Mahamudra form of the deity, and that realization cannot be altered by deluded appearances. With any one of these instructions one can attain the kaya of union in this life. Just by hearing the instructions of the *Vajra Verses* one can become enlightened as a sambhogakaya buddha in the intermediate state.

The Shangpa Kagyu lineage has the teachings of the dakini Sukhasiddhi, including the Six Yogas of Niguma as the profound path of skillful means, and the Mahamudra called the Pure Primordial Wisdom. There are also the instructions of the siddha Rahula called the Four Deities Practiced as One, and Maitripa's secret teaching of the practice of the Six-Armed Wisdom Mahakala. This lineage of experiential blessings continues to this day.

The Teachings of the Pacification Lineage

The word definition of *Shije,* or Pacification, is as follows. In all the other systems of teaching that were brought to Tibet, the students first turn away from a negative way of life, and then they purify their mental afflictions. This is the main way in which students train. But in the Shije tradition, first they purify the negativity of the body, such as sickness and physical defects, which arose from previous karma, and then they engage in yogic practices. In other words, first one relates with the result of the suffering, which shows up in one's body, and then one works on the cause of the suffering. This tradition is called the Dharma Which Pacifies Suffering, and its name reflects its general approach, which is the same as the *Prajnaparamita Sutra,* which contains "the mantra that pacifies all suffering," and teaches that "the suffering of the three types of suffering is pacified."

The noble dharma called the Pacification of Suffering has as its essence the teachings of the Prajnaparamita. It is closely related with the Vajrayana, and is a special instruction that condenses all the teachings of the sutras and tantras. The founder of this system is the great lord of siddhas, Pha Dampa Sangye. After becoming accomplished in the unborn nature of clear, melodious speech, he gave countless teachings in inconceivable and profound ways according to various students' inclinations, capacities, and intentions. Therefore, this tradition cannot be said to be only one kind of teaching.

In general, he guided his students according to his own personal experience, with the three vows as the foundation, yogic practice as the path, and beneficial activity as the result. In addition, he taught the three trainings through the three cycles of the *Torch of Pacification,* in accordance with the students' capacities as lesser, medium, or supreme.

The Shije teachings came to Tibet in three stages: earlier, middle, and later. The main one remaining these days is the later transmission, which came through Jangchup Sempa Kunga. Its pith instruction is the Prajnaparamita and it is related with the Vajrayana. Its root comes from the tantras, and it introduces the ultimate essence. It is supported by many methods that create favorable conditions, and it is an instruction where the entire teaching of the Buddha can be practiced on one seat at one time.

In terms of how to practice this, those who are not yet ripe become ripened by receiving the four empowerments of extraordinary, profound signs. Following that, those who are not yet experienced become experienced by practicing the White, Red, and Black Instructions. Those who are not yet realized become realized by taking the blessings of the lama as the path. Those who have not cut their doubts eliminate them by assimilating the meaning of the words in their mindstream.

The real instruction is called the Seven Pith Instructions for Completion in One Sitting, which is composed of the White Instructions, the Red Instructions, and the five parts of the Black Instructions. First, the White Instructions are for highly developed beings who directly see the uncontrived true nature of the mind beyond perceiver and perceived, and who can become instantly enlightened. This is called the Instruction for Seeing Naked Awareness. Medium-level students practice the Red Instructions, which are specifically called the Crucial Point of Cutting at Once with Devotion. By perfecting the path of the four kayas of the lama, the students purify the essence element in relation to the body, speech, mind, and all together, and they accomplish the four kayas according to Thögal, or Direct Transcendence.

Students of lesser capacity are taught the Black Instructions of how to enter and accomplish the five paths in stages. These are called the Pith Instructions Which Cut with Subtlety. The Black Instructions can be broken down into the stages of the five paths. First, on the outer level of the sutra vehicle of characteristics, there are eight instructions gathered into one root teaching. The five paths are practiced in one sitting, and through the general mind-training, or lojong, one completes the path of accumulation.

Second, there are instructions according to the Mother tantras in order to forcefully hold the moving vital energy of the body. In this way the five paths are practiced in one sitting, and one engages in the path of junction, the path of ascetic practice. Third, also related to the Mother tantras, there is the instruction on using the experience of bliss, so that the four mudras are practiced in one sitting. Through this one cuts through to the path of seeing.

Fourth, for the instruction on the ultimate essence, the four yogas or four samadhis are practiced in one sitting, so that the path of meditation is enhanced with the realization of One Taste. Finally, through the instructions on the Six-Branched Practice of Vajra Yoga, self-liberating awareness is accomplished in one sitting, and through this one attains the result, the path of no more learning.

The Teachings of the Chöd Lineage

The lineage of Cutting, or *Chöd-yul*, is a branch of the Pacification lineage. The meaning of the word *Chöd*, or Cutting, is given in Aryadeva's small treatise, the *Fifty Stanzas:*

It cuts the root of the mind;
It cuts the root of the five poisonous emotions
And the extreme views, which become the causes for meditation;
As well as conduct accompanied by inadequacy, hope, fear,
And pride—because it cuts all of these,
It is defined as Chöd, or "cutting."

Aryadeva also explains the meaning of *yul,* or "object":

What is being cut are the mind poisons, which are the cause. These arise from pursuing unwholesome objects of perception. The yogi focuses closely on these objects, including the habitual tendencies, and cuts them, right then and there.

So the name *Chöd-yul* is based on the action done in this practice.

The Chöd teachings have a male lineage and a female lineage, and these days the female lineage is more prominent. The *Prajnaparamita Sutra* forms the basis of its view, and it also has the special skillful means of the Vajrayana, so it is said to mix the realizations of both sutra and tantra.

The main body of this path is practicing the four points of the teachings. These are listed in the *Compendium of Sutras:*

There are four reasons why bodhisattvas become very learned and
powerful,
And cannot be overpowered or moved by the four demonic forces.
These are because of abiding in emptiness, not forsaking sentient
beings,
Acting in accordance with their words, and receiving the blessings of
the buddhas.

To explain how one puts these four points into practice, first, one abides in the view of emptiness. The first step is to stop seeing the aggregates of one's continuum as a self, and then to stop perceiving objects and other sentient beings as substantial things or as having real characteristics. In this way one continually abides in the meaning of selflessness.

The second point is to not give up on sentient beings. In relation to form beings, one is especially kind to those who are miserable, such as the sick; and in relation to formless beings, like the gods and ghosts, one is not malicious. With great compassion, one directs beings away from thoughts and actions that would hurt others, and one leads them on the path of enlightenment.

Third, to act according to what has been said, one stops acting recklessly and behaves in accordance with one's bodhisattva vow. Fourth, to receive the blessings of the buddhas, one takes refuge in the three jewels, and then supplicates the root and lineage gurus with strong devotion.

With these as a basis, one becomes a suitable vessel to practice the instructions and receive the extraordinary empowerments. The actual instructions incorporate the sutra tradition, the tantra tradition, and the combined realization of both of them. As the core of all these teachings, as the uncommon preliminary practice, one accumulates merit through offering one's body, and through devotion and prayers one makes sure that blessings are received.

Then, for the main practice, one follows nothing but the rigpa awareness to search for the secret of the mind. When one has it cornered, then one learns how to rest in that. Through the instruction called Opening the Door of Space, one is introduced to the true meaning of the Prajnaparamita. In meditation, one remains in the ineffable nature free of thoughts and words, and accomplishes the dharmakaya in one sitting. In post-meditation, the four demonic forces are cut by living without expectations and doubts, accepting and rejecting, the grasper and the grasped.

Whatever seems difficult to cut is fearlessly struck down. Even if one could cut them at one stroke in a frightening place, instead one wanders to various haunted, isolated places to stabilize and enhance one's practice. Through the practice of visualizing that one is offering one's body as food, one alternates doing the peaceful and wrathful feasts, including the White Distribution, the Red Distribution, and the Multicolored Distribution. By equalizing the concepts of good and bad in this way, the outer gods and ghosts, as well as one's inner ego-clinging, are recognized as selfless. At that moment it is evident that the Chöd practice is accomplished. Finally, one attains the three types of confidence, and all the paths and stages are spontaneously perfected.

The teachings on Shije and Chöd are contained in texts such as Pha Dampa Sangye's *Trilogy on Purity* and the *Torch of Pacification,* and the teachings of the three masters who followed Pha Dampa Sangye: Ma Chökyi Sherap, So Gendun Bar, and Kam Yeshe Gyaltsen. Also, these teachings are part of Dampa Kunga's system in his *Book on the Five Paths,* and in the text called the *Heart Practice of the Twelve Buddhas.* There are also many other texts on the Pacification teachings, such as those concerning the dharma protector Aghora.

These are several cycles of texts specific to the Chöd practice, such as the *Great Verse;* the *Great Composition of Precepts;* the *Further Composition, Questions and Answers;* the *Quintessential Composition, the Root of the Dharma;* the *Eight Common, Eight Extraordinary, and Eight Specific Appendices of Machik;* the *Treatise on Developing a Hair's Tip of Wisdom;* and the *Heart Essence of Profound Meaning.*

There are also various systems of Chöd practice—the Surmang tradition; the Gyalthang tradition; the Chöd practice and instructions of the third Karmapa, Rangjung Dorje; Togden Namdak's notes and instructions on wandering in isolated places; Taranatha's instructions called the *Essence of the Crucial Meaning;* Shamar Könchok Yenlak's Chöd instructions called the *Rain of Whatever Is Desired;* and the many writings by Karma Chagme. Altogether, there are many Chöd texts in all schools of Tibetan Buddhism.

The Six-Branched Practice of Vajra Yoga

The Six-Branched Practice of Vajra Yoga comes from the *Kalachakra Tantra.* What is hidden within the vajra words of the Anuttarayoga tantras, such as Chakrasamvara and Hevajra, is clearly stated in the Kalachakra. In all the root tantras of Kalachakra, such as the *Supreme Primordial Buddha,* the highest, profound meaning is directly shown to have a single intention. The Six-Branched Practice of the Yoga of Mahamudra is accepted as being unsurpassed and the ultimate completion stage practice.

To name the Six-Branched Practice, the root *Kalachakra Tantra* states:

> *Withdrawal and Mental Stabilization,*
> *Life-Force Energy and Retention,*
> *And Recollection and Concentration*
> *Comprise the Six-Branched Practice.*

The first two, Withdrawal and Mental Stabilization, are the yogas of the vajra body. They purify the central channel and accomplish all aspects of the vajra body. The second two, the Life-Force Energy and Retention, are the yogas of vajra speech. The Life-Force Energy practice brings the vital energy of the left and right channels into the central channel, and the Retention practice stabilizes that. Through these two, all aspects of vajra speech are accomplished.

Recollection is the yoga of the vajra mind. On the basis of the three mudras, the bodhichitta melts and is held without attachment, and in this way all aspects of the vajra mind are accomplished. Concentration, or samadhi, is the vajra pristine wisdom in which bliss free from attachment is inseparably united with the bodily kaya. Through this union, all aspects of vajra wisdom, including the union of bliss-emptiness, are accomplished. They are accomplished through the four stages of practice: approaching, closely approaching, accomplishment, and great accomplishment.

These six practices are also included in the three goodnesses. Withdrawal and Mental Stabilization are good in the beginning, the Life-Force Energy and Retention are good in the middle, and Recollection and Concentration are good in the end. The two that are good in the beginning accomplish extraordinary Shamatha and Vipashyana meditation. The two that are good in the middle integrate the vital energy with the mind and open the four chakras. The practices that are good in the end bring attainment of the changeless, primordial wisdom body.

By using these six branches as one's practice, at the beginning one partially experiences the vajra wisdom, and gradually one receives the full blessings of the descent of vajra wisdom, in which visions, experiences, and signs arise. The mind naturally remains nonconceptual, the body trembles, and the speech utters various expressions. By staying with these experiences without attachment or aversion, no matter what they are like, the knots of the body, speech, and mind gradually loosen. In the end, the essence, particles, and vital energy of the six chakras are purified, and one attains the kaya of the wisdom of the sixth buddha-family, that of Vajradhara.

As for the scriptural teachings coming from this lineage, the essence of the Kalachakra instruction on the Six-Branched Practice is called the Hearing Lineage of the Kalachakrapada. This is contained in various texts such as Shavaripa's small treatise and its commentary. There are many root texts and different sadhanas, such as the sadhana of the Nine Deities of Kalachakra with its supplemental practices. There is a commentary on the Six-Branched Practice called *Meaningful to Behold,* a commentary on the medium-size Six-Branched Practice called *Revealing the Vajra Words,* and many other commentaries on Kalachakra practice, which are still available today.

The Approach and Accomplishment of the Three Vajras

This tradition gets its name from the way it is practiced. It says in the *Guhyasamaja Tantra*:

> Make your body like your mind, make your mind like your body, and make your mind like it is expressed in words.

At the time of the ground, a relationship is established between the vajra body, vajra speech, and vajra mind so that they are inseparable. At the time of the path, one practices the yoga of the inseparable three vajras; and at the time of the result, there are special instructions so that the secret of the three vajras is actualized.

The *Vajra Verses* say:

> *Training the channels purifies the defilements of the body,*
> *Training the vital energy purifies the defilements of the speech,*
> *And attaining bliss without emission destroys the habitual patterns*
> *of the mind.*

Through the progression of the four joys, the knots of the four
channels are released.
By reversing sinking into unconsciousness, the sleep of ignorance is
cleared away.
Even nonattachment falls apart and the mind of aggression is
exhausted.
Since attachment is purified, one is liberated in great bliss.

This system is also based on the Kalachakra, so it includes the Six-Branched Practice of Vajra Yoga. Those six practices correlate with these three vajras. To purify the channels of the body, as part of the approaching stage practice, one practices the yoga of Withdrawal on the points of the body. The activity of Withdrawal is the cause and Mental Stabilization is the result. Through those, the vajra body is established.

To purify the vital energy of speech, one's preliminary practice is the vajra recitation. Then, the practice of the Life-Force Energy is the cause, and practice of Retention is the result. The activity of these two become the stage of accomplishment, and the vajra speech is established through all four practices of Withdrawal, Mental Stabilization, Life-Force Energy, and Retention.

To purify the essence element of the mind, the branches of practice are associated with the stage of great accomplishment. First, the practice of Recollection reveals all the worldly paths. A highly capable practitioner will purify the essence element through inner heat practice; a medium-level practitioner will do it within his own body; and a lesser practitioner will do it through another's body as a consort. Then, the yoga of Concentration reveals the transcendent path. There are two aspects: nondual great bliss with a reference point, and nondual great bliss without a reference point. When one's mind remains one-pointed in the bliss of intrinsic awareness, the pure essence that is usually emitted from the body is retained without release. Through the practices of Recollection and Concentration, the vajra mind is established.

When the three vajras are practiced properly, the gross, subtle, and very subtle obscurations of body, speech, and mind are purified. As a result, one attains the three kayas in one lifetime in one body.

As for the teachings of this practice lineage, the root texts of the path of skillful means were bestowed by four dakinis. There are also the *Vajra*

Songs of Aspiration, the commentary on the approach and accomplishment practices called the *Wish-Fulfilling Jewel,* the Ngöndro ritual texts, Dawa Senge's commentary on the approach and accomplishment practices, the Heart Essence text on how to practice approach and accomplishment in one sitting, and the commentary on that written by Drugpa Padma Karpo. These and other texts on the Three Vajras are studied and practiced to this day.

6

RANGTONG AND
SHENTONG MADHYAMAKA

An Overview of Madhyamaka

THE BUDDHIST TEACHINGS that spread in Tibet were a union of the sutras and tantras. In relation to the Sutrayana aspect of Tibetan Buddhism, there is a saying that its conduct follows the Sarvastivada Vinaya and its view is the Madhyamaka philosophy. All four schools of Tibetan Buddhism agree that Madhyamaka, or the Middle Way, is the highest philosophy. To summarize Madhyamaka, one could say that the ground is the union of the two truths, the path is the union of the two accumulations, and the result is the union of the two kayas. All the schools concur on this. However, within the view of Madhyamaka there are inner differences. These differences revolve around how the relative and ultimate truths are understood.

In terms of the relative truth, some people distinguish three views within the Madhyamaka: Sautrantika Madhyamaka, Yogachara Madhyamaka, and the Madhyamaka that accepts the common consensus. To distinguish these three, Jamgön Kongtrul says in the *Treasury of Knowledge* that the Sautrantika school asserts that external reality does exist on the relative level. This was taught by Bhavaviveka and others. The Yogachara school asserts that external reality does not exist, even conventionally. This view comes from Shantarakshita and others. The third group makes no philosophical statements as to whether the relative world exists or not. They do not question the way ordinary people conceive of external reality. This is the view of Chandrakirti and others. So, these three categories of Madhyamaka are based on their understanding of the relative truth.[1]

Then, for the ultimate truth, there are two schools of Madhyamaka: those who assert the ultimate is the illusory nature, and those who make no assertions. To explain further, the first says that the illusory nature is established when the perceiver of an object experiences a perception of that object as being unreal. This view was put forth by Kamalashila, Shantarakshita, and other proponents of the Svatantrika Madhyamaka school. Their view is clearly explained in Mipham Jamyang Gyatso's commentary on Shantarakshita's *Ornament of the Middle Way*. This commentary by Mipham Rinpoche is often considered the most important philosophical text of the Nyingma lineage in Tibet, particularly for those who follow Mipham Rinpoche's understanding of the Shentong Madhyamaka view.

The second way describes the ultimate as being when appearance is seen to be free of all elaboration and that is fully seen again. It is decisively seeing appearances as free of existing or not existing. This view was held by Buddhapalita and others.

There are several other ways of categorizing Madhyamaka philosophy. Acharya Shantarakshita distinguishes two ways of understanding relative truth: one that sees the relative as consciousness, and one that sees the relative as habitual tendencies. Acharya Maitripa has two categories of the ultimate truth: in his first category the ultimate is illusory and nondual; it is seeing that everything is an illusion. In his second category all phenomena are completely nonabiding; there is not even the concept of an illusion.

The Kashmiri pandita Lakshmi forms three divisions: Sautrantika Madhyamaka, Yogachara Madhyamaka, and Prajnaparamita Madhyamaka. The differences between them are in the way the ultimate is said to be empty, and especially in the way the relative truth is defined. Each of the schools is a little bit different, and there are many different ways in which the relative and ultimate truths are explained.

According to Jamgön Kongtrul, there are the two general categories of Sutrayana Madhyamaka and Tantrayana Madhyamaka. Within Sutrayana Madhyamaka he describes two further categories, Rangtong, "empty of self," and Shentong, "empty of other." This chapter focuses on how the Rangtong and Shentong understand the Middle Way philosophy, and how their views differ. We will begin by surveying the view of Rangtong Madhyamaka and how it developed.

Rangtong Madhyamaka

Wisdom, a Root Text on the Middle Way is the foremost text by Nagarjuna. Different interpretations of this text led to the formation of the various Madhyamaka schools, particularly the Prasangika, or Consequence, school and the Svatantrika, or Autonomy, school. The Prasangika Madhyamaka school follows the commentary entitled *Buddhapalita,* which was written by the scholar Buddhapalita, and the *Clear Words* by Chandrakirti. Other important treatises for the Prasangika system are Chandrakirti's *Entrance to the Middle Way,* Shantideva's *Way of the Bodhisattva,* and Atisha's root text and autocommentary called the *Entrance to the Two Truths.*

THE SVATANTRIKA TRADITION

The Svatantrika school follows Bhavaviveka's *Lamp of Wisdom,* which is his commentary on *Wisdom, a Root Text on the Middle Way.* Bhavaviveka's followers Jnanagarbha, Shantarakshita, and Kamalashila are known as the Three Rising Suns of Svatantrika, and their adherents make up the Svatantrika school. Some of their important texts are Jnanagarbha's root text and autocommentary called *Distinguishing the Two Truths;* Shantarakshita's root text and autocommentary called the *Ornament of the Middle Way;* and Kamalashila's *Ninefold Volume, the Light of the Middle Way,*[2] and his *Stages of Meditation: The First Treatise, Intermediate Treatise, and Final Treatise.*

These texts were introduced in Tibet through the translations by Pandita Jnanagarbha and Chokro Lui Gyaltsen of Nagarjuna's *Wisdom, a Root Text on the Middle Way* and Bhavaviveka's *Lamp of Wisdom.* The study and practice of Svatantrika Madhyamaka developed in Tibet through the teaching of Shantarakshita. Later, during the second spreading of the dharma in Tibet, Ngok Lotsawa Loden Sherap studied and taught the *Lamp of Wisdom* and many other Madhyamaka treatises. He taught these to the seat holders of Sangphu Monastery, and particularly to Chapa Chökyi Senge and his students who were called the Eight Great Lions. All of them upheld the Svatantrika system.

Later on, the great master Ma-we Senge Rongtön Sheja Kunzik reestablished the Svatantrika tradition in Tibet. In the nineteenth century,

Mipham Jamyang Gyatso started a special way of teaching Shantarak-shita's *Ornament of the Middle Way*, which is still spreading. The way Mipham explained the *Ornament of the Middle Way* goes beyond the Svatantrika view and becomes more like Yogachara Madhyamaka. Because of this commentary, many scholars say that the philosophical position of the Nyingma school is based on Svatantrika Madhyamaka.

THE PRASANGIKA LINEAGE IN TIBET

The Prasangika school was established in Tibet by Patsap Lotsawa Nyima Dragpa. He went to Kashmir and studied for twenty-three years with the two sons of Sajjana and other teachers. He translated into Tibetan the texts *Wisdom, a Root Text on the Middle Way;* the *Entrance to the Middle Way;* Aryadeva's *Four Hundred Stanzas on Madhyamaka;* and their commentaries. He brought these back to Tibet and estab-lished this tradition through studying and teaching them. His main students, called the Four Sons of Patsap, were Gangpa Sheu, who was very learned in the words; Tsangpa Dregur, who was very learned in the meaning; Maj Jangtsön, who was learned in both; and Shangthang Sagpa Yeshe Jungne, who wasn't learned in either the words or the meaning. Together with their own students they firmly established the Prasangika school in Tibet on the basis of Chandrakirti's treatises. By explaining, writing, and debating on his works, they opened wide a path for future students to follow.

All the ways of teaching Prasangika Madhyamaka in Tibet came from this source. It was especially through Shangthang Sagpa, the one who was said to be unlearned but was actually quite good, that the future gen-erations of Prasangika scholars developed. These included the holders of Patsap's center at Sangphu Monastery; the scholars of the Sakya lineage; the great master Butön Rinpoche; Je Rendawa, who was the teacher of Tsongkhapa Lozang Dragpa; and Tsongkhapa himself. Since that time these teachings have been held by the Gelugpa lineage, Karmapa Mikyö Dorje, Padma Karpo and his followers in the Drugpa Kagyu lineage, and many others. There are countless learned masters in all four schools of Tibetan Buddhism who regard the Prasangika as the heart essence of Madhyamaka philosophy. Through teaching, writing, and debating they have spread this teaching to the present time without degeneration. The main practice lineage of this system of Madhyamaka came from Atisha Dipankara to his students who became the Kadampa lineage, and from there it spread to all the schools of Tibetan Buddhism.

There are several ways of defining the difference between the Prasangika and Svatantrika systems. According to Kongtrul Yönten Gyatso:

> *These schools differ in the way the ultimate view is generated in one's being.*
> *There is no difference in what they assert the ultimate nature to be.*

In his autocommentary to the *Treasury of Knowledge* Kongtrul elaborates:[3]

> After Bhavaviveka saw Buddhapalita's commentary on *Wisdom, a Root Text on the Middle Way,* he criticized it and established his own system. Then, Bhavaviveka's system was refuted by Chandrakirti, who upheld the view of Buddhapalita. This is how these two systems developed. The difference is in how the view of the ultimate truth is generated in one's being. There is no difference in their assertion of the actual nature of the ultimate truth. All the great scholars who are unbiased say that both of these schools are authentic Madhyamaka.

THE COMMON VIEW OF PRASANGIKA AND SVATANTRIKA

These two schools share common views on many points. For both Prasangika and Svatantrika, the main things to be eliminated by practicing the path are the two obscurations—the afflictive emotions and the subtle, habitual ignorance. It is said that through cultivating understanding, you realize the selflessness of the person and the selflessness of phenomena. In analyzing the perceiver, you find two aspects: that which appears, and that which makes imputations about the appearance. It is not correct to negate what appears. As long as your ignorance and habitual tendencies have not been purified, the illusory appearances to the six senses do not cease. Even if you try to stop them, it cannot be done, and it is not necessary to negate them. All the problems that arise are not because of the appearances, but because of attachment to the appearances. Nagarjuna says in *Reversing Disputes:*

> *Some people think an illusory woman*
> *Created by a magician is a real woman.*
> *The initial illusion can be dispelled*
> *If a second illusion removes that misunderstanding.*

In his autocommentary to the same text, Nagarjuna explains:[4]

> Some people think that a magically created woman, who is empty by nature, is a real woman. Because they misapprehend her as real, desire arises to be with her. Then, the Buddha or his disciples can create an illusion which clears up that misapprehension. In the same way, even though my words are empty and illusory, they can reverse the misunderstanding that all things are not empty by nature. Just like the magically created woman, people take phenomena and my words to be real, but that misunderstanding can be reversed.

When a magician creates a beautiful girl, he does not become attached to her. In the same way, when something appears but you are not attached to it, then you are not fettered by the appearance. Children think something magically created is really there, so they get attached to it, and when there is attachment, the afflictive emotions increase. Intentionally negating appearance is a big mistake. Emptiness should not become a reason for things to disappear; in that case, emptiness would be understood as nothingness. If you meditate on emptiness in that way, you will fall into the extreme of nihilism.

Therefore, what Madhyamaka refutes are the imputations—the labels and assumptions about appearances. All of those who uphold the Madhyamaka approach agree that a permanent, singular, and independent self is not established even as relative truth. They also agree that the object of refutation, the imputed self, does not exist, even on the relative level. However, Madhyamaka does not negate what is accepted by worldly people as the interdependent arising of causes and conditions on the relative, perceptual level, although on the ultimate level they do refute the existence of interdependence. So there are two levels of refutation—one at the relative level and one at the ultimate level.

Nothing more is being done than to merely refute the perceiver as inherently existent and real. As Nagarjuna says:

> This understanding is that there is no essence; it is not the elimination of arising.

And Nagarjuna says in *Reversing Disputes:*

> *If I made some assertion,*
> *Then I could be at fault.*
> *But since I make no assertions,*
> *I am free of faults.*
> *If something is observable*
> *As an object of direct perception, and so forth,*
> *There would be something to establish or refute.*
> *But since I do not have that, I cannot be criticized.*

So, no matter what imputation is made about a thing, the thing does not exist in that way. In summary, the Prasangikas use nonaffirming negations, which merely eliminate what is imputed. They merely remove what is to be refuted. A nonaffirming negation is a mere separation from conceptual elaboration and establishes nothing else.

THE FIVE GREAT REASONINGS OF MADHYAMAKA

Emptiness free of extremes is proved by the two basic aspects of logic: refuting and establishing. Madhyamaka has five great reasonings: the first four are connected with refuting misunderstandings, and the fifth is connected with establishing correct understanding. In terms of what is refuted, first, causes are analyzed and invalidated through the reasoning called "the diamond fragments." Second, results are analyzed and invalidated through the reasoning called "the production and cessation of existence and nonexistence." Third, causes and results are analyzed together and invalidated through the reasoning called "the production and cessation of the four alternatives." Fourth, the nature itself is analyzed and invalidated through the reasoning called "free of one and many," and fifth, emptiness is established by analyzing appearances through the reasoning of interdependence.

The first four reasonings eliminate the misunderstandings posited by materialists who say that things exist by their own nature. They are sometimes called "the four reasonings that get rid of the extreme of existence." The first of these reasonings comes from the *Rice Seedling Sutra,* the fourth comes from the *Lankavatara Sutra,* and the second and third are found in many sutras. Now I will go through these four reasonings and give a very brief overview of each.

The first great reasoning, "the diamond fragments," examines the cause of an existent thing. For example, if you say that a plant grows, then what is its cause? There are four possibilities: it arises from itself, from something else, from both itself and something other, or without any cause at all.

In brief, if it causes itself to grow, then it would have to grow all the time. As long as the plant was there, it would grow endlessly; there would be no reason or cause for it not to grow.

If the cause is something other, that means the cause would have to be something totally different from the plant. The absurd consequence of a thing arising from something completely separate is that, for example, darkness could come out of light. There would be no connection between the cause and the result because they are totally distinct.

If a thing like a plant is caused by both itself and something else, then the faults indicated by each of the previous reasonings still apply. If the cause is neither itself nor something else, that is not possible because it could not be born. A plant cannot suddenly be there without any causes.

This reasoning of the "diamond fragments," which analyzes the cause, points to interdependent arising. The Buddhist view is that things appear due to many causes and conditions coming together. This reasoning refutes the notion that something existent could arise from itself, from another truly existent thing, from both of them, or without any cause at all.

The second great reasoning analyzes the result through "the arising and ceasing of existence and nonexistence." Here the question is whether or not the result exists in the cause. For example, if you say that a plant grows, is the plant there at the time of the seed or not there at the time of the seed? If the plant is there at the time of the seed, then the plant already exists and does not arise from the seed. If the plant is not dependent upon the seed, then the cause or seed is not needed.

On the other hand, if the plant is not present at the time of the seed, then the seed does not have the plant in it. The seed does not function at the time of the plant growing, and the plant does not function at the time of the seed being there. So where is their causal connection? Traditionally, this is compared to the horns of a rabbit: the cause does not have the result just like a rabbit does not have horns.

If you say that the plant is both existing and not existing at the time of the seed, that would be impossible—logically, either it is there or it is not. In addition, saying the result is both there and not there has the faults of both of the previous arguments. Then, for the final alternative, that the result is neither existent nor nonexistent at the time of the cause, that too is impossible. How could a plant actually arise if not from a seed or some sort of cause?

The third great reasoning analyzes the cause and result together, using the reasoning of "the arising and ceasing of the four alternatives." When you cannot find a singular thing that truly exists, it automatically negates the possibility that many of those things truly exist. Therefore, the four alternatives cannot truly be there: (1) that many results come from one cause, (2) that one result comes from many causes, (3) that one result comes from one cause, and (4) that many results come from many causes.

This reasoning establishes the unborn nature of phenomena, and points to a correct understanding of interdependence. Interdependence is not merely that cause and result operate. Cause and result do not function because things are really there; they function because things are magical illusions. There are many similar statements in *Wisdom, a Root Text on the Middle Way,* such as "there is no birth, no cessation, and no dwelling."

The fourth great reasoning analyzes the nature itself with the reasoning of "free of one and many." This fourth reasoning further clarifies the third reasoning, which was called "the arising and ceasing of the four alternatives." When you examine something like a plant, since you cannot find even one plant that is independently existing, it is impossible for there to be many plants that are independently existing. This reasoning establishes the unreality of apparent phenomena. You begin by examining a single thing and see that it can be broken down into smaller pieces, thereby negating singular existence. This analysis automatically refutes multiple existence as well, since there must be one before there can be many. This reasoning of "free of one and many" is regarded as the root reasoning of all the Buddhist philosophical systems for negating the true existence of things.

As I mentioned earlier, emptiness free of extremes is proved by the two main aspects of reasoning—refutation and establishment. The previous four reasonings clear away misunderstanding, so they are part of the category of refutation. Now we will look at the fifth great reasoning, which is connected with the establishment of emptiness.

Emptiness is established through analyzing mere appearance with the great reasoning of interdependence. This reasoning is found in the *Sutra Requested by the Naga King Madröpa.* Using the logic of interdependent arising clears both extreme views of nihilism and eternalism. The extreme of nihilism is eliminated because the relative, perceptual level is not nonexistent. The extreme of permanence is eliminated because everything depends on many causes and conditions. The reasoning of interdependence is known in Madhyamaka as "the king of reasonings" because it establishes the emptiness of reality. There is no disagreement between the various schools of Madhyamaka about these reasonings and the ultimate truth.

DISTINCTIONS BETWEEN PRASANGIKA AND SVATANTRIKA MADHYAMAKA

If there is no disagreement about the way of reasoning, then what are the differences between Prasangika and Svatantrika? As I have said, there is no difference at all in the way they posit the ultimate truth, but there are a few differences in the way they posit the relative truth. For the relative level, the Svatantrika school uses terminology similar to the Chittamatra, or Mind-Only, school, and the Sautrantika, or Sutra-Follower, school. However, according to the Prasangika school, the Chittamatra and Sautrantika descriptions of both the ultimate and the relative are incorrect. Chandrakirti's *Entrance to the Middle Way* states:

There is no way to attain the peace of nirvana
Other than by following the path of Arya Nagarjuna.
Followers of other schools corrupt both the relative and
   ultimate truth,
So they have no way to accomplish liberation.

The Prasangika masters do not follow the tenets of Chittamatra and Sautrantika concerning the relative truth; they say that the relative truth follows the conventional thinking of ordinary people. In other words, the Prasangikas assert that the ultimate truth accords with the perception of enlightened beings, and that the relative truth accords with the perception and terminology of worldly beings.

So, Prasangika and Svatantrika have different ways of positing the relative truth. In their statement of the relative, the proponents of Svatantrika say that the relative level is conventionally true. This contrasts with the Prasangika, who do not accept the relative as even conventionally true. In the *Entrance to the Middle Way* Chandrakirti says:

The way you accept the dependent nature as being real
Is something that I would not assert even on the relative level.
Although things are not there, I say they are there
Just to go along with the perceptions of worldly beings.

Therefore, the Prasangikas accept the relative truth only because others see it as true; it is not asserted from their own point of view.

Also, when they debate, there is a difference between Svatantrika and Prasangika as to whether they put forth their own assertions or not. The Svatantrikas do put forth assertions, at least on the relative level, because they say one must show reasoning about what is correct and incorrect, and give examples to prove what is true. The Svatantrikas say it is wrong for the Prasangikas not to make any assertions and simply negate others' views, because that is just attacking others without having anything better of their own to propose. They think that one first needs to use valid cognition to establish emptiness and the unborn nature, because merely criticizing others' views is not enough to establish emptiness.

The Prasangikas respond to this criticism by saying: "Since we have nothing to posit, then we do not need a way to establish it." The *Entrance to the Middle Way* states:

> *Both refuting and establishing are only negation*
> *Because in reality there is nothing to establish and nothing to refute.*

When the Prasangikas say, "Actually, there is nothing to negate, not even the tiniest particle," then the question is asked, "Then why do you negate things?" The Prasangikas reply, "It is not because we feel hatred for others' views or we just like to debate, but those with wrong views are caught in ignorance and clinging. We have nothing to establish; we are just trying to eliminate others' wrong views."

According to the Prasangika approach, they negate others' assertions to clear up misunderstanding. The true nature cannot be understood through the logical analysis of refuting and establishing. The natural state is free of all fabrications; it cannot be an object of conceptual examination. The *Entrance to the Middle Way* states:

> *Samsaric beings are bound by their concepts,*
> *Whereas yogic practitioners without concepts will be liberated.*
> *Learned beings say that the result of analysis*
> *Is the collapse of mistaken thinking.*

There are some other differences between Prasangika and Svatantrika, and various Tibetan scholars have their individual views about what the distinctions are. However, I will not elaborate on these here.

AN OVERVIEW OF THE PRASANGIKA ANALYSIS

Among the four schools of Tibetan Buddhism—Sakya, Geluk, Kagyu, and Nyingma—the great majority of those who uphold Rangtong Madhyamaka agree that the Prasangika school has the ultimate view. All four schools emphasize the approach of Prasangika Madhyamaka. So at this point I will give a summary of the Prasangika view according to the understanding of Jamgön Kongtrul.

The supreme scholar of Prasangika Madhyamaka was Chandrakirti, whose works on Madhyamaka are the classic texts for the Prasangika approach. He said that one should not assert a position of one's own, but use the reasoning of negation merely to show the internal contradictions in others' views. In Prasangika there is no attempt to establish or negate anything about one's own system, but for the sake of others, one simply negates wrong views by means of the four types of valid cognition and the four reasonings.

The four types of valid cognition are: (1) valid cognition based on what is known in the world, (2) direct perception, (3) inference, and (4) scriptures based on the authentic experiences of highly realized beings. The four reasonings are: (1) to use an inference drawn from what is known in the world, (2) to show the contradictory consequence of what is asserted, (3) to offer an equally valid reason that reaches the opposite conclusion, and (4) to show a reason is invalid because it merely reiterates the thesis.

These four special reasonings of the Prasangikas can be applied to each of the four alternatives already mentioned to examine how an existent thing cannot actually arise. In other words, does an object, like a plant, arise from itself, from something other, from both self and other, or from neither self nor other? Since these are the main reasonings used in the Prasangika approach, I will show how they are applied to the positions of various Indian philosophies by quoting Jamgön Kongtrul from his *Treasury of Knowledge*:[5]

> To begin with, the Samkhya philosophy of India claims that a thing arises from itself. This means that a thing can arise only if it is there at the time of its cause. Or put the opposite way, if the thing is not there at the same time as its cause, then it cannot be born. They use the example of being able to extract oil from a sesame seed because the oil is already there at the time of the seed. One cannot extract oil from sand, because oil is not already present.
>
> To negate that, from among the four special reasonings, the Prasangikas begin with the second, showing the contradictory consequence of the Samkhyas' statement. They use the following syllogism: There is no purpose in a thing being born since it is already present at the time of its cause. If it is already there, then it cannot, and need not, be born again.

If the Samkhya proponent says this reasoning is somewhat acceptable but it does not cover everything, then the
Prasangika opponent responds with another reason. The
consequence of arising from itself would be endless birth;
the thing would repeatedly reproduce itself. When people
say that something has arisen, that means it was not there
before. This is an example of the third type of reasoning,
the reasoning of equal weight, where one's reason has no
greater or lesser weight than the opponent's reason, but
comes to the opposite conclusion. With the example of
extracting oil from a sesame seed, the oil was not already
there in the form of oil. If it was, there would be no need to
extract it from the seed.

The Samkhyas reply that they agree, the potential oil in the
seed and the extracted oil are not the same. The oil is the result
and therefore it arises; it is born, so to speak. When the oil is
extracted it is not an unending birth; it just arises once when
the seed is pressed. The Samkyas give another example: a pot
is made from clay. Even at the time of the cause, which is the
clay, there is the potential of it becoming a pot. There was no
visible pot, but when the clay is shaped it becomes a pot. The
pot does not produce pots, but the clay produces pots, and the
pot is clay.

The Prasangikas reply: "How can you say that a pot is
there when only clay is there? To say that there is an unseen
pot in the clay is absurd. When the pot is invisible, no pot
is there." This is the fourth type of reasoning: showing that
the reasoning is invalid because the reason given is the same
as what is to be established. It is simply a reiteration of the
assertion, saying that the assertion is a reason, when no reason is actually given. So, any phenomenon, whether outside or inside the mind, does not arise from itself if the
phenomenon is already there. And if it is not already there,
one cannot assert that it is there. This is something everybody understands, so it accords with the first reasoning, an
inference that is drawn from what is known by people in the
world. This is an example of how the Prasangikas apply

these four reasonings to the first alternative of how something could arise from itself.

Next is an overview of how these reasonings are applied to the second alternative, that a thing arises from something other than itself. This view was put forth by the Buddhist Vaibhashika, or Substantialist, school. For example, they would say that a sprout arises from a seed, and that these are different entities. The Prasangikas reply that they cannot be totally different things, because for one to arise from the other there must be a connection between them; and if there is a connection between them, then they are not totally distinct. If they do exist separately, then one cannot be affected by the other. So, this is the reasoning of showing the contradictions.

If the Vaibhashikas say that this is not always true, then the Prasangikas reply that if the cause and result have no connection but are totally separate things, then it would follow that anything could come out of anything. Even something opposite could arise, for example, darkness could come from light. This is using a reasoning of equal weight that reaches the opposite conclusion. The Vaibhashikas reply that some things have the capacity to cause growth and other things do not have that capacity; everything cannot produce everything. The Prasangikas reply that this is adding a special condition, rather than simply asserting that things arise from separate entities. Therefore, sprouts are not caused by seeds, because these are essentially two different things.

Next, the Jain school of Indian philosophy put forth the view that a thing arises from both itself and something other than itself. Their example is that the pot comes from the clay, which is coming from itself, but it also comes from the potter, his thread tool, the water, and so forth, which makes it also coming from other things. The Prasangikas reply that logically, if something cannot come from itself and also cannot come from something other than itself, then how could it come from both of them? Each of these possibilities has already been shown to be invalid. Therefore, something cannot come from both itself and another. The *Entrance to the Middle Way* states:

> It is not reasonable that something arises from both itself
> and others
> Because that would entail both of the faults previously
> stated.

The fourth possibility, arising from neither self nor others, was asserted by the Charvaka school of Indian philosophy, who are known as the Hedonists or Nihilists. They assert that things arise without any cause. To negate that, the Prasangikas ask, if there are no causes, then why are things there at certain times and not there at other times? They say that if something without a cause could be perceived, then, for example, people could perceive flowers growing in the sky, because there is no cause for that to happen. This is using the reasoning of equal weight. If the Charvakas say there is a difference in that the flowers in the earth are there, but the flowers in the sky are not there, then the Prasangikas reply that the flowers are in the earth because of causes for them to be there. Therefore, things in the world do not arise without causes and conditions. Something arises when its causes and conditions are present, and when those are absent, the thing does not arise. This is using inference based on what is known in the world.

THE THREE SPECIAL POINTS OF CHANDRAKIRTI

Most Tibetan scholars regard Chandrakirti as the definitive commentator on Nagarjuna's five Madhyamaka texts known as the *Collection of Reasoning*. According to Jamgön Kongtrul in his *Treasury of Knowledge*, Chandrakirti's philosophy is characterized by three special points:

> The conceptual mind is necessarily a deluded mind.
> Both the accurate and the mistaken relative truth are equally
> functional.
> The two truths are defined as deluded and undeluded.

Briefly, these are the tenets of the ultimate commentator on the Collection of Reasoning.

As it says, the first special point is that the conceptual mind is utterly deluded.

Then, for Chandrakirti's second point, the *Commentaries by Bodhisattvas* states:

In the contexts of dreaming and being awake,
There is no difference in how things function.

So, the pure relative truth perceived by yogis and the impure relative truth perceived by ordinary people are not different in that they both function.

His third special point is explained in the *Entrance to the Middle Way:*

Whether things are seen correctly or mistakenly,
They are true in that they function, but they are perceived in
*   two ways.*
Seeing things rightly is suchness, the ultimate truth;
Seeing things mistakenly is the relative truth.

The two truths can be categorized by saying that what is true for the person whose mind is deluded is the relative truth, and what is true for the person whose mind is undeluded is the ultimate truth. These three points are considered to be the unique tenets of Chandrakirti.

THE EIGHT SPECIAL POINTS OF TSONGKHAPA

As for other special tenets of the Prasangika school, Tsongkhapa and the great Gelugpa scholars propose what are called the Eight Great Theses of the Prasangika. Four of them are stated as negations and four are stated as affirmations. The first four, the negations, apply even on the relative level: (1) they do not accept that things have inherent characteristics; (2) they do not accept any reasonings that assert what is true; (3) they do not accept self-awareness as direct perception; (4) they do not accept the alaya. The latter four theses that the Gelugpas attribute to the Prasangikas are affirmations: (1) they accept that there is some outer reality, in other words, there is interdependence and everything is not simply the mind; (2) from among the two obscurations, clinging to true existence is the obscuration of the afflictive emotions, not the subtle habitual obscuration; (3) they accept that the absence of something is in itself a thing; and (4) when the shravakas and pratyeka-buddhas attain the realization of an arhat, they realize the selflessness of phenomena.

There is a great deal of debate on these eight theses, particularly the third affirmation, that the absence of something is a thing. This point is very sensitive to the Gelugpas, and has been one of the main topics of debate since the time Tsongkhapa proposed it. These eight theses were specifically addressed by Serdok Panchen Shakya Chogden. He and his followers say the Prasangikas would accept that arhats realize the selflessness of phenomena to some extent, but as for Tsongkhapa's other seven theses, the Prasangikas never even dreamed of them. Many refutations have been applied to these points. In particular, the Sakya lineage holder, Gorampa Sönam Senge, compiled eighty contradictions to refute Tsongkhapa's eight theses. Recently, these eighty contradictions were extensively used by the Sakya khenpo, Khenpo Rinchen, who was a great logician of the twentieth century, in his debates with the Gelugpas.

THE FIVE SPECIAL POINTS OF KONGTRUL

Jamgön Kongtrul did not affirm or negate any of Tsongkhapa's eight theses, but formulated his own presentation of the Prasangika view in five main points. These five are delineated in the following root verse and autocommentary from the *Treasury of Knowledge:*[6]

> *Conceptual imputations are abandoned; all things are merely designations.*
> *Compounded phenomena are deceptive; nirvana is not deceptive.*
> *The root of samsara is clinging to true existence, which generates the obscuration of the afflictive emotions.*
> *Since the first three yanas have the same way of seeing reality, there is only one path of seeing.*

*All phenomena dissolve such that one's enlightenment only appears
for the perception of others.*

In his autocommentary, he explains these five points more fully:

1. In their own system and in relation to the world, the Prasangikas
   do not engage in reasoning or conceptual definitions of what is
   validly cognized and what is not validly cognized. They completely
   abandon making these distinctions, saying that they are irrelevant.
   On the relative level, there is no phenomenon, whether outer or
   inner, or cause or result, which truly exists on its own. Everything
   is imputed by the mind and exists merely as a designation. The
   horses and cows seen in the waking state and the horses and cows
   seen in a dream are equally unreal.[7]
2. If something is compounded, there is no activity in the first
   instant of its existence, but in the second instant it has changed
   and is no longer there. If one analyzes through reasoning, compounded things cannot be established as existent. Anything we
   identify is deceptive and false because it is constantly dissolving.
   There is no mutual ground for what is compounded and what is
   validly established. If one analyzes more deeply, even nirvana and
   anything that might be beyond it are not truly established. However, if one does not go that deep but only analyzes a little bit,
   then enlightenment is not deceptive; there is some truth there. As
   it is said:

   Nirvana alone is true.
   This was taught by the Buddha.

   So, enlightenment is the only thing which is somewhat true; everything else is compounded and therefore unreal.
3. The root cause of samsara is holding things to be real. This is the
   obscuration of the afflictive emotions. It is the perception of things
   as truly existing, and includes everything that follows from that,
   such as attachment and other mental afflictions. It is not correct
   to say that the perception of the three spheres of subject, object,
   and action is the subtle habitual obscuration. Fixating on real

things in terms of a perceiving subject and perceived object is not the habitual obscuration; it is only the obscuration of the afflictive emotions. As the *Entrance to the Middle Way* states:

> As long as there is clinging to the five aggregates,
> There is clinging to the self.

So, clinging to things as true is definitely the root cause of samsara. Since this is part of the obscuration of afflictive emotions, the shravakas and pratyekabuddhas who become arhats must realize the egolessness of phenomena as well as the emptiness of the self.

4. For the first three yanas of the shravakas, pratyekabuddhas, and bodhisattvas, there are no distinctions at the level of the path of seeing, in terms of the sixteen moments, the fifteen moments, the twelve moments, the four moments, and so on. For all of them, it is the same level of seeing the true nature. As the *Entrance to the Middle Way* states:

> The wisdom that sees suchness is not different nor changing.

So, the Prasangikas accept that the path of seeing is the same for practitioners of all three lower vehicles.

5. The form kaya of a buddha and the buddha-activities are beyond comprehension by our thoughts and words. They are like the wish-fulfilling jewel or the Garuda Stupa. After the Garuda Stupa was built, it continued to bestow blessings without having any concept of doing so. Once one is enlightened, one need not have the intention to benefit beings; it just happens due to one's past aspirations and the positive karma of sentient beings. So, enlightenment appears only to the perception of others. Aryadeva wrote of what it is like from a buddha's perspective:

> When one awakens from the sleep of ignorance,
> All aspects of samsara are no longer visible.

So, at that time all the consciousnesses and phenomena have dissolved, and a buddha appears only for the perception of others.

TAGTSANG LOTSAWA'S WAY OF
TEACHING PRASANGIKA MADHYAMAKA

In general, when teaching the Madhyamaka root texts of Nagarjuna and Aryadeva, most scholars use the system developed by Tagtsang Lotsawa and his followers who explain the texts in three levels: for those who have not done any analysis, for those who have done a little analysis, and for those who have done a thorough analysis. As it is said:

At the first level, one eliminates nonvirtue,
At the second level, one eliminates self-clinging,
At the final level, one eliminates all bases for having a view.

To explain these in more detail, first, the ground with its aggregates, elements, and sense bases, the path with its conduct and methods, and the result with its kayas and enlightened activities, all exist for people who have not done any analysis. These aspects of the dharma are taught according to worldly terminology and conventional ways of seeing. Most of these aspects are already well-known in the world or could be known. This is how many teachers explain the relative truth of the world and the relative truth that appears to realized yogis in meditation and post-meditation. Even without analysis, these teachings are very beneficial.

At the second level, correct reasoning is presented for those who have analyzed a little bit. After negating the existence of the individual self and the self of phenomena, then one establishes the unborn nature, emptiness, and the ultimate truth.

Third, for those who have analyzed deeply there is a final, ultimate stage of explaining Prasangika Madhyamaka. The *Entrance to the Middle Way* states:

Right from the beginning, in the unborn nature
There is nothing to be refuted and nothing to be established.
At the level of the unborn, there is no distinction of
Attaining nirvana or not attaining nirvana.

The unborn nature itself is also not there,
Because there is no thing which is unborn.
There is no relative and no absolute.
There are no buddhas and no beings.

There is no view and nothing to meditate on.
There is no conduct and no result.
The mind is the meditation;
The mind free of concepts rests in its own place.

There is nothing that recognizes and nothing that is distracted.
There are no characteristics, and the meditation is very clear.

This quotation shows the ultimate view, in which all fabricated characteristics have completely dissolved.

Shentong Madhyamaka

THE SOURCES OF SHENTONG

As mentioned earlier, Jamgön Kongtrul divides Sutra Madhyamaka into the two categories of Rangtong, "empty of self," and Shentong, "empty of other." The Shentong view is the essence of the third-turning teachings on buddha nature, which are elaborated in twenty different sutras. These sutras were explained by the regent and future buddha, Lord Maitreya, in the latter four of his *Five Treatises of Maitreya*. These latter four treatises are the *Ornament of the Mahayana Sutras*, *Distinguishing Phenomena and the True Nature*, *Distinguishing the Middle and the Extremes*, and the *Sublime Continuum*.

The holders of the Shentong view also claim as their source the third-turning teachings written by Arya Nagarjuna called the *Collection of Praises*. In these texts Nagarjuna taught this view at three levels: praising the nature and knowing the nature at the level of the ground; praising skillful means and wisdom at the level of the path; and praising the individual three kayas and the view of the nature at the level of the result.

Commentaries on these treatises and this system of teaching and learning were fully expounded by Asanga and his brother Vasubandhu, the master Chandragomin, and their followers. Later on, Shantipa and others spread this approach even more widely. In Tibet, many of the third-turning sutras and shastras were translated during both the earlier and later spreadings of Buddhism in Tibet.

During the later spreading, the main teaching lineage for the latter four treatises of Maitreya came down from Ngok Lotsawa, and the main practice lineage came down from Tsen Khawoche. The great translator Ngok Lotsawa received teachings on Maitreya's latter four treatises and their commentaries from the Kashmiri master Sajjana, and Ngok later taught these extensively in Tibet. Tsen Khawoche, who was a student of an early tertön in Tibet, Drapa Ngönshe, also received the teachings from Khache Sajjana on the *Sublime Continuum* and other treatises. Tsen Khawoche passed on these teachings to Changrawa and others, and this teaching lineage continued for a long time. The writing of Situ Chökyi Jungne describes the approaches of Ngok and Tsen Khawoche:

> The lineage of Ngok Lotsawa explains Maitreya's teachings as Madhyamaka, and the lineage of Tsen Khawoche explains them as Chittamatra. In Tsen Khawoche's writing, consciousness is asserted to be free of the duality of perceiver and perceived; it is self-aware, self-luminous, truly established, and the cause of buddhahood.

In this way Situ Chökyi Jungne affirmed that Tsen Khawoche followed the Chittamatra view when he asserted consciousness to be self-knowing and truly established.

In general, Indian scholars such as Vasubandhu, Dignaga, and Sthiramati explained the books of Maitreya as being Chittamatra treatises, and this interpretation spread widely. There was also a lineage of explanation that stemmed from the great siddha Maitripa, which was conveyed as a special hearing lineage for highly capable students. This lineage evolved in Tibet through Su Ga-we Dorje and Tsen Khawoche, who passed this teaching on to the siddha Yumowa, who was the first author to write on the latter four books of Maitreya according to the Shentong view. Then, Dölpopa Sherap Gyaltsen, who was born in the Water Dragon year of 1292, commented on Yumowa's writing, and he is considered to be the founder of the Shentong tradition. It is generally understood that before Dölpopa there was no terminology of "Rang-tong" and "Shentong."

Later on, Serdok Panchen Shakya Chogden, Jetsun Taranatha, and many others expounded the special points that constitute the Shentong philosophy. However, Kongtrul says that previously, Karmapa Rangjung Dorje and Longchenpa had already clearly stated the main points of Shentong. Although Rangjung Dorje and Longchenpa did not use the terminology of Shentong, Jamgön Kongtrul says they asserted the same definitive view. Later on, Minling Terchen Gyurme Dorje and his brother Lochen Dharma Shri, along with Situ Chökyi Jungne and their followers, called the Shentong view "the tradition of Great Madhya-maka, the definitive meaning that goes beyond Chittamatra." They held the Shentong view very dearly, and they clarified it and spread it.

THE VIEWS OF SHAKYA CHOGDEN AND DÖLPOPA

It is said that even within the Shentong tradition there are slightly different ways of teaching it. Jamgön Kongtrul summarizes these in two main views, those of Silung Panchen Shakya Chogden and Jonang Kunkhyen Dölpopa Sherap Gyaltsen. First, Shakya Chogden teaches two levels of Shentong: that the first three books of Maitreya reflect Yogachara Madhyamaka, and the last, the *Sublime Continuum,* reflects the definitive, ultimate Madhyamaka. These two approaches to Madhyamaka have no real difference in their views; the difference is that the first three books of Maitreya do not mention some of the points covered in the *Sublime Continuum,* and they teach that ultimately there are three distinct yanas—the Shravakayana, the Pratyekabuddhayana, and the Bodhisattvayana.

The *Sublime Continuum* teaches that ultimately there is only one yana, and that each yana leads to the next one. Because there are different levels of disciples, the *Sublime Continuum* discusses the ordinary disciples' level of ignorance and habitual tendencies, as well as the extraordinary disciples' level of rebirth through undefiled karma. Disciples begin by clearing their doubts through study and contemplation, and gradually actualize the true meaning through meditation. In the *Sublime Continuum* these three ways of cultivating wisdom are all stages of a single path and not segregated into separate yanas.

Generally, most Tibetan scholars would agree that teaching the three yanas as totally separate is not in keeping with Madhyamaka. However, the masters who hold this position say that a teacher is not excluded from the Madhyamaka system just because he teaches that arhats can enter parinirvana without remainder and never enter the Mahayana path. They say that the system of Madhyamaka is defined on the basis of its view, not on the basis of how the path to enlightenment is defined. The master Kamalashila gives three points that define the Madhyamaka view: all phenomena are of one taste in being empty, all sentient beings have buddha nature, and everyone has the capacity to become enlightened. Even those who teach the three yanas as separate would agree on these three points.

Jamgön Kongtrul contrasts Shakya Chogden's understanding with that of the great Jonangpa, Dölpopa, who says that the five books of Maitreya have no difference in their view. Most Tibetan scholars think that the *Ornament of Clear Realization* is a Rangtong text, but Dölpopa disagrees. He also does not think there is a lesser level of Shentong for the shravakas and pratyekabuddhas who hear and contemplate the teachings, and a greater level of Shentong for the bodhisattvas who actualize the teachings in meditation. Dölpopa says there is only one level of Shentong, that no one would say that ultimately there are three separate yanas since all beings have the potential for full enlightenment.

Dölpopa says that many Tibetan scholars think the first three books of Maitreya are not Madhyamaka but Chittamatra, and in particular, the part of the Chittamatra school called the False Aspectarians. He says that the designations of False Aspectarians and True Aspectarians were imputed by the Tibetans. The treatises of Maitreya do question whether the mind that appears as subject and object is true or false, but there were never separate tenet systems in India called the False Aspectarians and the True Aspectarians.

Silungpa Shakya Chogden strongly posits the *Sublime Continuum* as a Madhyamaka text. He reasons in this way:

> There is no scripture or reasoning that establishes the *Sublime Continuum* as a Chittamatra text, and within the *Sublime Continuum* there is no scripture or reasoning given which validates that assertion. If one can apply scripture and reasoning from outside sources to establish one point and criticize

another, then there is no teaching that can be established as totally Madhyamaka. Maitreya and Asanga say that the view expressed in the *Sublime Continuum* is Madhyamaka, and that should be enough to establish it as Madhyamaka, since there could not be a higher authority on the text than its authors.

Nagarjuna's texts are established as Madhyamaka because Bhavaviveka and Kamalashila say that Nagarjuna was an arya, a highly realized being, who was predicted by the Buddha. If that reasoning is valid, then since Maitreya and Asanga were also aryas and predicted by the Buddha, then it is appropriate for the *Sublime Continuum* to be Madhyamaka as well.

In the *Sublime Continuum*, from among the three natures, the perfected nature is said to be the ultimate truth. If someone says that a reference to the perfected nature shows this text is not Madhyamaka, that is not a sufficient reason. There are many Tibetan scholars who say that the emptiness which is a nonaffirming negation is the ultimate truth. But then that understanding would similarly not qualify as Madhyamaka, because according to Madhyamaka the definition of ultimate truth is being free of all elaborations.

According to Maitreya and Asanga's own system, there are no other treatises except the *Sublime Continuum* which give the real Madhyamaka view. This is said within the *Sublime Continuum* itself, as well as in other texts such as the *Four Collections* and Asanga's two compendia, the *Compendium of Abhidharma* and the *Compendium of Mahayana Commentaries*. Furthermore, the third-turning teachings clearly state that one should not take literally the sutras which say that all phenomena are essenceless. Taking them too literally would make one a nihilist, because that view lacks wisdom and clear light.

The Shentong View of the Ground Madhyamaka

In general, all the Madhyamaka systems accept the view that the ground is the union of the two truths, the path is the union of the two accumulations, and the result is the union of the two kayas. There are small differences in the way the two truths are stated by the different groups of Madhyamaka, such as Prasangika, Svatantrika, Rangtong, Shentong, and so on. To clarify the Shentong view, I will give Jamgön Kongtrul's explanation of the Shentong way of describing the ground as the union of the two truths.[8]

> The two truths are the relative truth and the ultimate truth. First, to clarify the relative truth: consciousness exists on the relative level as impure, mistaken perception of the arising of various appearances. Although appearances are there, the way they are grasped dualistically, as a subject who is perceiving objects, is merely imputed by the mind. These imputations do not exist, even as relative truth. Therefore, relative truth is free of the two extremes of true existence and true nonexistence. Since consciousness is there on the relative level, then the extreme of nihilism is avoided; and since the perceiving subject and perceived objects are not true, and all interdependent arising is merely imputation, then the extreme of eternalism is avoided.
>
> Next, the ultimate truth is the primordial wisdom of emptiness free of elaborations. Primordial wisdom is there in its very nature and is present within the impure, mistaken consciousness. Even while consciousness is temporarily stained, it remains in the wisdom nature. The defilements are separable and can be abandoned because they are not the true nature. Therefore, the ultimate truth is also free of the two extremes of nihilism and eternalism. Since emptiness is truly established, then the extreme of nihilism is avoided; and since all phenomena and concepts of subject-object grasping do not truly exist, then the extreme of eternalism is avoided. It is said in *Distinguishing the Middle and the Extremes:*
>
> > *Impure conceptual mind exists.*
> > *But duality does not exist in that;*
> > *Emptiness exists in that*
> > *And that exists in that.*
> >
> > *That is not empty nor nonempty.*
> > *That is how everything is explained.*

In relation to what exists, does not exist, and exists,
That is the path of the Middle Way.

In addition, the *Treasury of Knowledge* says:

The relative is merely deluded appearance, empty of
nature.
The true nature is unchanging and not empty of nature.

The perceiving subject and perceived objects of the relative level are only deluded appearances arising; they have no reality of their own. Deluded appearance is empty of its own nature, and it is impossible for something to be established on the basis of another's nature. Deluded appearances are empty all the time, so there are no things that are not empty.

The primordial wisdom nature, the dharmata, always exists in its own nature and never changes, so it is never empty of its own nature and it is there all the time.

THE SHENTONG UNDERSTANDING OF THE THREE NATURES

The *Treasury of Knowledge* also says:

Although the imaginary nature does not exist at all, the
dependent nature exists on the relative level.
The perfected nature does not exist on the relative level,
but it exists on the ultimate level.

If this is true, then what about the statements in the sutras that the dharmadhatu, the sphere of reality, is also empty? Yes, it is said that everything is empty, because everything that is other than primordial wisdom—which means everything that is fabricated or an aspect of subject-object perception—is empty. Every characteristic placed on primordial wisdom is empty. That is why we say that everything is empty or emptiness.

In general, the Shentong school categorizes all phenomena into the three natures of the imaginary, the dependent, and the perfected nature. First, the imaginary nature is defined as whatever is grasped by mental designations. This includes nonentities, like the sky; objects that one thinks about; and the relationships between names and objects, such as grasping the name as being the object, or mistaking the object for the name. Characteristics such as outer and inner, center and edge, big and small, good and bad, directions and time—all the things that are imputed by the mind and that can be grasped by the mind—are the imaginary nature.

The second of the three natures, the dependent nature, is defined as just awareness or as consciousness, which arises as the basis for the perceiving subject and perceived objects. It is called "dependent" because appearances are dependent on the habitual tendencies created by ignorance.

The third nature, the perfected nature, is defined as self-aware, self-luminous, and free of all fabrications. It is the dharmata, or nature of reality; the dharmadhatu, or sphere of reality; the tathata, or suchness; and the ultimate truth—it has many synonymous names.

The imaginary nature and dependent nature are equal in being untrue, deluded appearances, relative, and false. They are classified separately because the imaginary nature is not there, even on the level of relative truth, but the dependent nature is there as relative truth. The perfected level is not there on the level of relative truth but is there on the level of the ultimate truth.

> These three exist as imputed, exist as substantial, and
>   exist as unfabricated.
> They are the emptiness of the nonexistent, the existent,
>   and the ultimate.
> Their characteristics, arising, and ultimate essence do
>   not exist.

As the root verse summarizes, the imaginary nature exists through imputation, the dependent nature exists as substantial, and the perfected nature does not exist in these two ways but is beyond fabrications. The imaginary nature is the emptiness of what does not exist, the dependent nature is the emptiness of what does exist, and the perfected nature is the emptiness of the ultimate.

Jetsun Maitreya explains:

> *If you understand the emptiness of what is nonexistent,*
> *And likewise the emptiness of what is existent,*
> *And the emptiness of the nature,*
> *Then it is said that you understand emptiness.*

Furthermore, in the imaginary nature, the characteristics are essenceless; in the dependent nature, what arises is essenceless; and in the perfected nature, the ultimate is essenceless. There are three aspects of the essence and three aspects of essencelessness. Through these, all phenomena are taught to be natureless.

The *Treasury of Knowledge* goes on to say:

> *Therefore, every phenomena is pervaded by emptiness.*
> *The perfected nature in its essence is not connected with*
> *   relative phenomena.*
> *It is without characteristics, the concept characterized,*
> *   and the basis for the characteristics.*
> *It is posited as free of fabrications, permanent,*
> *   indivisible, and omnipresent.*
> *The other presentations in Shentong concur with the*
> *   Chittamatra view.*

As the root verse says, according to the system of Shentong Madhyamaka, all phenomena are pervaded by emptiness and essencelessness, and the perfected nature is established as true. If the perfected nature is true, then one might wonder whether it arises, dwells, or ceases. Does it come or go or change? Does it have directions or times? Is it one or many? No, none of these.

If those qualities were there, then it would not be true. The perfected nature is never connected with the phenomena of the relative level. It does not arise, dwell, or cease, it does not come or go, it is not one or many, it is not cause or effect. In its very nature, it is free of characteristics, the concept characterized, and the basis for the characteristics. It is free of all elaborations, such as directions and times, so it is permanent by nature. It is indivisible and cannot be divided into separate parts. It is the nature of everything, so it is ever present and all pervasive.

Most other aspects of the Shentong presentation of the ground, path, and result generally accord with the Chittamatra system.

SHENTONG IS NOT THE SAME AS CHITTAMATRA

Since the Shentong Madhyamaka system and the commentaries of the Chittamatra masters are both based on the same third-turning sutras, many scholars say that Shentong is Chittamatra and is not Madhyamaka. So we will look at why Jamgön Kongtrul says the Shentong view is not the same as the Chittamatra view. The *Treasury of Knowledge* says:

> *The False Aspectarians within Chittamatra say that the*
>   *nature of consciousness is established as true*
> *And within the realm of the mind. In Shentong,*
>   *primordial wisdom*
> *Is posited as true but uncompounded.*
> *The Shentong view is free of the fault of saying that the*
>   *ultimate is an entity.*

To explain this root verse, there are two groups within Chittamatra, which are called the False Aspectarians and the True Aspectarians. According to the False Aspectarians, the nature of the all-ground consciousness is established as true. Most Tibetan scholars believe that Chittamatra says the all-ground consciousness is within the experience of the unenlightened mind. If one asserts that, then one becomes a Vaibhashika, or Substantialist, rather than a follower of Madhyamaka.

Shentong Madhyamaka certainly does not assert that. In this system, the sphere of buddha nature is asserted as true, but it is beyond ordinary consciousness. Not only do the Shentongpas assert the presence of the very nature of primordial wisdom free of elaborations, but that the primordial wisdom free of extremes is uncompounded. So, they do not incur the fault of asserting that the ultimate truth is a substantial entity.

TARANATHA'S REFUTATION OF SHENTONG AS VEDANTA

Some of the assertions made by the Shentong masters seem to disagree with the Madhyamaka view and agree with the statements of non-Buddhists, particularly those of Vedanta. There have been many misunderstandings and refutations of this philosophy in Tibet. In order to clear up these misunderstandings, I will quote some points extracted from the teachings of Taranatha, which Jamgön Kongtrul quotes in the *Treasury of Knowledge*. Taranatha says:[9]

Some scholars cite the *Lankavatara Sutra*, which says:

If buddha nature has all the marks and signs, then isn't it the same as the atman of the non-Buddhists? In reply, the Buddha said, "It is not the same because it is emptiness."

They say that the buddha nature is not true, because if it had all the signs and marks, it would be just like the non-Buddhist traditions. They say buddha nature is not established as anything; it is like space.

I would reply that their identifying emptiness as meaning "untrue and nothing whatsoever" is a fault coming from attachment to their own tenet system. In addition, the sutras say that this view is not the same as the non-Buddhist view because the signs and marks are established as emptiness but are not established as nonexistent. Explaining the buddha nature with its radiant, perfect marks and signs as a provisional teaching is simply a mistaken, worldly misunderstanding.

Some critics say that the Shentong assertion that buddha nature is permanent makes it a non-Buddhist system. When they say that, they are rejecting the Tathagatagarbha sutras. It is illogical to declare that "permanent" must mean that something always continues. If that was enough to make something permanent, then all compounded phenomena would be permanent, since even samsara and dualistic grasping always continue.

Another related criticism says that if the buddha nature was first impure and later becomes pure, then it must be impermanent. From the perspective of the sphere of absolute reality, it was not initially impure and later purified; whether it seems impure or pure depends upon the mindstreams of the individuals. Just because an individual's perspective changes, that does not mean the true nature changes.

When they argue that it is unreasonable for the mindstream of sentient beings to contain the primordial wisdom of the buddhas, they are contradicting the direct statement of the Buddha: "Because the wisdom of the buddhas abides in the multitude of sentient beings."

They also disagree that sentient beings' mindstreams have the enlightened qualities. For example, they say that if sentient beings have the ten powers in their mindstreams, such as the power to discriminate what is appropriate and inappropriate, then it follows that they should be omniscient about what is appropriate and inappropriate. This is a wrong understanding of what is being said. We are not asserting that sentient beings' mindstreams are enlightened. If so, then saying that a buddha and the buddha qualities abide in the mindstreams of sentient beings would be analogous to saying that if a buddha abides on a throne, then the throne must be omniscient. There is no way that the eight consciousnesses in the mindstreams of sentient beings are enlightened. The enlightenment that abides in sentient beings does not abide in the relative sense like the contents in a container. It abides as the true nature in the ultimate sense.

THE MAIN DIFFERENCES BETWEEN RANGTONG AND SHENTONG

In the *Treasury of Knowledge,* Jamgön Kongtrul presents the main differences between Rangtong and Shentong. He says:[10]

> For both Rangtong and Shentong the relative level is
>   empty,
> And in meditation, all fabricated extremes have ceased.
> However, they differ in their terminology about whether
>   dharmata is there or not there in post-meditation,
> And in the ultimate analysis, whether primordial wisdom
>   is truly established or not.
>
> Shentong says that if the ultimate truth had no established
>   nature
> And was a mere absolute negation, then it would be a
>   vacuous nothingness.
> Instead, the ultimate is nondual, self-aware primordial
>   wisdom.
> Shentong presents a profound view which joins the sutras
>   and tantras.

For both Rangtong and Shentong Madhyamaka, all phenomena included in the relative truth are established as emptiness, and in meditation there is the cessation of all fabricated extremes. Their views do not differ on these points.

However, in relation to post-meditation, to clearly distinguish the tenet systems, merely in terms of the way they use terminology, Shentong says that the dharmata, the true nature, is there, and Rangtong says the dharmata is not there. In the ultimate analysis, using the reasoning that examines the ultimate, Shentong says nondual primordial wisdom is truly established and Rangtong says primordial wisdom is not truly established. These two statements delineate their main differences.

In relation to the three natures, the holders of the Shentong philosophy say that the imaginary nature and the dependent nature are the relative truth, and that the perfected nature is the ultimate truth. Seeing things as not truly established, as mere absolute negations and vacuous emptiness, is true for the relative level, but the emptiness of the ultimate nature is not like that. The ultimate nature is primordial wisdom, which is devoid of subject-object discrimination, but is self-awareness. The Shentong tradition is very similar to the enlightened intent of the great tantras. It has reached the pinnacle of Madhyamaka, and its profound view is a bridge between the sutras and the tantras.

EQUAL RESPECT FOR THE TRADITIONS OF NAGARJUNA AND ASANGA

Many earlier and later Tibetan scholars, as well as many of the Indian panditas, dissociated this system from Madhyamaka and said it belongs in Chittamatra. Not only that, but they held this system as being greatly inferior to the Madhyamaka treatises of Nagarjuna.

The Buddha's teaching is like the sky, and the two great charioteers, Nagarjuna and Asanga, adorn it like the sun and moon. The scriptural traditions of other Buddhist masters cannot compare with theirs. The supreme paths of the two charioteers do not contradict each other, but are supportive—one is mainly outer and the other is mainly inner. Therefore, it is good to study, contemplate, and meditate on them with equal dedication and respect.

The great master Shakya Chogden also says that the teachings by Asanga and Nagarjuna are both necessary. He says:

> *Without the treatises taught by Asanga, which include the system of*
>   *the alayavijnana*
> *And the presentation of the three types of emptiness,*
> *How could one explain the ground of purification and the purifier*
>   *taught in the vajrayana scriptures,*
> *And the presentation of the three aspects of outer, inner, and other*
>   *in the* Kalachakra Tantra?
>
> *How could one explain nondual primordial wisdom and the way*
>   *everything is empty of essence*

Without the explanations of the Prasangika and Svatantrika
  treatises?
How could one quit clinging to the concept of profound and clear
  primordial wisdom as being true,
And give up clinging to the sublime deities?

The Madhyamaka philosophy of the Buddha's teachings has two aspects: the ultimate essence of the definitive meaning as presented in the texts of Maitreya, and the ultimate essence of the definitive meaning as presented in the texts of Nagarjuna. In the first aspect of Madhyamaka, which comes from Maitreya's texts, the primordial wisdom is free of the dualistic grasping of subject and object. This view is explained in his two "ornament" texts—the *Ornament of Clear Realization* and the *Ornament of the Mahayana Sutras;* in his two "distinguishing" texts—*Distinguishing the Middle and the Extremes* and *Distinguishing Phenomena and the True Nature*—as well as in the *Sublime Continuum.* The treatise *Distinguishing the Middle and the Extremes* is the text that establishes this view as Madhyamaka philosophy, and *Distinguishing Phenomena and the True Nature* is the text that shows how to bring this view into one's personal practice.

The second aspect of Madhyamaka, which comes from Nagarjuna's texts, negates all fabricated extremes, and it is simply an absolute negation or a negation in which nothing is affirmed. This view is explained in Nagarjuna's texts called the *Collection of Reasoning.* However, the understanding expressed in Nagarjuna's *Collection of Praises* is the same as the teachings of Maitreya.

The main expounders of these two systems of Madhyamaka are Nagarjuna and Asanga. The Rangtong system establishes both the relative truth and the absolute truth as empty of nature. The Shentong system establishes only the relative truth as empty of nature, and through that it automatically eliminates elaborations about the ultimate truth. There are two other systems particularly worthy of note: that of Haribhadra, whose Rangtong interpretation of Maitreya's *Ornament of Clear Realization* was very influential; and the system of Jigme Chökyong Shap, who interpreted Nagarjuna's *Collection of Reasoning* as Shentong. All four of these systems are within the Madhyamaka path and their treatises are considered to be authentic.

The Rangtong system is accepted as Madhyamaka by the great masters of Prasangika and Svatantrika. Nagarjuna explains the emptiness of the Rangtong view by saying:

Whatever arises interdependently
Is taught to be emptiness.
Whatever is dependently imputed
Is the path of Madhyamaka.

The Shentong system is accepted as Madhyamaka by Asanga and his brother Vasubandhu. Maitreya explains the emptiness of the Shentong view, with its three types of emptiness, when he says:

In relation to what exists, does not exist, and exists,
That is the path of the Middle Way.

The Tibetans think that from among the four philosophical schools of Buddhism—Vaibhashika, Sautrantika, Chittamatra, and Madhyamaka—that the Madhyamaka school generally refers to the systems of Prasangika and Svatantrika. From among those two, Prasangika alone is superior. Chandrakirti says:

That which was just explained [the Prasangika view] is very profound and frightening, and it is realized only by those accustomed to it from past lives. Even those who study extensively cannot fully comprehend it.

There are two possible responses to this quote. The first merely confirms the assertion. For instance, if someone uses the reasoning that Rangtong Madhyamaka is the highest Madhyamaka because Chandrakirti says so, then one could say that Shentong Madhyamaka is the highest because Asanga says so. Asanga says that the Rangtong view understates the ultimate nature, making it less than it is, and this is the view put forth by overbearing people who just talk loud. Therefore, if one tries to identify the most definitive meaning, the same authority that is given to the texts of Chandrakirti to prove or disprove something could be given to the texts of Asanga. Actually, Asanga would be more authentic because in the sutras Buddha predicted that Asanga would be the master who defined the provisional and definitive meanings. Chandrakirti, who is a great Mahayana master, does not accept the Shentong scriptures as part of Madhyamaka. But then the arya Asanga, who is also an undisputed master of Mahayana, says that Rangtong is not the scriptural tradition of Madhyamaka. In conclusion, determining which philosophical school is the highest is basically a matter of debate.

There is a second possible response to the quote from Chandrakirti. When teaching the intention of Nagarjuna, the Rangtong system is supreme; and when commenting on the intention of Maitreya, the Shentong system is the most profound. The scriptures and reasoning of each system cannot refute the other. Otherwise, we would have to give more weight to Asanga's texts and logic, because he had reached the spiritual level of an arya, a bodhisattva on the bhumis, and he was predicted in the sutras as the one to clarify the definitive meaning. Also, he was the first to found a philosophical system within the Mahayana. Chandrakirti does not say that Asanga does not understand Madhyamaka; he merely says that Asanga does not explain the intention of Nagarjuna.

DISTINGUISHING VIJNANAVADA AND CHITTAMATRA

It is also relevant to distinguish between the Chittamatra school and the Vijnanavada school. *Establishing the Two Systems as One* states:

> Many Tibetan scholars teach that the Chittamatra and Vijnanavada are the same in meaning, but those scholars are deluded in stating that awareness and primordial wisdom are pervaded by the conceptual mind and mental factors, and deluded in not distinguishing between consciousness and wisdom. This misunderstanding comes from not having thoroughly studied the terminology of the third-turning teachings.
>
> For those of you who assert that Chittamatra and Vijnanavada are the same, it is said in scripture:
>
> > *Other than the dharmadhatu, the sphere of reality,*
> > *There are no existent phenomena.*

A sutra says:

> *The sphere of beginningless time*
> *Is the domain of all phenomena.*

A tantric scripture says:

> *I pervade all of this*
> *And do not see any other nature of beings.*

And another tantra says:

> *Outside of the precious mind*
> *There are no buddhas or sentient beings.*

Rather than just reciting the words of the tantras, if you contemplate their meaning, you will understand that it is unreasonable to say that Chittamatra and Vijnanavada are the same.

It is clear that the Vijnanavada scriptures say that the dharmadhatu must be understood as nondual wisdom, as the natural dharmakaya. The Vijnanavada doctrine is not Chittamatra; it is a much higher view because it is also in the tantras.

There are also quotations from the sutras that establish that the Shentong view is Madhyamaka. For instance, it says in the *Ultimate Emptiness Sutra:*

> When a thing is not there, there is the emptiness of that thing,
> but what remains is there. This is the Madhyamaka path, the
> view of emptiness, genuine and unmistaken.

There are many similar quotations in the sutras. Also, it says in the *Ornament of the Middle Way:*

> *Therefore, form and so on are the mind itself,*
> *They are not asserted to be external.*
> *Based on the Chittamatra view,*
> *One should understand that there are no external,*
>   *substantial things.*

> *Having that system as a basis, then on top of that,*
> *One should fully understand selflessness.*

In the *Entrance to the Three Kayas*, Nagamitra says:

> *That which is called "the path of Madhyamaka"*
> *Is none other than mere awareness.*
> *Once one has analyzed with reasoning,*
> *Nothing else is acceptable.*

And Shantarakshita says in the *Ornament of the Middle Way*:

> *Here I will explain the two truths,*
> *In conjunction with valid cognition and scripture,*
> *As they are taught by Maitreya and Asanga*
> *And agreed upon by Nagarjuna.*

In this way, both Shentong and Rangtong are free of the fault of not being Madhyamaka. They accord in espousing a view free of all fabricated extremes. Not only that, but in most schools of Tibetan Buddhism there were masters who were lineage holders of both systems, and nobody looked upon them as having wrong views.

Tantra Madhyamaka

As mentioned at the beginning of this chapter, Jamgön Kongtrul broadly categorizes Madhyamaka into Sutra Madhyamaka and Tantra Madhyamaka. Having discussed Sutra Madhyamaka, we will complete this chapter with a synopsis of Tantra Madhyamaka. Kongtrul Rinpoche says in the *Treasury of Knowledge*:

> *In the profound view of Tantra Madhyamaka, the nature*
> *of all phenomena*
> *Is naturally clear light, distinguished by great bliss.*
> *The primordial wisdom that is the union of clarity-*
> *emptiness and bliss-emptiness*

Is clearly taught in the texts such as the Five Stages *and
the* Trilogy of Commentaries by Bodhisattvas.

For the Madhyamaka that comes from the tantras, the most
important aspect is nondual wisdom, which makes Tantra
Madhyamaka more in accord with Yogachara Madhyamaka.
The nature of the mind, which is clear light, free of all fabrications and characteristics, is the self-aware, true nature of all
phenomena, and it is timelessly and spontaneously that way.
This understanding is clearly elaborated in the third-turning
teachings of the Buddha, and it is established and practiced in
the tantras.

Furthermore, being naturally clear light and distinguished
by great bliss, the emptiness aspect is designated by the syllable E and the compassion aspect by the syllable VAM. This
pristine wisdom is the union of clarity and emptiness, bliss and
emptiness, and so forth. This meaning is clarified and elaborated in tantric commentaries such as the *Five Stages* and the
Trilogy of Commentaries by Bodhisattvas, and should be understood through those teachings.

The general understanding of Tantra Madhyamaka has two aspects:
one related with creation stage practice, and one related with completion stage practice. Within the creation stage, there are also two aspects:
first, the bases for generating the deity; and second, after the deity has
been accomplished, the way of concluding without fabrication. First,
the bases for generating the deity are the seed syllables and symbolic
implements, which arise from nondual primordial wisdom. They arise
from emptiness and are no other than the dharmadhatu wisdom. This
view accords with the teaching of Shentong Madhyamaka.

In the second aspect of the creation stage, the way of concluding the
accomplishment of the deity without fabrication, one begins by establishing the deity as clarity-emptiness. In this context, clarity refers to
clearly seeing all the characteristics and details of the deity and its mandala, and emptiness refers to not conceptualizing or clinging to the
deity at all. If one clings to the characteristics of clear appearance,
one will not transcend samsara. On the other hand, it is not simply a

matter of stopping thoughts. Through the mere absence of thoughts one can transcend suffering, but one will not reach the state of union, so that approach is still poisonous.

One needs to practice clarity and emptiness in union. While the deity clearly appears it is empty, and while the deity is empty it clearly appears. In the pith instructions, particularly in the Sakya lineage, the union of clarity and emptiness is called "the inseparability of samsara and nirvana." At that time, one sees perceived objects as the union of appearance and emptiness and the perceiving consciousness as the union of clarity and emptiness. When one arises from this stage of meditation, without losing the pride of the deity, one then engages in the outer yogic practices. This is an overview of the creation stage practice.

Next, the Tantra Madhyamaka of the completion stage practice also has two parts: letting go of attachment to the creation stage, and the real wisdom of the completion stage. The first is when the entire mandala of the deity and environment is no longer maintained but is dissolved, and the practitioner remains in a state without reference point. This is the same approach as in Rangtong Madhyamaka, and it is supreme in dissolving the elaboration of thoughts. However, this is not the real wisdom of the completion stage practice because it is not the experience of self-aware primordial wisdom.

The real wisdom of the completion stage has three aspects: what is to be experienced, the methods through which one experiences it, and the stages of actualizing it. What is experienced is self-awareness simultaneous with the wisdom of great bliss. The method through which this is experienced is the process of blessing oneself, also called the wisdom of self-awareness. This is nonconceptual, undeluded wisdom, which is the view free of poison.

However, simply generating this experience does not mean that one has reached the level of an arya or the first bhumi, because this is just the example wisdom. This experience is called the wisdom that is the union of bliss and emptiness, or the wisdom that is the coemergent melting in bliss. This explanation is according to the general tantras; its special presentation is found in the *Kalachakra Tantra*, but that will not be explained here. The main difference between Sutra Madhyamaka and Tantra Madhyamaka is in the perceiving subject or practitioner; there is no difference in terms of the perceived objects, which are in themselves free of all extremes.

To summarize the main points of all the Madhyamaka schools, Jamgön Kongtrul says in the *Treasury of Knowledge:*

> *Whatever appears in relative truth is not denied,*
> *And the natural state is free of all fabricated extremes.*
> *This is the ground.*

> *With profound wisdom, one abandons all grasping at*
> *characteristics,*
> *And with compassion, one accumulates what is positive*
> *for the benefit of others. This is the path.*

> *By accomplishing the peace of the dharmakaya, and*
> *through the form kayas,*
> *One acts without concepts to benefit beings. This is*
> *the result.*
> *All the teachings of Madhyamaka are condensed in*
> *this way.*

All the main points of the various systems of Madhyamaka can be summarized in this way. By not denying any of the relative appearances, one is free of nihilism. Since the natural state, the ultimate truth, is free of all fabricated extremes, then one is free of eternalism. This is the Ground Madhyamaka, the union of the two truths.

Through the wisdom of prajna, by not holding on to any phenomena or characteristics, one is free of eternalism. Through compassion, by accumulating a great collection of positive deeds for the benefit of others, one is free of nihilism. This is the Path Madhyamaka, which is the union of the two accumulations.

Through attaining the dharmakaya, which is the pacification of all conceptual complexity, one is free of eternalism. Through the endless activity of the two form kayas to benefit both supreme and ordinary beings, one is free of nihilism.

This is the Result Madhyamaka, which is the union of the two kayas.

This presentation of Ground, Path, and Fruition Madhyamaka is said to incorporate the entire teaching of Madhyamaka.

7

THE TRADITIONS OF THE NYINGMA AND SARMA TANTRAS

A DISTINCTION IS OFTEN MADE in Tibetan Buddhism between the two traditions of the Nyingma, or old tantra system, and the Sarma, or new tantra system. One can find treatises where these two systems are critical and cynical about each other. The old tantra system is mainly held by the followers of the Nyingma school, and the new tantra system is mainly held by the followers of the three other main schools of Tibetan Buddhism—the Kagyu, Sakya, and Geluk. In this chapter we will look at these two traditions, noting their distinctions and examining the controversies as they are presented by Jamgön Kongtrul.

The Nyingma tantras are part of the Early Translation tradition, which includes all the translations done from the time of the dharma king Songtsen Gampo in the seventh century until the time Atisha Dipankara came to Tibet in the eleventh century. Particularly during the time of the dharma king Trisong Detsen, in the eighth century, great panditas such as Shantarakshita, Padmasambhava, and Vimalamitra were invited to Tibet, and they worked with a hundred Tibetan translators, such as Vairochana, Kawa Paltsek, Chokro Lui Gyaltsen, and Shang Nanam Yeshe De. They translated all the sutras and tantras that they could obtain, and they caused them to be disseminated widely. Later, Jowo Je Palden Atisha's arrival in Tibet marked the beginning of the New Translation tradition.

Classifications of the Tantras

The teachings of the Early Translation tradition contain the three pitakas of the Sutrayana level and six tantras of the Vajrayana level.

The three pitakas are held in common by both Nyingma and Sarma, so there is no dispute about that. The difference between Nyingma and Sarma is in which tantras are followed. The Sarma tradition has four categories of tantras: Kriya, Charya, Yoga, and Anuttarayoga. The Nyingma tradition has six categories of tantras within nine yanas. Kriya, Upaya, and Yoga are called the three outer tantras, or the Yanas of Vedic Austerities, while Maha, Anu, and Ati are called the three inner tantras, or the Yanas of the Skillful Means of Mastery. When one adds the Shravakayana, Pratyekabuddhayana, and Bodhisattvayana, which are called the Yanas of Causal Characteristics, to the six tantras just mentioned, that makes nine yanas.

Just the way the tantras are counted is not a basis for dispute. There are many numbering systems for the tantras, such as two, three, four, five, six, seven, and countless tantras. I will cite a few of these. For example, the *Vajra Essence Ornament Tantra* classifies them in two parts when it states:

> *By understanding the distinction of outer and inner,*
> *One understands the differences in the tantras.*

The same tantra also divides them into three:

> *The Kriya Tantra, Upayoga Tantra, and the Yoga Tantra—*
> *There is nothing like these teachings on wisdom mind.*

Upayoga Tantra is another name for Charya Tantra. It is said to combine two tantras, Kriya Tantra and the Yoga Tantra.

Then, the *Vajra Tent Tantra* classifies four tantras:

> *Kriya Tantra is for lesser ones,*
> *And Non-Action Yoga Tantra is for those above that.*
> *Yoga Tantra is for excellent beings,*
> *And Anuttarayoga Tantra is for those even above that.*

The *Entrance to the Meaning of the Anuttarayoga Tantra* also lists four tantras:

There are known to be four entrances to the resultant Vajrayana vehicle: Kriya Tantra, Charya Tantra, Yoga Tantra, and Anuttarayoga Tantra.

Most of the tantras and their commentaries teach four categories. However, the *Compendium of Vajra Wisdom* has five:

O Bhagavan, what is the extent of the tantras? There are the Yoga Tantra, Upayoga Tantra, Charya Tantra, Kriya Tantra, and Parikalpana Tantra.

And the *Vajra Tent Tantra* adds a sixth:

The Yogini Tantra is called the sixth tantra.

The *Torch of the Three Methods* also presents six:

There are six tantras: Kriya, Mula, Charya, Yoga, Yogini, and Anuttarayoga.

There is also a way of presenting seven tantras in the New Translation tradition. Atisha Dipankara writes in his autocommentary on the *Lamp of the Path of Awakening*:

As for what are called the tantras, such as Kriya and Charya, they are the Kriya Tantra, Charya Tantra, Parikalpana Tantra, Upayoga Tantra, Yoga Tantra, Mahayoga Tantra, and Anuttarayoga Tantra.

Commonalities of the Nyingma and Sarma Tantras

No matter which numbering system is used, the Kriya, Charya, and Yoga tantras are common to both the Nyingma and Sarma traditions. They have no disagreement whatsoever on the nature of those tantras, the meaning of the words, the classifications, the empowerments for entering them, the samayas and vows to be observed, the realization of the path, the siddhis to be accomplished, or the levels, paths, and results. Concerning this, Jamgön Kongtrul says in his autocommentary to the *Treasury of Knowledge:*[1]

> The nine yanas begin with the Shravakayana, Pratyekabuddhayana, and Bodhisattvayana, which are called the Three Sections with Characteristics. They are also known as the Yanas Leading away from the Origin of Suffering, since they lead to liberation through one's abandoning the mind poisons. Then, the three outer tantras begin with Kriya, which means "action." The second is Upaya, which means "method," and is also called Charya, which means "conduct." The third tantra is Yoga, which means "practice." Practitioners of these three tantras focus on cleanliness, bathing, and austerities, and their conduct must accord with the Brahmanic tradition. That is why these are known as the Yanas of Vedic Austerities. Since the classification of these six yanas is held in common by the new and old traditions, there is no need to discuss them further here.

Furthermore, some of the Anuttarayoga tantras, such as Guhyasamaja and Yamantaka, which are usually regarded as Sarma tantras, are held in common with the Nyingma tradition. On this point Jamgön Kongtrul says:[2]

> During the Early Translation period there was a translation included in the eighteen Nyingma tantras which is called the *Guhyasamaja Mind Tantra,* and it was translated by someone named Che Tashi. During this time there were commentaries on the *Guhyasamaja Tantra* as well as a teaching system on it that stemmed from the Indian teacher Vajrahasa.

In another place in the *Treasury of Knowledge,* Jamgön Kongtrul says:[3]

> In particular, within the Yamantaka cycle, the tantras and the stream of pith instructions for Red Yamantaka, Black Yaman-

taka, and Vajrabhairava were collected by the great acharya Shridhara and others, so that this lineage gradually spread. This teaching came to Tibet to some degree, and Songsten Gampo, the emanated Tibetan king of the seventh century, is known to have composed practice liturgies on Yamantaka. So, the Yamantaka texts were the first tantras to come to Tibet.

Around the time when the monastic system spread through Tibet, the *Yamantaka Vijaya Tantra* was translated, and the empowerments, explanations, instructions, and practices were introduced with it. Nupchen Sangye Yeshe spread the Yamantaka teachings and many vidyadharas became accomplished through his Yamantaka lineage. These are more or less the earliest Vajrayana practices and teachings in Tibet.

During the later spreading of the dharma in Tibet, the teachings on the real Manjushri, or Yamantaka, came through several great masters: Chogdru, Nagtso, Rongzom, Chal, Ra, Kyo, Shang, and Nyö. Among these, Ra Lotsawa's tradition is supreme in terms of both teaching and practice.

So, the Sarma tantras are held in common by both the Early and New Translation traditions. Not only did the Nyingmapas spread the Sarma tantras through explanation and practice, but they never criticized them. Also, the Nyingmapas have held the teaching lineages of *Chanting the Names of Manjushri* and the *Kalachakra Tantra* with particular respect.

Distinctions in the Nyingma and Sarma Tantras

Well then, what is the main difference between the Nyingma and Sarma tantras? Mipham Jamyang Gyatso says:

> The tantras that are usually considered Sarma tantras, such as Guhyasamaja, are actually common to both the new and old traditions. What is not held in common are the three inner tantras, which are called the Nyingma tantras; these are the basis for dispute.

The New Translation tradition makes no distinctions in relation to the sutras, only in relation to the tantras. The three inner tantras have some unique terminology, but there seems to be another reason for differentiating the old and new tantras. Shechen Gyaltsap Padma Namgyal explains this in his *Commentary on the Aspiration for the Longevity of the Nyingma Teachings:*

> After King Langdarma suppressed the Buddhist teachings, Lu-me and others reestablished the sangha. The Vinaya lineage remained unbroken, but some sanghas created their own versions of the teachings, so there were different views and disagreements. Shamthap Ngönpochen and Acharya Marpo translated the *Path of Desire,* and these teachings spread to the sanghas in Ngari in western Tibet. The ngagpas, or lay Vajrayana practitioners, did not have teachers, and they started to spread their own fabricated versions of the dharma. Also, many of them started practicing the Union and Liberation teachings as they were literally written in the tantras.[4]
>
> Most Tibetans became disgusted with this distortion of the teachings. In the eleventh century, when the new translations were spreading in Tibet, Lha Lama Yeshe Ö, the king of western Tibet, wrote an official letter to the ngagpas. In it he explained the gradual path of the Sutrayana, and forbade them from doing the tantric practices of Union and Liberation unless they truly understood the Sutrayana and did the practices with great care. This is not something that the Nyingmas need to defend; rather, it is an instruction for us. The great translator Rinchen Zangpo also wrote a treatise called *Refuting Misunderstandings about the Vajrayana,* which is very similar to the Yeshe Ö's letter. It is not a refutation of the Nyingma lineage.
>
> Around the time of Rinchen Zangpo, in the eleventh century, many Tibetan practitioners went to India and the new translations began to appear. They were unable to receive or translate what was not commonly known at that time; they translated only the most well-known texts. Then, for a period of time there was a lot of jealousy and competition between

the Sarma and Nyingma teachers, trying to assert their superiority. Their minds became disturbed by the demon of pride, and there was discord between the teachings and the teachers. The Sarma teachers alleged that most of the three inner tantras were composed by the Tibetans and had not come from India.

In particular, a proclamation letter was sent out, which was supposedly written by the translator Gö Khugpa Lhatse. In it he said that if one examines the words of the Nyingma tantras, one finds they were composed by the Tibetan translators. When he went to India, he did not find the Nyingma tantras, and when he asked his Indian teacher about those tantras, the pandita merely said, "My son, this is not true." Except for these few deceitful words based on jealousy, this proclamation letter gave no reasons, even as big as a sesame seed, for why the Nyingma tantras are not authentic. There were similar letters from Shiwa Ö and Drigung Paldzin which became seeds for refuting the Nyingma teachings. Competitive teachers used these to spread criticism of the Nyingma tradition. Ignorant people heedlessly followed along, and without any reason they maintained the view that the inner tantras are not genuine.

The initial disputes about the Nyingma and Sarma tantras seem to have focused on individuals rather than the dharma. It is clear that some people pretended to hold the Nyingma tantras while acting completely contrary to the dharma. For example, they would indulge in alcohol and sex and claim that they were following the Nyingma way. On the other hand, some translators of the Sarma tradition, while trying to remove incorrect tantras, also wanted to highlight the new teachings they had brought from India, so they said things against the holders of the Nyingma tradition, whether they were truly critical of their teachings or not. So, there were people on both sides who claimed to be holders of their traditions, and yet lacked understanding and blindly went along with the crowd. It is easy to understand how this competitiveness led to the discord of sectarianism.

Although the Sarma followers criticized the Nyingma tantras, I have never seen any criticism by the Nyingma followers of the Sarma tantras. Here, I will present some refutations of the Sarma criticism of the three inner tantras, which were made by some Nyingma lineage holders and unbiased scholars from the other schools.

Mipham Rinpoche's Rebuttal of the Criticism of the Nyingma Tantras

The first of these rebuttals comes from the teaching of Mipham Jamyang Gyatso. This is quoted by his heart student, Shechen Gyaltsap, in his *Commentary on the Aspiration for the Longevity of the Nyingma Teachings.* Mipham Rinpoche says:[5]

> Regardless of whether those proclamations were factual, I will examine them a little bit. You intelligent and unbiased ones, please investigate thoroughly what is truthful. If there is something that goes against the dharma and we understand that it is anti-dharma, then of course we should refute it. If it is not against the dharma, then we should not accumulate the bad karma of rejecting it. For instance, some panditas said that the Nyingma tantras were not found in India. But Tibet is very far away, and how could a translator, traveling on foot, find all the teachings then existing in India? Think of how one or two people, walking through Tibet looking for teachings, could never find them all, and Tibet is much smaller than India.
>
> Also, it is uncertain whether all the Buddha's teachings could be found in one place, even in the big centers like Nalanda Monastery because, generally speaking, there are countless sutras and tantras. For example, during the three periods when the Abhidharma teachings were attacked, sutras such as the *Avatamsaka Sutra* and the *Heap of Jewels Sutra* were unavailable. Or consider the long *Prajnaparamita Sutra*, which was not found in India and had to be brought from the land of the nagas by Nagarjuna.
>
> If certain texts were not present in a particular library that the Tibetans visited, it is childish and small-minded to conclude that those texts cannot be Buddha's teachings. A catalog listing all the Buddha's teachings was unheard of in India; his

teachings were never gathered in one place and published together. Although some texts were collected, how could all of them be collected? For example, it is said that after the Brahman king Pushyamitra damaged the Buddhist teachings, Buddhist monks from different countries collected the scriptures of the Tripitika and brought them together in Mathura. However, they could not find the text called the *Sublime Basis,* one of the four bases of the Vinaya, so they could not form a complete collection.

In terms of the Vajrayana, there is no translator who ever saw all the Sarma teachings in India. It is said that the *Chakrasamvara Tantra in a Hundred Thousand Stanzas* is not found in the human world. The texts of Kriya, Charya, and Yoga tantras, which are mentioned in the *Chakrasamvara Samvarodaya* and the *Compendium of the Wisdom Essence,* were also not present in India and are difficult to find.

During the Early Translation period the Tripitika teachings were also translated, but later on no one compared these translations in the same way that the tantras were compared. Later on, only rarely could someone read Sanskrit well, so how could they know if all the tantras were there or not? Since the time of the Buddha, all the Vajrayana teachings have not been written in books and kept in libraries. The Buddha predicted that the tantras would come later on.

When the seal on the tantras was broken by Vajrapani, who compiled the tantras along with the wisdom dakinis, then the great siddhas gradually brought them out. For instance, after the *Guhyasamaja Tantra* came to King Indrabhuti it went to the land of Uddiyana, and from there it went to India. The histories say that later on, Lalitavajra was still searching for teachings on Vajrabhairava, and even later, the great Kalachakrapada, Acharya Pindopa, brought the *Kalachakra Tantra* to India. These examples help us understand why one would not find all the tantras together. Even if all the important texts were in India when the Tibetan translators came, it is possible that the texts were not shown to those people, since the texts had been sealed.

Therefore, just because some lotsawas roaming around India on foot could not find certain texts in a particular library does not mean those teachings are not authentic. That resembles the story of the frog in the well who didn't believe that the ocean could be bigger than his own place. It is as Sakya Pandita says:

> If someone says, "This extends only so far,"
> And infers that is as far as anything could go,
> It contradicts what the Buddha said.
> One should examine the Buddha's intentions, which
>   are limitless.

Sakya Pandita adds:

> If you thoroughly investigate what that person is saying, you will find a sectarian view.

If someone uses the reasoning that the old tantras are not the Buddhadharma because one or two translators did not see them, then one could similarly reason that the new tantras are not genuine because the great siddhas and panditas like Padmasambhava and Vimalamitra did not see them and translate them.

The proclamation letter from Gö Lotsawa states that the Yamantaka cycle of teachings were composed by Nup Sangye Yeshe, and the *Great Space Liberation Tantra* and other Dzogchen texts were written by Vairochana. In reply to the statement that the Nyingma tantras were written by the translators, I want to ask Gö Lotsawa and the others: what proof do you have for this? If these are just words with no reason behind them, then this is a serious allegation. If you do have a reason, there are only four ways that you could know this. Either you personally saw the translators write down the texts, or you heard about this from someone else, or you know this through your personal analysis, or you know it through your clairvoyance.

Let's look at these four possibilities. First, it is impossible that you actually saw them, because those lotsawas were not alive at the same time as you. Second, if you say that it is because someone told you so, from whom did you hear it? For example, why didn't the previous great translators like Rinchen Zangpo hear this and mention it? What about the statements of Jowo Je Atisha? Among the later renowned panditas he is indisputably great; he is the incomparably kind protector of all Tibet. Atisha praised the Nyingma tantras and never said they were composed by Tibetans. If you did not hear this from great masters like these two, then from which reliable source did you hear it? If you tell us, then we can examine whether their words are right or wrong, but it seems no one can say what their sources are. Saying without any reason that the Nyingma tantras were written by the translators must be mere jealousy. Who would take those words for the truth?

For the third possibility, if you know this by examining the tantras with your own intellect and reasoning, how could you decide which teachings are Indian and which are Tibetan? As an object of comprehension, it is hidden from us who did or did not compose them; the authorship cannot be established from the teachings themselves.

The fourth possibility is that you understand this through your own higher perception. If you claim to have unmistaken clairvoyance and say that the *Guhyagarbha Tantra* was written by Ma Rinchen Chok and the *Yamantaka Appearance in the Mirror Tantra* was written by Nup Sangye Yeshe, then what you say is wrong. The Sanskrit originals were later found and retranslated by the lotsawas and panditas, so all your allegations are crushed in one blow and your clairvoyance is proved wrong. This makes your words resemble those of the skeptics who accused Buddha Shakyamuni of deceiving his followers with magic.

Another aspect to consider is that the great translators of the past were highly realized beings. Why would they write false tantras? Tell me what their motivation would be. They had no need to tear down the edifice of Buddha's teaching in Tibet because it wasn't even established at that point. If they truly wanted to harm Buddhism and write something new, then why didn't they write their own sutras as well? Why only tantras? It is illogical that they would have translated the sutras genuinely and then falsified the tantras.

Their motivation couldn't be their personal gain, because at that time the king gave strict orders that all the texts should be divided into numbered sections, and even tiny mistakes in the wording were not tolerated, much less the falsification of whole texts. Many great panditas and siddhas were there to witness this, including the great dharma king Trisong Detsen, who was the very nature of Manjushri. They were all residing there and hearing the teachings; it wasn't a situation where someone had something to gain from falsifying the scriptures.

From another angle, I would like to question Paldzin about his allegation that after Ma Rinchen Chok composed the *Guhyagarbha Tantra*, Ma was punished by the king and went into hiding for twelve years. This statement does more to prove how difficult it would have been to falsify the tantras than to prove that Ma did that. Paldzin, your own words are more of a contradiction than a substantiation. Generally speaking, the king was so strict that if Ma had to hide for twelve years for composing one tantra, then what would have happened to Nup and Vairochana who supposedly composed much more than that?

Look at it this way—the king didn't know about it and Guru Padmasambhava didn't hear about it. Or if they did know and understand what was happening, then why would Ma have been punished? You shouldn't make statements that contradict your own assertions. If the panditas, siddhas, and kings at that time were unaware of those compositions, and centuries later you say that it happened, only childish people who can't think might believe you. Anyone who can analyze even a little bit would not believe it.

And what about the later tantras that your tradition follows? It could equally be alleged that you and the translators of your era made them up. This sort of talk cannot prove or disprove anything, so there is no point in saying such things.

To put forth something as the Buddha's teaching when it is not the Buddha's teaching is a cause for going to the hell realm, because it is faking the dharma. The early translators, who were very learned and highly realized, would never have done such a thing, so it is clear that your words are only defamation.

Even though you say the Nyingma tantras did not come from India, there is proof that they did. Although you allege that Ma Rinchen Chok composed the *Guhyagarbha Tantra*, later Khache Panchen found the original Sanskrit text in Samye Monastery. He gave the text to Tatön Ziji, who passed it on to Shage Lotsawa, and then it went to Chomdende Rigpe Raltri. He edited the translation and translated two chapters that were not included before. Rigpe Raltri also wrote a commentary called the *Floral Ornament of the Guhyagarbha Practice,* and then he spread that teaching. The *Guhyagarbha Tantra* found later was also translated by Tharpa Lotsawa. Lowo Lotsawa Palden Jangchup found the same text in a Nepalese monastery, and Drigung Lotsawa Manika Shrijnana translated it in the place called Zurkhar Gadenling.

There is another proof that your allegations are false. There are quotations from the *Guhyagarbha Tantra* in the commentary written by Vajrahasa, in the commentary written by Indian pandit Vishvamitra on the later *Guhyasamaja Tantra,* and in the commentary written by Indranala on the *Equalizing Buddhahood Tantra.* Similarly, although it is claimed that Nup Sangye Yeshe composed Guru Padmasambhava's heart teaching, the *Yamantaka Appearance in the Mirror Tantra,* this tantra was mentioned by the master Shantarakshita as a Charya Yoga Tantra. Also, Acharya Shridhara said that it was Kriya Yoga, and so it must have originated in India.

There are other examples which show that the Nyingma tantras were undoubtedly already in Sanskrit in India and Uddiyana. Gö received the *Yamantaka Udagi Tantra* from Prince Meghavegin of India, including the sadhana, practices, and scriptural tradition. These teachings became known as the Gö Tradition of Udagi. This lineage went to Ngok Khawachen, as part of Gö's miscellaneous teachings, and it still exists today. There are also many Nyingma teachings that were retranslated and corrected later. For example, the Samyak Heruka practice called One Fire, One Skull was translated into Tibetan by Panchen Shakya Shri and Tropho Lotsawa, and Sakya Pandita made corrections on the *Vajrakilaya Piece of the Root Tantra.* So, some of these tantras were translated a second time from Sanskrit to Tibetan, but these examples show that they were not made up by Tibetans.

To supplement the above arguments by Mipham Rinpoche, here is a short quotation from the very learned and accomplished Orgyenpa:

> I said to the lay Vajrayana practitioners of Tibet concerning the many Sanskrit manuscripts in Nepal, "You all go to Mangyul, on the border of Tibet and Nepal, and I will bring the Nyingma panditas and Sanskrit texts there. I will be the translator and we will translate them." But the ngagpas were too distracted by their families and it was not accomplished. Even now there is much more to be translated.

Furthermore, in the main temple of Nalanda University, the translator Su Ga-we Dorje saw the paintings of the tantra texts raining down from the sky, which is the way some of the Nyingma tantras had appeared. Also, among the books of the Indian panditas, some of the Tibetan translators saw a short sadhana of the Eight Sadhana Teachings. When they asked the panditas about this, they were told, "I don't know, I don't know; it belongs to the old lamas." The panditas talked about how it was kept secret.

Not only that, but when Gö Khugpa Lhatse believed that Nupchen Sangye Yeshe composed the Nyingma texts on Yamantaka Lord of Life, he personally experienced a strong negative effect from having attacked the Nyingma teachings, so he went to India to find some deep teachings that would help him. There, Pandita Krishna Samayavajra gave him the teaching of Yamantaka Lord of Life, the same one the Nyingmapas had.

It was Gö Lotsawa himself who translated the text on Yamantaka Lord of Life that is now in the Tengyur.

Gö Lhatse was a very learned translator, but he made many allegations about the Nyingma teachings. It is rumored that at one point Gö was kicked out of the Zur lineage community, and that made him sick at heart. He was known to have a bad disposition and he also made accusations against Gayadhara. When he was a student of Drogmi Lotsawa, he became very upset when Drogmi did not give him certain teachings. Gö Lotsawa is quoted as saying before he went to India, "If I cannot become an excellent scholar, I will lose face with that vowbreaker Drogmi." So, it was his style to speak badly of people, even his own teacher.

Thukan Chökyi Dorje's Refutation

Another refutation of criticism of the authenticity of the Nyingma tantras comes from the great Gelugpa scholar, Thukan Chökyi Dorje. In his response to the criticism made by his teacher, Sumpa Khenpo Yeshe Pal, Thukan Chökyi Dorje says:[6]

> My teacher gave several reasons why some of the Nyingma teachings are not authentic, and his criticism can be summarized as follows: some of the mantras are not totally Sanskrit but have Tibetan words with them, so the mantras are both Sanskrit and Tibetan. Those Nyingma texts also contain some colloquial Tibetan expressions, terminology connected with the Chinese astrology of the elements, and words from the Shang Shung language. Another reason to discount the Nyingma tantras is that they are not found in the Kangyur. He said that some of the Bönpos of Tibet and some of the lay tantrikas of China are certainly stupid, so to obtain offerings from those people and eat well, the translators wrote the Nyingma tantras and said they came from the Buddha and Padmasambhava. These are his reasons for rejecting the early tantras.

To my teacher's criticism I would reply: If the Nyingma teachings go beyond the Four Seals of the Dharma, then they are outside the teachings of the Buddha and should be abandoned. However, I don't think that is the case. Your criticism does not mention that their meaning is incorrect. If there is no fault with the meaning, and only a few of the words are not right, then it is inappropriate to reject them. The Buddha himself said that one should not rely on the words, but rely on the meaning. In the authentic sutras, shastras, and tantras of India and Tibet there are many instances of imperfect words. For instance, the *Stainless Light*, the commentary on the *Kalachakra Tantra* states:

> In the tantras some of the stanzas are repeated and some of the stanzas end at the wrong point; in some places the grammatical particles are missing and in other places the vowels and consonants are separated wrongly, and so on. This was done so that those who are skilled in language would let go of attachment to good wording and rely on what the words mean. It is also like that in other texts. To understand the tantras, one must follow the oral instructions of one's master.

We should reject treatises opposed to Buddha's teachings, even if they are beautifully written by Buddhists. If what they say contradicts the dharma, those treatises should be abandoned. For example, the collected writings of Khedrup Sangye are full of poor wording, but the teaching is precisely the instructions of Je Tsongkhapa, so learned and realized beings do take those writings to heart. In support of this, Sakya Pandita says:

> *There are many dharma traditions known to be*
> *In the hearing lineage and the word lineage.*
> *If their teachings accord with the tantras, then it is*
>   *appropriate to accept them.*
> *If not, then they are false compositions.*
>
> *If the teachings that come from dreams,*
> *Visions of the deities, and similar sources*

Are in accord with the sutras and tantras,
Then there is no problem in accepting them.

But if teachings do not concur with the sutras and tantras,
Then they should be known as the blessing of the Maras.

Thukan Chökyi Dorje continues his reply to his teacher's criticism:

In the past, you too have used this quotation as a guideline.
One should determine the correctness of a teaching by comparing its meaning to the sutras and tantras, not merely its
words. In terms of the meaning, if the main points are not
mistaken, even though there may be small errors, then it is
not a false treatise. Sakya Pandita says:

Therefore, if a teaching is a little bit confused, it is all
right.
One needs to examine whether the main points are
confused or not.

Now, as for the mantras, if there are Tibetan syllables
mixed with the Sanskrit, one need not consider them incorrect. One can find Tibetan syllables in authentic, undisputed Sarma tantras as well as in the oral instructions of the
Kadampa, Sakyapa, and Gelugpa masters. I can give several
examples. In the *Vajrapani Tantra Directly Showing the
Secret,* translated by Bavalachandra and Lendar Tsultrim,
there are mantras that include both Sanskrit and Tibetan
words, such as:

MARAYA RAKTA NGUP NGUP
MARAYA KEM CHOM CHOM
MAHA MANU MARAYA TUP TUP

There is a similar example in another Vajrapani Tantra, the
Last Tantra of the Ferocious Ocean of Activity:

RAMA NAGA SHIK / NAGA CHER

Also, in Jowo Je Atisha's pith instructions, the Hayagriva
mantra has mixed Sanskrit and Tibetan syllables:

GYALGONG TSE LA A SHA DOM RE LA TRAGTUNG
NYING TRAK VAJRASADU SAMAYA JAH

And furthermore, you said in your own words:

In our own Gelugpa tradition, the oral instructions on the
Six-Armed Mahakala, which were edited and corrected by
Khedrup Je, and also in the *Eight Chapter Tantra,* it says:
SÖ SVAHA. . . .

In the mantra of the Mother it says:

BHYO MAMO NAGMO BHETALI

Also there are many Tibetan words in the very secret mantras
for accomplishing the wind energy, which were collected by
Khedrup Je, such as:

SER SER KHUK KHUK NYING TRAK LA BE

In glorious Sakyapa's *Golden Teachings,* the Black Manjushri
mantra has:

OM TRA SÖ / CHU SÖ / DUTTA SÖ / NYING GO A CHÖ / KHA
LA JVA

The mantra of the dharma protectors Putra Brother and Sister is similarly mixed:

A LI A LI MA DZAH DZAH / SHAM SHAM LI DE / A SHVA DE
MO MUK PU TRI A LI MA

There are many examples like these. Also, some of the tantras,
like Chakrasamvara, say that they were taught in the language
of the barbarians.

Generally, it is uncertain in which language of the buddhas a mantra has been blessed. For example, the mantra of
the protector Putrabhadra was originally written down in the
language of Shang Shung, and the text was buried in Samye.
When this terma was revealed, the great lotsawa Rinchen
Zangpo practiced this liturgy. At first he translated the
mantras into Sanskrit, but he found that they had no special
power. Then, he went back to saying them in the original

Shang Shung language, and he was able to accomplish the mantra. This caused Rinchen Zangpo to say, "Guru Padmasambhava is the knower of the three times," and to praise him. This story is found in Sakyapa Kunga Nyingpo's volume on the dharma protectors. So, for certain reasons, a mantra is more powerful in the language in which it was blessed; if it is put into another language, it does not have the same power. This story illustrates that.

If a text is not found in the Kangyur collection which was translated into Tibetan, that does not prove it is a false teaching. The Kangyur collection of the Chinese contains many texts which were never translated into Tibetan. For example, we know of the *Heroic Samadhi Sutra* which was translated by Changkya Thamche Khyenpa from the Chinese language into Tibetan, and the *Thought Tantra of Yamantaka,* which was translated by Pandita Chözang and found to be very similar to the Vajrabhairava visualization of the Gelugpa lineage. The *Sutra of the King of Giving Instructions* is another sutra in the Chinese Kangyur which is not in the Tibetan, and many of the Pali sutras are also not in the Tibetan Kangyur. So, it should be apparent that just because a text is not in the Tibetan Kangyur does not mean it is not authentic.

Atisha's Statements on the Early Tantras

From what I have said so far, it should be clear that the inner tantra teachings of the Early Translation tradition cannot be proven to lack an authentic source or to be written by Tibetans. Now, I would like to give some special historical evidence to establish that the Early Translation tantras did come from India.

All the tenet systems and schools of Tibetan Buddhism, such as the Sakya, Geluk, Kagyu, and Nyingma, accept and revere Jowo Je Palden Atisha, who is peerless in both India and Tibet. In his life story there is a passage about the time he went through the library of Samye Monastery and saw many Sanskrit texts that he had never seen before. Atisha said:[7]

There are many secret tantras that the humans do not know about. The dakinis opened the doors to many temples in the sky and showed me many tantras, but these texts in Samye were not there. The Mahayana and Secret Mantrayana are limitless; one can never find an end to them.

This caused Atisha's pride to be humbled, and he rejoiced and praised the king of Tibet. He said further:

The way the teachings spread in Tibet did not happen elsewhere, even in India. On three occasions there were terrible fires in India, and maybe these texts burned then. There are many Sanskrit books here that are not in India.

Atisha searched through them, copied them, and sent them to India. He also said:

The reason there are more Sanskrit texts in Tibet than in India is that Acharya Padmasambhava went into the sky, and from the lands of the devas and nagas, and from Nalanda University and elsewhere, he took all the tantras and brought them to Samye in Tibet.

Atisha is one of the greatest scholars and realized masters. He is chief among the masters who cleanse any defilements that might get incorporated into the Buddha's teaching. If all the special tantras of the Early Translation were not in accord with the teachings of the Buddha, or if they were composed by the ignorant Tibetans, then Atisha would have said, "These do not exist in India; they were fabricated in Tibet." But he did not say that; instead he praised these texts, copied them, and sent them back to India.

The tantras of both the earlier and later translation periods are established as being the teachings of the Buddha and authentic scriptures. The tantras of both periods are part of the Anuttarayoga tantras. Also, on the basis of the *Kalachakra Tantra*, the special teachings of Dzogchen, such as Thögal, can be established as the ultimate path.

Specific Criticism of the Dzogchen Teachings

Not only have the texts of the Nyingma tantras been criticized as inauthentic, but the Dzogchen practices that they contain have also been denigrated. The Nyingma lineage considers the Clear Light Great Perfection as the ultimate of all instructions. To remove mistaken criticism of this teaching, I am including a long excerpt from the *Commentary on the Aspiration for Longevity of the Nyingma Teachings* by Shechen Gyaltsap Padma Namgyal. This excerpt consolidates and presents criticisms of the Thögal teachings, and gives the corresponding refutations made by the noble masters of the Nyingma lineage. Shechen Gyaltsap begins by stating the criticism:[8]

Some critics say, "You claim that the appearance of the Thögal visions and the spontaneous radiance of clear light are very deep. However, in order to point out the rigpa vajra chains, you have the students do things such as look at the sun, press on the eyeballs, cover the eyes, make sounds that obstruct hearing, bind the nerves, and wear a mask. We question whether that experience is a direct perception of the true nature of reality, a direct perception of a temporary meditation experience, or a sensory direct perception.

"If it is a direct perception of the true nature of reality, the Thögal visions are a display of naturally appearing primordial wisdom, because they are within the experiential domain of the dharmata. They should be naturally clear and should not need these special conditions to be experienced. If the visions are experiences of wisdom rather than the objects of the sense consciousnesses, then you should not need those various conditions.

"If it is a direct perception as a meditation experience, then it is a temporary experience due to meditation and a sign of reaching a stage on the path. But it couldn't be that, because even without meditating, if you set up the right conditions, the visions appear. The third possibility is that the clear light is a sensory direct perception, but if so, then it cannot be the direct perception of the true nature of reality. If the direct perception of the dharmata could be perceived by a sense consciousness, that would make a laughing stock of the dharmata.

"Furthermore, you say the colors which appear from the various conditions actually abide inside your heart; that the nature of the mind abides as the five colors. When they radiate, they are seen outside when you look at the rays of the sun. If the visions are a display of something naturally present in your heart, then even if you don't look at the rays of the sun, they should still be seen, but they aren't. If you say they need to be evoked by certain conditions, that entails the presence of three minds: a mind that is the basis for the arising and abides as light in the heart; another mind that is the arising itself in the form of the vajra chains that appear in the sunlight; and a third mind, the visual consciousness that perceives the vajra chains. If you assert three minds, then your philosophical position is completely foreign to the Buddhist understanding.

"There is no difference at all between your view and the Hindu view. When you say that the nature of the mind is in your heart in the form of five-colored light, that is the same as a view of permanence, a view of the self, the enjoyer, the creator, and an independent mind. The Hindus say that the atman is in one's heart, and it is like an egg when it is large and like a sesame seed when it is small. If your view is different, then you need to explain it.

"The supports for the light—the heart and the internal organs—are definitely there, but nothing besides the organs is seen inside the body. Even if it is certain that there is light in your heart center, there is no certainty that the light rays come outside. If you look directly at the rays and lights and use them as supports to concentrate and keep the view in meditation, that is not a problem. But it would be much better and deeper to use whatever arises as the support for your meditation, rather than imagining lights in your heart. If you know how to apply the view in meditation, then it makes no difference whether you are seeing light rays or a heap of vomit.

If you have genuine understanding, then either of those can be liberating; if you don't, then either of them is a cause of bondage. What pure reasoning can you present for your claim that the direct vision of spontaneous presence is very deep?

"Furthermore, your Nyingma treatises say that the circles and small circles seen in Thögal are the sambhogakaya realms, and when you see them you are seeing the sambhogakaya. Are they real buddha fields or not? If not, then it is useless to say they are buddha fields; if you say they are real, then both scripture and reasoning deny that.

"The scriptures say that a practitioner must be at the sixth bhumi to have the power to see a sambhogakaya buddha realm. To see your sambhogakaya buddha field does not require even the first bhumi! If you point it out to an ordinary person, they immediately see it, and that person is an impure individual. If it is a real sambhogakaya buddha field, then the buddha fields become more expansive as people advance on the spiritual path. At the end of the path there would be zillions of buddha fields. However, in Dzogchen the highest attainment is called the Exhaustion of Phenomena in the Dharmata—all appearances dissolve just like ropes being gathered up and removed. So, in your system, at the end nothing remains to be seen, including the buddha fields. What you see in Thögal is just an experience on the path, which makes your buddha fields impure. So your assertion is refuted by both scripture and reasoning. What do you say to that?

"If you think there is a similarity between the direct perception of the dharmata, which we talk about, and the signs such as smoke which are taught by other traditions like the *Kalachakra Tantra*, we have no problem with that. The experiences such as smoke are signs that one's meditation is stabilizing. They do not depend on outer conditions; it doesn't matter whether the eyes are open or closed, or whether it is night or day. But you say that the rigpa vajra chains are invisible when your eyes are closed or there is no sun. Since they need particular conditions, they are not at all the same. Even if they are similar, the signs like smoke are merely signs on the path, similar to the reasoning of where there is smoke, there is fire. We do not consider those signs to be a supreme meditation. It is just the outer shell of experience; you have to discard them to attain liberation. That is how we understand it.

"You say that the direct perception of the dharmata is a pure experience, a supreme meditation state, and that one is liberated by seeing it. Therefore, signs like smoke and the direct perception of the dharmata are not similar; they have different implications. Your system also seems the same as the Bön teachings. They have many instructions on looking at lights. They say that if one's body enters the light, then one attains the eternal body without remainder; and if the light enters into oneself, then one attains the eternal body with remainder. I don't see a difference between your experience of light and theirs. What reasoning do you use to distinguish your experience from theirs?"

Shechen Gyaltsap's Refutation of the Criticism of the Dzogchen Teachings

Then, Shechen Gyaltsap systematically refutes each of these objections, beginning with a discussion of the inseparable nature of compassion and emptiness.

EMPTINESS, COMPASSION, AND CLEAR LIGHT

Shechen Gyaltsap says:

> Here are some brief answers to these objections. To begin with, the essence of the Buddha's teachings is emptiness endowed with the very nature of compassion. The *Stainless Light* states:
>
> > When one talks about the nonduality of emptiness and compassion, the compassion is free from all concepts and reference points. The emptiness is endowed with all the supreme qualities, and one completely knows the past,

present, and future at all times. This is the definitive teaching of the Buddha.

In talking about the inseparability of emptiness and compassion, emptiness is not a common sort of emptiness, like a house without people in it, nor is it the emptiness found through logical examination. It transcends these. The completely pure wisdom of the buddhas is clear light; it is the form of emptiness endowed with all the supreme qualities. *A Brief Teaching on the View of Manjushri* states:

> The emptiness that is found when the aggregates are
> analyzed
> Is like a banana tree, without any essence.
> But the emptiness endowed with all the supreme qualities
> Is not like that; it is unchanging,
> Unborn, and unceasing.
> In the way that one sees phenomena,
> The entity of emptiness is also empty,
> So this is not an analysis of the aggregates.

This quotation is talking about the clear light. What is the clear light? The *Wisdom Essence Tantra* states:

> "Bhagavan, what is the clear light? Where does it exist?"
> The Bhagavan replied: "The clear light is the circles abiding in the space of the sky. Through them you discover Mahamudra."

The *Five Stages of Guhyasamaja* states:

> The Mahamudra which is always dependent upon
> The buddhas of the five families,
> Arises as five-colored light,
> Similar to a rainbow in the sky.

Another Guhyasamaja commentary, the *Circle of Liberation*, states:

> That which holds the form of Mahamudra
> Is like an illusion and a rainbow.

> *It purifies the mindstreams of myself and others,*
> *So it is called "complete clarity."*

THÖGAL VISIONS AS DIRECT PERCEPTION

Shechen Gyaltsap continues:

As these quotes point out, the clear light which is seen has characteristics. For example, Nagarjuna's *Sixty Stanzas on Reasoning* states:

> *Those whose minds are groundless*
> *Have transcended existence and nonexistence.*
> *They meditate on the meaning of characteristics*
> *Which are profound and nonconceptual.*

Also, Naropa says these characteristics are omens that presage the fruition of suchness. In other words, if you think that the signs, such as the lights and circles, are merely external things, that is not so; they merely appear in the mind. They arise from your own mind, like the reflection of a form in a mirror.

The Thögal visions are not phenomenal entities outside the appearances of sentient beings' minds. They are direct perception itself, free of all concepts and delusion. Since they are direct manifestations of nonconceptual mind, they are not the appearances of discursive thinking produced by habitual tendencies.

The vajra chains do not appear because of dysfunctional sense faculties, like seeing two moons due to faulty vision, or because one's mind consciousness is dysfunctional. They are not things that appear to the sense consciousnesses, because they are not sense objects. They are manifestations of the uncontrived mind consciousness. Acharya Aryadeva explains the mind consciousness as having three appearances, and Acharya Drowazang Nyingpo's *Commentary on Suchness* discusses the manifestations of uncontrived mind in this way:

If one asks, "What is this? Is this entity suchness or not?" it is said to be beyond words. It is an appearance of the nature of the alaya consciousness; it is the essence that is not an entity and that pervades all of space. Through meditating on this noble thing, primordial wisdom arises.

To elaborate on this, the Thögal visions are the appearance of the real alaya which is the absolute universal ground, not the alaya consciousness which is one of the eight consciousnesses. They are not deluded appearances, but appearances of direct perception; they are not mere signs. They are the nature that is highly praised as "union"—the union of emptiness and compassion—and they become the great kaya of a buddha. The *Hevajra Tantra* states:

> *The higher realms, the underworld, and the upper world*
> *Become a single form in one instant.*

This is the main point to be kept secret in the Vajrayana, so it is a difficult matter to discuss with those who lack devotion and wisdom.

Now, we should discuss the meaning of direct perception. If you take a path without valid cognition you will go the wrong way and be deceived. Here, we are establishing these visions through valid cognition. Valid cognition has two aspects: direct perception and inference. The Secret Mantrayana has the same two types of valid cognition that are taught by Acharya Dharmakirti. The *Kalachakra Tantra* states in the chapter on practice:

> Observing the deity has two aspects: direct perception and inference. When direct perception is joined with suchness, the sambhogakaya forms arise, like the many stars in the sky. When there is not direct perception, the inference of the deity is like a dead body—it is imputed and not suchness. Those whose minds have not matured and who cannot see the deity directly should look at a representation, such as a painting, and use that for the object of meditation.

The direct perception taught here is not the ordinary direct perception by the sense faculties. Nor is it the yogic direct perception experienced by the shravakas and pratyekabuddhas. It is a special direct perception that is established through the direct perception of the yogis who are meditating on inner suchness. This direct perception also does not distort appearances in the various mistaken ways of knowing phenomena. It perceives what is called "suchness," the basis which does not change throughout the stages of the path, from being a deluded sentient being up to being a buddha. The *Oral Instructions of Manjushri* states:

> All phenomena, starting with form
> And extending to omniscience, have a nature
> Which is completely pure, like the mandala of the sky.
> Their nature is wisdom—profound, clear, and nondual.

> It is not a nonentity nor the meditation on a nonentity,
> Yet it is separate from all entities.
> It is not encompassed by the dhatus and ayatanas.
> It is naturally clear light.
> It is primordially pure, like the sky.

> It is dissociated from nonexistent phenomena.
> It has no phenomena or true nature.
> It is not an entity; it is similar to space.
> It is free from all words and letters.

> This is the essence of all phenomena,
> Of all directions and times.
> It is neither body nor speech
> Nor mind. It is not the desire realm,
> The form realm, or the formless realm.

> It is none of the four elements,
> So it abides nowhere.
> Therefore, it is equality.
> Great Vajradhara is like that.

> It is the supreme nature of all phenomena.
> It is something to be practiced through skillful means.

It is devoid of all concepts.
It is great abundance, difficult to fathom.
The nature ripens as the radiance
Which fully manifests Mahamudra.
It is the supreme nature of nonduality.
Even great Vajradhara
Cannot express this great form.

These words describe the direct perception that sees inner suchness. The *Commentary on the Vajra Heart* describes direct perception as follows:

> Sensory direct perception, mental direct perception, yogic direct perception, and self-aware direct perception have the corresponding characteristics of being that which shows, that which engages, that which arrives, and that which experiences.

So, what is the nature of direct perception? It is nonconceptual and undeluded consciousness that sees all phenomena as clearly as the stars in the sky. This happens by meditating on suchness, the practice of unified emptiness and compassion, through the five eyes—the flesh eye, the divine eye, the wisdom eye, the dharma eye, and the buddha eye. The *Commentary on the Vajra Heart* states further:

> Here, that which is meditated upon, the thing in the sky, is like a dream; it is beyond the nature of material particles. To understand that fully, what is meditated upon is the nonentity of things. It is seeing the reflections of the mind free of concepts. Because it is nonconceptual and undeluded, it is called direct perception.

SIMILAR VISIONS IN THE SARMA TEACHINGS

Next, Shechen Gyaltsap gives several quotations from tantras and commentaries followed in the Sarma tradition, which describe visions of light. He says:

What skillful means are used to see in this way? The *Chakra-samvara RI GI A RA LA Tantra* states:

> While staying quietly in a solitary place,
> And abandoning all dualistic thinking,
> By rolling the eyes upward
> And letting the mind be between the eyebrows,
> A good practitioner will first see it
> In the form of limitless darkness.

Also, the same text describes the manner of seeing:

> First, what one sees is darkness;
> Second, white and smoke;
> Third, fireflies;
> Fourth, a rainbow-colored flower;
>
> Fifth, the wisdom of a cloudless sky.
> Genuine awareness is released from perceptions of self
>   and other.
> The practitioner continually accustomed to these visions
> Will become one with single-pointed mind.

The *Vajra Tent Tantra* states:

> First, the appearances resemble clouds.
> Second, they are like smoke;
> Third, fireflies;
> Fourth, a flaming lamp;
> And fifth, the constant appearance
> Of a cloudless sky.

And the *Guhyasamaja Tantra* states:

> First, one sees a mirage;
> Second, smoke;
> Third, fireflies;
> Fourth, a flaming lamp;
> And fifth, unclouded appearance.

Aryadeva's *Lamp of Concise Practice* states:

What one sees first is a collection of five-colored light rays, which are like a mirage. The second, called "appearance," is like light rays of the moon. The third, "the increase of appearance," is like the rays of the sun. The fourth, "the attainment of appearance," is like darkness. Then, in an instant one is freed from that darkness, and the characteristic that appears is constant clear light. The nature of ultimate truth is seen with the eye of primordial wisdom.

CORRELATION OF THE SARMA TEACHINGS WITH THE FOUR LAMPS OF THÖGAL PRACTICE

Next, Shechen Gyaltsap compares the Sarma visions with the stages of Thögal. He says:

In the previous quotations from the Sarma practitioners and scriptures, the first, the miragelike appearance, is a collection of five-colored light rays. In Dzogchen, the first lamp of Thögal practice is the Lamp of Pure Space, which is described as appearing like blue silk or a peacock's feather. The quotes show that there is no difference between the first vision of Thögal and what is said by Aryadeva and the Sarma tantras.

The other visions mentioned by Aryadeva and the Sarma tantras resemble other Thögal visions, such as the rigpa vajra chains, those resembling the eyes of a fish, and shiny white circles. These visions get larger, like the three circles that become twenty-five circles, and so on. These are called the Appearances of the Direct Perception of Dharmata, which is the first of the four stages of Dzogchen practice.

In addition to the five Thögal visions already described by the Sarma tantras, there are the five appearances that are seen in the daytime, which make ten altogether. These ten are described in the Sarma text, *A Brief Teaching on Empowerment,* which states:

There are appearances of smoke, a mirage, the sky,
A flaming lamp, the moon, the sun,

Darkness, a big circle,
And clear light having various forms.

Seeing clear light having various forms is the same as the second stage of Dzogchen practice—the Appearances of Increasing Experience. The Dzogchen teachings say that the forms of light have five distinct colors and look like a long roll of felt, like a vertical stick, like a net, like brocade, and like yak-hair fabric. Then, the light expands to pervade all phenomena, all appearances and possibilities, and the light is clear even if one is not looking for it. Within the circles one sees various forms of the buddhas, sometimes peaceful and sometimes wrathful. After that, one reaches the third stage of Dzogchen practice, the Appearances of Awareness Reaching Its Full Measure. This correlates with the words of the *Kalachakra Tantra*:

> With a mind free from clinging, like space, and without blinking one's eyes, one enters the vajra path. From within emptiness, one sees the smoke, the mirage, the clear stainless sky, the lamp, the flames, the moon, the sun, the vajra, the excellent aspects, and the circles. Within those circles, one sees many sambhogakaya forms of the buddhas, in varying aspects and places.

Also from the *Kalachakra Tantra*:

> The practitioner should look with staring eyes at the center of a cloudless sky. One should continue to look until one sees stainless light radiating in a form like yak-hair fabric.

Another criticism is that if the sambhogakaya forms seen in the Thögal visions dissolve at the time of buddhahood, then those forms are not really visions of the sambhogakaya. Here again, we can find corresponding quotations from the New Translation tantras and teachers. For example, the glorious siddha Shavari says:

> *After you have perfected the ten signs,*
> *Then the large circles appear.*
> *In the large circles of various colors,*

Figures appear like yak-hair fabric.
In the circles you will see the beings of the six realms
And many very fine forms of the nirmanakaya
And sambhogakaya buddhas.
This is clear light having various forms.

When the mind dissolves in that,
All aspects of the meditation have been accomplished.

This culmination is the same as the fourth stage of Dzogchen practice, the Exhaustion of Phenomena in the Dharmata.

REFUTATION OF THÖGAL AS SENSORY DIRECT PERCEPTION

Shechen Gyaltsap goes on to discuss the relationship between Thögal and direct perception:

> These Sarma quotations are describing the direct perception of the dharmata. The timeless true nature is primordial wisdom, which is self-radiating and naturally clear. This has been established by the previous quotations. However, there is another criticism: if one can see the true nature with one's eyes, that makes a laughing stock of the dharmata. But that criticism contradicts the words of Naropa, who says:
>
> > *When one's mind is free from all grasping at characteristics,*
> > *And one's eyes are looking halfway up,*
> > *And the wind energy is brought into the central channel,*
> > *At that time the vajra fire and smoke will appear.*

This is direct experience; these appearances are experienced by a practitioner while meditating on the path. As the Lamdre *Vajra Verses* by Virupa say:

> This is called "the appearances experienced in meditation by a yogic practitioner."

Sensory direct perception is explained in terms of the eyes, which are called the Far-Reaching Water Lamp in the Thögal teachings of the Four Lamps. The eyes are the door through which the appearances happen, but the Thögal visions are not sensory direct perception. This is because the wisdom of the buddhas is primordially self-radiating as the very light of the five wisdoms, and that wisdom transcends the eyes seeing and the objects seen. Also, you can see the Thögal visions in the darkness when you cannot even see your own hand reaching out, and you can see them in the bardo when you have no bodily eyes, so they are not just sensory direct perception. *A Brief Teaching on Empowerment* states:

> *They are not seen by your own eyes*
> *And also not seen by others' eyes;*
> *Seeing the unborn*
> *Is like seeing the son of a virgin.*

The *Commentary on the Praise of Chakrasamvara* states:

> Because they are experienced by the covered as well as uncovered eyes, they are not form, and yet they are not other than form. Also, they are not the eye consciousness.

As the *Commentary on the Vajra Heart* says, these visions can be seen as the four kinds of direct perception in the following way. The engaged objects, what are seen by a practitioner of the completion stage, are many circles and colors. These are seen through sensory direct perception. Then, the magical displays of forms appear, and they are reflected in the mind and the sky, like reflections in a clear mirror. The entire three worlds appear, and many brilliant, stainless light rays radiate. So, it is with mental direct perception that one sees the reflections of the mind as the indestructible circles, and from that one gains confidence. Then, one has the experience of Awareness Reaching Its Full Measure, and that is the yogic direct perception, which leads to actualizing self-aware primordial wisdom. When the final stage of Dzogchen occurs, the Exhaustion of Phenomena, all appearances dissolve beyond the duality of perceiver and perceived, and this is self-aware direct perception.

When one is shown these appearances through relying on supports such as covering one's eyes with colors or masks, or looking through crystals or at the rays of the sun, that is not the real wisdom awareness. In this system of teaching there are three methods of introduction: through symbols, meanings, and signs. When one is introduced to the real meaning by relying on symbols, these are known as symbolic representations. We never assert these as being the wisdom of direct perception.

SARMA QUOTATIONS ON WISDOM LIGHT IN THE HEART

Then, Shechen Gyaltsap quotes some Sarma teachers and texts that reflect the Nyingma understanding of clear light. He says:

The primordial wisdom that exists in one's heart has the nature of clear-light emptiness. It is not viewed as being the self or atman, like the eternalistic non-Buddhists say. The *Hevajra Tantra* states:

> *Great wisdom resides in the body;*
> *There is no Buddha somewhere else.*
> *Those obscured by the darkness of ignorance*
> *Attempt to find the Buddha in something other than*
> *   the body.*

The *Sambhuti Tantra* states:

> *Inside the heart, which is like a lotus seed,*
> *Are eight petals and a center.*
> *Within that center, the channel of the seed*
> *Has the essence of a lamp.*

> *It is like the flower of a plantain tree,*
> *Spreading underneath this entrance.*
> *Inside of that is the hero,*
> *The size of a sesame seed.*

And the great Brahmin Saraha says:

> *Learned scholars teach the scriptures*
> *Without realizing that wisdom exists in the body.*

Vajraghanta says:

> *The single circle is unchanging,*
> *Always remaining in the heart.*
> *Wisdom definitely arises*
> *For people who meditate on that.*

One can find many further explanations of this in the tantras and commentaries. Its essence is primordial wisdom, free from particles of matter and moments of time. Having the form of the sky, it is the vajra of space pervading space. Transcending all objects of elaborations and characteristics, it is the equality of union. Because it does not change throughout the three times, it transcends the extremes of being permanent or impermanent. Therefore, it is designated as self-arising wisdom and the great permanence.

THE NYINGMA UNDERSTANDING OF THE ULTIMATE MEANING

Next, Shechen Gyaltsap gives a long verse summary of the ultimate meaning according to scholars who fully understand the profundity of the sutras and tantras. He says:

> *The natural state as it is, the middle way, pervades all of samsara*
> *   and nirvana.*
> *For samsaric beings it appears as the ground.*
> *For the bodhisattvas it appears as the path.*
> *For the pure beings it appears as the result.*
>
> *These three are the way it appears, not the way it is.*
> *The naked natural state is seen only by the buddhas.*
> *Those on the path partially see it—*
> *They see a mixture of the way it is and the way it appears.*

The natural state is always in union.
The way it is as the ground is the same way it is as the result.
The natural state is Madhyamaka, the middle way.
If one proceeds in accordance with that, it is the path of
  Madhyamaka.

Called the union of relative truth and absolute truth,
The union of appearance and emptiness, the union of clarity and
  emptiness,
The union of skillful means and wisdom, the union of emptiness
  and compassion,
The union of bliss and emptiness, the union of the illusory body and
  clear light,

The union of the kayas and wisdoms, and so on—
All these distinguish the union of the path
From the dharmata, the union of the way it is.
The paths are not true, they are like magical illusions.

What is called the ultimate, the union of space,
Is the dharmakaya, the real buddhahood.
It is the buddha nature, it is the dharmadhatu.
Its nature is emptiness, free of elaboration; it is the Prajnaparamita.

It is everywhere and pervades everything, so it has no parts.
It pervades the past, present, and future, so it has no time.
All the qualities of a buddha, such as the major signs and
  minor marks,
Are self-arising, primordially accomplished, and therefore
  permanent.

In the sutras the dharmadhatu and the Buddha are said to be
  permanent.
In the tantras they are said to be endowed with all the supreme
  qualities.
The main point in asserting that the buddha nature is permanent
Is to reach the way it is, which is unchanging bliss.

The qualities of the buddhas are self-arising and spontaneously
    present
Because that is how the dharmata is.
The nature is unchanging, yet all the aspects arise
While it remains primordially permanent. This is so marvelous!

Although all the qualities are naturally there, the nature does not
    have parts.
While the nature remains unchanging, it arises all the time.
Although it arises as the three worlds, it is free of elaboration.
The great bliss is self-aware, and yet free of feeling and experience.

The qualities of the buddhas pervade all phenomena.
The single wisdom and all phenomena are equal.
All phenomena, without exception, are known clearly and
    distinctly.
There are no extremes whatsoever in that awareness.

The nature of the dharmata is the dharmakaya,
So the dharmakaya is endowed with all the qualities.
The dharmakaya is wisdom that is aware of all phenomena,
So it is also established as having all the aspects.

It is said that the dharmadhatu has no divisions in its essence.
Yet at times it is taught as if
Each phenomenon exists with its own dharmadhatu.
By joining these two understandings, one knows why the supreme
    qualities are present all the time.

Form and the other objects are not conceptualized; one does not
    dwell in form.
Existence and nonexistence are not conceptualized; one does not
    dwell in existence or nonexistence.
Speaking in this way is free from the deluded relative level.
Because the nature transcends impermanence and all extremes, it is
    established as permanent.

The nature of the dharmadhatu, the expanse of reality, never changes,
And buddhahood always exists within beings.
One might think that if the nature is permanent, it is an entity,
*   an extreme.*
To remove this doubt, the nature is taught as being empty and free
*   of elaboration.*

When something is said to be "empty," it is never taught
As just nothing or as something untrue.
From the relative point of view, it is empty of nonexistence or
*   nonbeing.*
From the ultimate point of view, it is empty of conceptualized
*   objects.*

The ultimate is said to be empty of itself.
This is said so that the mind will not fixate
And conceptualize the ultimate.
It is not empty in the sense of primordially nonexistent or
*   primordially nonbeing.*

The essence, suchness, has all the qualities.
Suchness does not change, so it is permanent as well as bliss.
This is very clearly taught in the tantras.
It is said that the sutras point toward this understanding.

In terms of being partless and all-pervading like space,
Some say it is unfeasible that the nature is obscured and unobscured
*   while being partless.*
But those aspects appear to different viewpoints; from its own side
The dharmadhatu is neither obscured nor unobscured.

Consciousness which perceives the nature
Exists in different situations, which is why distinctions of obscured
*   and unobscured are taught.*
Because the perceivers are different,
There are said to be distinctions in what is perceived.

Actually, it is one's mind that is veiled by obscurations.
But to that mind, it is the dharmata which seems obscured.
It is like a city shrouded in mist,
Whose inhabitants think the sun is veiled by clouds.

When the clouds are blown away by the wind passing over
the earth,
One understands that what obscured the sun has been cleared away.
Similarly, in accordance with the students' understanding,
It is taught that suchness is attained once it is free of defilements.

Buddhahood exists ultimately
Because buddhahood is the ultimate.
Buddhahood could not be other than the ultimate,
Because it is impossible for the qualities to be present if the basis for
the qualities is not there.

Is the buddhahood that will be attained the true nature or not?
If not, then what good would it do to attain a deluded appearance?
If it is the true nature, then the buddhahood one attains
Was also the true nature when one was a sentient being.

It is the true nature from the time one is an ordinary person
To the time one is a buddha, so it is unchanging and permanent.
The three times, such as before and after, ultimately do not exist.
The three phases are ways of seeing with the mind.

The true nature abides unaffected by time.
Delusion and samsara arise through concepts.
The antidote is meditation on the nonconceptual path.
Since the thoughts ride on the karmic winds,

If one meditates on the path that purifies the winds within its
nature,
One will actualize the result, the excellence that fulfills the purposes
of oneself and others.

Shechen Gyaltsap concludes:

> This explains how to distinguish between the way things are and the way things appear. All of this is rooted in the ultimate meaning, the union of E and VAM, which is coemergent and unchanging great bliss.

REFUTING THE THREE MINDS

Shechen Gyaltsap still has a few more criticisms of the Nyingma teachings to address. He says:

> The Nyingmapas reply to their critics: You assert that our understanding entails having three different minds—a mind that is the basis for the arising and abides as light in the heart; a mind that is the arising itself in the form of the vajra chains that appear in the sunlight; and the mind that is the visual consciousness that perceives the vajra chains.
>
> Your allegation comes from not understanding the eight consciousnesses, even in a general way; you sound extremely ignorant. Your misunderstanding is like saying that since the sun has rays, there must be two suns; or that to practice the six yogas one must have six separate minds—when meditating on illusory appearances one would have a mind which is the illusory body; when meditating on all phenomena as dreamlike, one would have a dream mind, and so on. Your argument has this kind of faulty consequence.
>
> The mind is not like that, rather it is like the great Brahmin Saraha says:
>
> > The coemergent nature of the mind is the dharmakaya.
> > The coemergent appearance is the light of the dharmakaya.
> > Therefore, mind and appearance are nondual and coemergent.
> > I pay homage to the mind, which is like a wish-fulfilling jewel.

Isn't the mind said to be like that? The appearances of light are experienced while in a meditative state; it is not like a child looking at paintings on a temple wall. You will understand this if you look carefully at the genuine instructions of the completion stages practice and the Six-Branched Practice of Vajra Yoga.

THE SIGNIFICANCE OF THE VISIONS

Shechen Gyaltsap goes on to say:

> Another thing you allege is that looking at the circles and light is equivalent to looking at a heap of vomit. This is a great misunderstanding. The circles are definitely the mandalas of the enlightened ones, and one is liberated just by seeing them. It says in the *Sutra of the Recollection of the Buddha:*
>
>> There is great significance in seeing this. This is the individual, self-knowing awareness of the wise.
>
> Also, it is said that by seeing the ten signs of Retention in the Six-Branched Practice of Vajra Yoga, one accomplishes various abilities, such as having all one's words come true. For those who possess the view, a heap of vomit does not ultimately exist, but still, no good qualities would arise from seeing it.
>
> If one asks about the profound main point of the first stage of Dzogchen realization, the Direct Perception of the Dharmata, it is the view which cuts the continuity of living in the city of samsara. Since it cuts the continuity of being born, one will not wander in samsara later on. It is said that those who see this crucial point of direct perception never return to the three realms.
>
> All the great siddhas of India traveled this path, which is clear from their songs of realization. It would take too long to write them all here, but I can quote a few examples. To begin with, Saraha says:

How wonderful! O bhusuku, you carefree yogi, there
    arises in the center of space,
O bhusuku, an incomparable, blossoming flower.
Get this precious, priceless blossom.
This flower is grown in the hermitage of emptiness.
This flower has many different colors.

And also from Saraha:

The yogi who has attained direct perception
Must understand these other signs.
When they are accomplished, there is no more delusion.
They are like the smoke of the dark path,
Staring eyes,
The head bent down,
The mind and mental factors not moving,
And the emptiness that sees emptiness.

Aryadeva says:

When the full moon rises,
The king of the mind is laid to rest.
The sound of the damaru drum of joy and compassion
Comes clearly to Aryadeva without reference points.

Shantideva says:

Once one has seen the profound dharma, then the
    negative path,
The path of darkness, is no longer seen.
When the flowers blossom in the pinnacle of the sky,
Then I, Shantideva, cut through delusion.

Another quote from Shantideva says:

By looking and looking until daybreak,
Shanti discovers the path with his inner lamp.

And from Krishna Samayavajra:

The five flowers arise and dissolve into that.
The joyful nature of mind is revealed in the sky.

Acharya Anupamarakshita says:

> *When you look into the stainless sky by opening the*
> *emanation eyes,*
> *There is the moist blossom of the enlightened mind,*
> *which is the basis of perception.*
> *It is free from the distinctions of existence and*
> *nonexistence, entities and nonentities.*
> *All the signs, like smoke, arise suddenly in the nature of*
> *emptiness.*

There are many more quotations like these. Another question you raise is how practitioners could see sambhogakaya buddhas since the sambhogakaya is seen only by the tenth-bhumi bodhisattvas. In reply, it says in the tantras:

> . . . of the dharmakaya, such as those having sambho-
> gakaya forms and the bodhisattvas in space. . . .

To explain this reference, the buddha forms abiding in the pure realms are also called the sambhogakaya. This term does not refer to the real sambhogakaya only, but to the buddha forms abiding in the pure lands. They are seen in these visions. The sambhoga, or "great enjoyment," explained here is another name for the dharmakaya. In one way of describing it, the forms in the colored circles are sometimes called the nirmanakaya, and the various sounds that appear are sometimes called the sambhogakaya. This is the explanation by the great lamas of the Six-Branched Practice of Vajra Yoga.

It is said in our own Dzogchen tradition:

> *By the appearance of Awareness Reaching Its Full*
> *Measure,*
> *One realizes the form of the sambhogakaya.*

For yogis at the stage of Awareness Reaching Its Full Measure, wherever they reside is a sambhogakaya pure realm and all their followers are a sambhogakaya retinue. However, before one attains this level, the place one resides is not a sambhogakaya place. Practitioners who have reached this level see their surroundings as a pure realm and their followers as a sambhogakaya retinue, but the other people around them do not see that, because one's perceptions are the display of the dharmata. The reason it is seen like that is explained in the sutras:

> Whether the buddhas arise or do not arise, at all times all sentient beings possess the buddha nature.

To establish this, the *Sublime Continuum* states:

> *Because the form of perfect enlightenment shines forth,*
> *Because suchness cannot be divided,*
> *And because the potential for enlightenment exists,*
> *All beings always possess the buddha nature.*

This nature is clearly taught with these three characteristics. In the *Sublime Continuum,* examples such as water, gold, and the sky are used to describe how the nature is primordially pure. The tantras concur, which can be seen from the following quotations from the Sarma tantras. To begin with, the *Kalachakra Tantra* states:

> Outside of one's body, there is no buddha who bestows liberation. Sentient beings themselves are buddhas. There is not some other great buddha who exists here in this world.

The *Vajra Tent Tantra* states:

> *Outside this precious mind,*
> *There are no buddhas and no beings.*

The *Two Segments Tantra* states:

> *The great primordial wisdom*
> *Abides within each being's body.*
> *Its manner is both dual and nondual.*
> *The primary nature is substantial and insubstantial.*
> *It remains stable as well as moving and pervasive.*
> *It abides as illusory form.*

The *Vajra Mirror Tantra* states:

> *That which abides in the hearts of beings*
> *Is unconditioned, naturally occurring wisdom.*
> *It is great bliss, the indestructible circle,*
> *All-pervading like space.*
> *It is nondwelling, the nature of the dharmakaya.*

Therefore, it should be clear that the Sarma tantras and the Nyingma tantras express the same understanding.

This concludes the refutations from Shechen Gyaltsap's *Commentary on the Aspiration for Longevity of the Nyingma Teachings.*

Jamyang Khyentse Wangpo's Explanation of the Ultimate

The main points of this discussion can be summarized in the following words of Jamyang Khyentse Wangpo:[9]

> *Svatantrika Madhyamaka's five great reasonings*
> *Establish that phenomena are unreal.*
> *They say that the ultimate truth is essenceless*
> *And the relative truth is the way things appear.*

> *Prasangika Madhyamaka completely discards all elaborations,*
> *Assertions, additions, and subtractions.*
> *They specialize in using logic to destroy*
> *Others' assertions by showing the internal contradictions in their*
> *   statements.*

> *Prasangika Madhyamaka and Dzogchen*
> *Are of one taste in showing the true nature*
> *Is inconceivable, beyond the intellect.*
> *One sees it only through well-established meditation.*

> *The pure and stainless Chittamatra school*
> *And the Shentong Madhyamaka are not the same.*

Mind-Only asserts that consciousness is the ultimate,
And Shentong states primordial wisdom is the ultimate.

The Lamdre school says that all appearances are the mind;
Whatever appears to the mind is illusory
And is established as unreal in its nature.
They make two categories: the interdependent and the ineffable.

So, one should not misunderstand,
Like the Vaibhashikas do,
That this understanding is the same as the Mind-Only view.
This error comes from not examining these views in detail.

This understanding is stated in the Vajra Tent Tantra:
"Outside the precious mind
There are no buddhas and no beings."
Also, the Sambhuti Tantra *states:*

"Upon examination, everything external or internal
Is found to be the mind.
There is nothing else
Other than the mind."

The reasoning for this
Was given by the protector Nagarjuna:
"One external object
Can be seen in many different ways.

"A form that appears beautiful to you
Appears differently to others.
The body of a woman
Seems unclean to an ascetic,

"Desirable to a lover, and edible to a dog—
It appears in three different ways."
This is the sort of reasoning he uses.
Specifically, saying that appearances are the mind

Is the same for Yogachara and Chittamatra.
But unlike Chittamatra, in Yogachara we do not accept that the
nature of mind is truly existent;
It is free from all extremes. Therefore our views are not the same.
It says in the Great Self-Arising Awareness Tantra

Of the Clear Light Great Perfection:
"From the heretical views of eternalism and nihilism
Up to the essence of the highest Vajrayana teaching,
The levels of the view are differentiated in detail."

And the root Hevajra Tantra *states:*
"To your students, first teach the Vaibhashika view,
Then teach according to Sautrantika.
Following that, teach the Yogachara view

And then the Madhyamaka."
Thus, the tantras clearly say to proceed in stages.
It is as the great yogi Virupa said.
In order for an individual to gradually enter the path,

The essential meaning is explained
In terms of the aggregates, sense bases, and consciousness.
This is similar to the two tenet systems of the shravakas,
And surpasses heretical views.

When consciousness without an object, and consciousness with
an object,
And the nonduality which is other than those,
Are taught as not having self-nature,
This teaching surpasses the Chittamatra.

The relative appearances are illusions
And the ultimate is not posited in any way.
This approach is higher than
The Madhyamaka positing the ultimate as essenceless.

Therefore, from the very beginning
The four extremes created by the mind are transcended.
Practicing according to the union of relative and absolute
Is the ultimate understanding of this path.

Moreover, when the ultimate discriminating-awareness wisdom
Radiates from the depths of one's being,
And not just through words,
It becomes of one taste with Dzogchen.

In summary, in the profound and secret Nyingtik teachings,
Rigpa is abruptly and forcefully introduced
To mature students who can immediately recognize it.
For them the Dzogchen teachings are particularly good.

The Lamdre, the Path with Its Result,
Is presented in a more gradual way.
If the distinctions between forceful and gradual teaching are
  understood,
Then the contradictions between the approaches dissolve into space.

ACKNOWLEDGMENTS

FOR THE TIBETAN EDITION, 1985

I BASED THIS WHOLE BOOK on the writings of Jamgön Kongtrul, whose Ri-me understanding is inseparable from that of Jamyang Khyentse Wangpo. I consulted the writings of some of their main students, such as Mipham Jamyang Namgyal Gyatso, Dodrupchen Jigme Tenpe Nyima, and Shechen Gyaltsap Padma Namgyal, as well as the writings of other learned and realized beings in all four schools of Tibetan Buddhism. My research was also based on study I have done at the feet of many great scholars and meditation masters, who answered my questions with great kindness. However, because of my inferior intellect I am unable to understand the true meaning of all these teachings. If there are any errors in my explanation, I confess them in the presence of the great learned ones.

I also want to mention that while writing this book I continuously received exceptional assistance and guidance from the professors at the library of the Central Institute for Higher Tibetan Studies in Varanasi, particularly from the Director of the Institute, Professor Samdong Rinpoche. I also consulted the Research Institute of Tibetology in Gangtok, Sikkim, and the library of the Sikkimese nobleman Barjnak Athing, where I was constantly provided with excellent conditions for research. I also want to thank my earlier and more recent spiritual guides: the late Khenchen Thubten Tsöndru, the Kagyu khenpo Yeshe Chödar, and especially the Khangdong Tertrul, Chi-me Rigdzin Rinpoche, who accepted the responsibility of giving me advice and help, and made corrections to the manuscript. To all these people I extend heartfelt and unending gratitude.

This book was completed in the city of Gangtok, in the hidden land of Sikkim, on the fifteenth day of the first month of the sixteenth sixty-year cycle of the Tibetan Female Water Pig year, 2110. In the Western calendar this date is February 27, 1983.

Ringu Tulku

For the English Edition, 2006

For the English edition of this book, I would like to acknowledge, first of all, the work of my cotranslator, Ann Helm, who did most of the work when we translated this book during teaching visits at Naropa University, 1999–2004. My thanks also go to two scholars who provided the original Sanskrit for many of the Tibetan names used in this book: L. D. Rabling for providing the titles of the Indian texts, and Zoran Lazovic for finding the names of the Indian masters. My heartfelt thanks go to Zenkar Rinpoche, Gene Smith, Cyrus Stearns, Sarah Harding, and Karl Brumholzl for their help at various levels. I also extend ongoing appreciation and gratitude to Emily Bower and the staff of Shambhala Publications for all their assistance in the production of this book.

Notes

All the citations below, except for the English translation of Kongtrul's autobiography, refer to Tibetan texts, for which the publishers' names, locations, and dates of publication are not available to be included here.

Homage

1. The Indian legend says that the noise of the flowing Brahmaputra River irritated Lord Shiva as it passed by, so he swallowed the river to keep it quiet. When there was no more water downstream, the gods and humans came to Shiva and asked him to please release it. Shiva did so through the top of his head. The allusion here is that Jamgön Kongtrul's knowledge flows from his head just like the Brahmaputra River flows from Shiva's.

Preface

1. A translation of Kongtrul's entire autobiography, including Tashi Chöphel's account of Kongtrul's passing and funeral observances, is now available in English as the *Autobiography of Jamgön Kongtrul*, trans. Richard Barron, Snow Lion Publications, Ithaca, N.Y., 2003.

Chapter 1

1. The *Biography of Jamyang Khyentse*, p. 65.
2. *Awakening Reverence for the View* by Rongzom Pandita, p. 10.
3. This quotation comes from Khenchen Kunpal's *Commentary on the Beacon of Certainty*, p. 15.
4. From the *Treasury of Knowledge*, vol. VAM, beginning on p. 559.
5. Jamgön Kongtrul's *Informal Discussion of the View* is found in his *Collected Works*, vol. TA.

Chapter 2

1. From Kongtrul's *Autobiography*, p. 66.

CHAPTER 4

1. This is from Shechen Gyaltsap's *History of the Dharma,* pp. 87–88.
2. This information comes from Kongtrul's *Treasury of Knowledge,* vol. E, p. 506.
3. This is mentioned by Jamgön Kongtrul in the *Treasury of Knowledge,* vol. E, p. 119.
4. The five great treatises are the *Commentary on Valid Cognition* by Dharmakirti, the *Entrance to the Middle Way* by Chandrakirti, the *Ornament of Clear Realization* by Maitreya, the *Treasury of Abhidharma* by Vasubandhu, and the *Vinaya Root Discourse* by Gunaprabha.
5. *Ali Kali* stands for the Sanskrit vowels and consonants, and means "words" or "speech."

CHAPTER 5

1. The *Sixteen Circles of the Kadampa* is also the name of a book, with an empowerment and teachings, but here it is a general reference to the main teachings of the Kadampa lineage.
2. The four bodhisattva practices and three knowledges are fully explained in the *Ornament of Clear Realization.*
3. This exposition of the Gelugpa teachings comes mostly from the writings of Jigme Samten, a very learned Gelugpa master of the nineteenth century.
4. When people take the empowerment, they agree to do the practice four times each day. Each session takes about one-and-a-half hours, and the practitioners are not supposed to stand up once they have started the session. This particular regime is characteristic of the Sakya tradition.
5. This way of explaining the name "Kagyu" comes from the *Collected Writings of Jamyang Khyentse Wangpo,* vol. TSHA, p. 456.

CHAPTER 6

1. From the *Treasury of Knowledge,* vol. E, p. 518.
2. The Tibetan translated here as *Ninefold Volume* is *bam po dgu pa,* literally, the "nine sections." A bampo is a way of measuring and sectioning a text by the number of words. A bampo is about five hundred stanzas, so this text is about forty-five hundred stanzas long.
3. From the *Treasury of Knowledge,* vol. E, p. 454.
4. From the *Great Exposition of the Stages of the Path* by Je Tsongkhapa, pp. 287–88, Tashi Lhunpo edition.
5. From the *Treasury of Knowledge,* vol. VAM, p. 535.
6. From the *Treasury of Knowledge,* vol. VAM, p. 550.
7. This disagrees with the fifth of Tsongkhapa's eight theses, which posits some external reality. However, this understanding also disagrees with the Chitta-

matra view, because for the Prasangika, the inner, mental phenomena are mere designations and do not truly exist.

8. This explanation is from the *Treasury of Knowledge,* vol. VAM, beginning on p. 555.

9. The next section is from Taranatha's *Essence of Shentong,* pp. 511–13. It is quoted within Kongtrul's *Treasury of Knowledge,* vol. VAM, beginning on p. 560.

10. From the *Treasury of Knowledge,* vol. VAM, beginning on p. 559.

CHAPTER 7

1. From the *Treasury of Knowledge,* vol. MA, p. 187.

2. From the *Treasury of Knowledge,* vol. E, p. 463.

3. From the *Treasury of Knowledge,* vol. E, p. 476.

4. Union involves sexual practices and Liberation involves the ritual slaughter of animals.

5. This is from Shechen Gyaltsap's *Commentary on the Aspiration for the Longevity of the Nyingma Teachings,* p. 35.

6. This is taken from *Polishing the Ketaka Jewel,* volume NA, p. 11.

7. These statements by Atisha come from the writings of Sogdogpa and Gyara Longchenpa, who both wrote lengthy responses to the criticism of the Nyingma teachings. They give a complete explanation of these points.

8. This quotation begins on p. 407 of Shechen Gyaltsap's *Commentary on the Aspiration for the Longevity of the Nyingma Teachings.*

9. From the *Collected Works of Jamyang Khyentse Wangpo,* volume KHA, p. 160.

SOURCES

These are the English and Sanskrit titles used in the text, along with the Wylie transliteration of the Tibetan and, if known, the Sanskrit title and the author.

Activity Garland Tantra (karma sa le).

All-Victorious Yamantaka Tantra (gshin rje rnam par rgyal ba'i rgyud; Skt. Yamarikrishna Tantra or Krishnayamarivijayatantra).

Arising of the Twelve Kilayas Tantra (phur pa bcu gnyis pa 'byung ba'i rgyud; Skt. Vajrakilayadipashatantra).

Armor against Darkness (mun pa'i go cha).

Array of Samayas (dam tshig bkod pa; Skt. Trisamayavyuharaja or Samayavyuha).

Ascertaining the Meaning of Suchness (de nyid rnam nges; Skt. Tattavavinishchaya) by Asanga.

Ascertaining the Meaning of Valid Cognition (tshad ma rnam nges; Skt. Pramanavinishchaya) by Dharmakirti.

Assembly of Secrets (gsang ba 'dus pa; Skt. Guhyasamaja).

Authentic Words (bka' yang dag pa'i tshad ma; Skt. Ajnasamyakpramana).

Autocommentary on the Treasury of Abhidharma (mdzod 'grel; Skt. Abhidharmakoshabhasya) by Vasubandhu.

Avatamsaka Sutra (phal chen).

Awesome Wisdom Lightning (ye shes rngams glog; Skt. Sarvatathagataguhyamahaguhyakoshakshayanidhadipamahprata-pasadhana-tantrajnanashcharyadyutichakra-nama-mahayana-sutra).

Barche Kunsel (*Heart Practice That Dispels All Obstacles*) (thugs sgrub bar chad kun sel) terma of Chogyur Lingpa.

Basic Transmission of the Vinaya ('dul ba lung gzhi; Skt. Vinayavastu).

Beneficial for Students (slob ma la phan pa) by Dharmottara.

Black Yamantaka Tantra (gshin rje gshed nag gi rgyud; Skt. Sarvatathagatakayavak-chittakrishnayamari-nama-tantra).

Blue Annals (deb ther sngon po) by Gö Lo Shönupal.

Blue Draft (reg zeg sngon po).

Bodhisattva Stages (byang chub sems pa'i sa; Skt. Bodhisattvabhumi) by Asanga.

Book on the Five Paths (lam lnga'i glegs bam) by Dampa Kunga.

Branch Terma Teachings (gter phran).

Brief Teaching on Empowerment (dbang mdor bstan).

Brief Teaching on the View of Manjushri ('jam dpal gyi lta 'dod mdor bstan pa; Skt. Pradarshananumatoddeshapariksha-nama).

Brilliant Lamp (sgron gsal; Skt. Pradipodyotana-nama-tika) by Chandrakirti.

Buddhapalita by Buddhapalita.

Chakrasamvara RI GI A RA LA Tantra (bde mchog ri gi a ra la'i rgyud).

Chakrasamvara Samvarodaya (bde mchog sdom 'byung).

Chakrasamvara Tantra ('khor lo bde mchog).

Chakrasamvara Tantra in a Hundred Thousand Stanzas (bde mchog 'bum pa).

Chanting the Names of Manjushri ('jam dpal mtshan brjod; Skt. Manjushri-namasamghiti).

Chetsun Nyingtik (lce bstun snying tig) terma of Chetsun Senge Wangchuk.

Chokling Tersar (mchog gling gter gsar).

Circle of Liberation (grol ba'i thig le).

Clear Compendium of the Five Stages (rim lnga bsdus gsal; Skt. Panchakramasam-grahaprakasha) by Naropa.

Clear Essence of the Three Yogas (rnal 'byor gsum gyi snying po gsal ba) by Rangjung Dorje.

Clear Expanse (klong gsal) terma of Ratna Lingpa.

Clear Words (tshig gsal ba; Skt. Mulamadhyamaka-vritti-prasannapada) by Chandrakirti.

Collected Kadam Teachings (bka' gdams glegs bam).

Collected Works of Dölpopa (dol po'i bka' 'bum).

Collected Works of the Great Tertön (gter chen bka' 'bum).

Collected Works of the King (same as *Collected Works of the Mani*) (rgyal po bka' 'bum) terma of Drupthop Ngödrup.

Collected Works of the Mani (same as *Collected Works of the King*) (ma ni 'ka' 'bum) terma of Drupthop Ngödrup.

Collected Works of the Sakya Lineage (sa skya bka' 'bum).

Collected Works of Taranatha (ta ra na tha'i bka' 'bum).

Collection of General Teachings (gtam tshogs; Skt. Kathasamgraha or Kathagana) by Nagarjuna.

Collection of the Nyingma Tantras (rnying ma rgyud 'bum).

Collection of Praises (bstod tshogs; Skt. Strotrasamgraha or Satvagana) by Nagarjuna.

Collection of Reasoning (rigs tshogs; Skt. Yuktisamgraha or Yuktigana) by Nagarjuna.

Combination of the Four Commentaries ('grel pa bzhi sbrags ma) by Tsongkhapa.

Commentaries by Bodhisattvas (byang chub sems 'grel; Skt. Bodhichittavivarana-nama).

Commentary on the Aspiration for the Longevity of the Nyingma Teachings (rnying bstan smon 'grel) by Shechen Gyaltsap Padma Namgyal.

Commentary on the Difficult Points, called Padma (dka' 'grel padma can; Skt. Hevajratantrapanjikapadmini-nama) by Bhavabhadra.

Commentary on Difficult Points of the Vinaya Root Discourse (mdo rtsa'i dka' 'grel) by Butön Rinchen Drup.

Commentary on the Distinctions (rnam dbye 'grel; Skt. Vibhangatika) by Buddha-guhya.

Commentary on the Praise of Chakrasamvara (bde mchog bstod 'grel; Skt. Laksha-bhidhanduddritalaghutantrapindarthavivarana).

Commentary on Suchness (de kho na nyid kyi 'grel pa; Skt. Tattvavritti) by Drozang Nyingpo.

Commentary on the Treasury of Abhidharma (mdzod 'grel; Skt. Abhidharmakosha-bhasya).

Commentary on Valid Cognition (tshad ma rnam 'grel; Skt. Pramana-varttika) by Dharmakirti.

Commentary on the Vajra Heart (rdo rje snying 'grel; Skt. Hevajrapindartha-tika).

Commentary Which Is Easy to Understand on the Abridged Prajnaparamita Sutra (sdud 'grel rtogs sla) by Haribhadra.

Compassion Practice Tantra (snying rje rol pa'i rgyud; Skt. Shri-herukakarunakrid-itatantraguhyagambhirottama-nama).

Compendium of Abhidharma (mngon pa kun btus; Skt. Abhidharmasamucchaya) by Asanga.

Compendium of All Practices (bslab pa kun las btus pa; Skt. Shikshasamucchaya) by Shantideva.

Compendium of Astrological Calculations (rtsis kun bsdus pa) by Rangjung Dorje.

Compendium of Established Teachings (gtan la dbab pa bsdu ba; Skt. Yogacharya-bhumivinishchayasamgraha) by Asanga.

Compendium of Mahayana Commentaries (theg pa chen po bsdus pa; Skt. Mahayana-samucchaya) by Asanga.

Compendium of Sadhanas (sgrub thabs kun btus) by Jamyang Khyentse Wangpo.

Compendium of Sutras (mdo sdud pa; Skt. Acharya-prajnaparamita-sanchaya-gatha).

Compendium of Tantras (rgyud bde kun btus) by Thartse Pönlop Loter Wangpo.

Compendium of Valid Cognition (tshad ma kun btus; Skt. Pramana-samucchaya) by Dignaga.

Compendium of Vajra Wisdom (ye shes rdo rje kun las btus pa; Skt. Vajrajnanasaa-mucchaya-nama-tantra).

Compendium of the Wisdom Essence (ye shes snying po kun las btus pa; Skt. Jnanasarasamucchaya) by Aryadeva.

Continuous Flower Garland (me tok phreng ba rgyud; Skt. Vinayakarika) by Sagadeva.

Dialectics (rtsod pa grub pa; Skt. Vinayakarika) by Vasubandhu.

Differentiating the Three Vows (sdom gsum rab dbye) by Sakya Pandita.

Discourse of One Hundred Actions (karma sha tam; Skt. Ekottarakarmashataka) by Gunaprabha.

Discourse on Valid Cognition or *Compendium of Valid Cognition* (tshad ma mdo; Skt. Pramana-sutra) by Dignaga.

Distinguishing Consciousness and Wisdom (rnam shes dang ye shes 'byed pa) by Rangjung Dorje.

Distinguishing the Middle and the Extremes (dbus dang mtha' rnam par 'byed pa; Skt. Madhyantavibhanga) by Maitreya.

Distinguishing Phenomena and the True Nature (chos dang chos nyid nam par 'byed pa; Skt. Dharma-dharmata-vibhanga-karika) by Maitreya.

Distinguishing the Three Vows (sdom gsum rab dbye) by Sakya Pandita.

Distinguishing the Transmissions of the Vinaya ('dul ba rnam 'byed; Skt. Vinaya-vibhanga).

Distinguishing the Two Truths (dbu ma bden pa gnyis rnam par 'byed pa; Skt. Satyadvaya-vibhanga) by Jnanagarbha.

Double Armor of Mahamudra (phyag chen go cha gnyis pa) by Atisha.

Drops of Logic (gten tshigs thigs pa; Skt. Hetu-bindu) by Dharmakirti.

Drops of Reasoning (rigs pa'i thigs pa; Skt. Nyaya-bindu) by Dharmakirti.

Eight Chapter Tantra (rgyud le'u brgyad ma; Skt. Ashtaparicccheda-tantra).

Eight Common Appendices of Machik (thun mong gi le lag brgyad).

Eight Cycles of the Lamdre Teaching (lam skor brgyad).

Eight Extraordinary Appendices of Machik (thun min gyi le lag brgyad).

Eight Specific Appendices of Machik (khyad par gyi le lag brgyad).

Eight Sadhana Teachings, the Assembly of the Sugatas (bka' brgyad bde 'dus) terma of Nyangral Nyima Özer.

Eight Sadhana Teachings, the Embodiment of the Sugatas (bka' brgyad bde gshegs kun 'dus) terma of Jamyang Khyentse Wangpo.

Eighteen Thousand Stanzas on Valid Cognition (tshad ma stong phrag bco brgyad pa; Skt. Pramanavarttikalamkara) by Prajnakaragupta.

Eliminating the Darkness of the Mind (yid kyi mun sel) by Chapa Chökyi Senge.

Eliminating the Darkness of the Ten Directions (phyogs bcu'i mun sel) by Longchen Rabjam.

Embodiment of the Master's Realization (*Lama Gongdu*) (bla ma dgongs 'dus) terma of Sangye Lingpa.

Embodiment of the Precious Ones (dkon mchog spyi 'dus) terma of Jatsön Nyingpo.

Embodiment of the Primordial State of Samantabhadra (kun bzang dgongs 'dus) terma of Padma Lingpa.

Embodiment of the Quintessence (yang snying 'dus pa) terma of Guru Chöwang.

Embodiment of the Sugatas (bde gshegs kun 'dus) terma of Minling Terchen Gyurme Dorje.

Embodiment of the Three Roots' Realization (rtsa gsum dgongs pa kun 'dus) terma of Jamyang Khyentse Wangpo.

Empowerments and Practices (dbang dang sgrub thabs) by Rangjung Dorje.

Enlightenment of Mahavairochana Tantra (rnam par snang mdzad mngon par byang chub pa'i rgyud; Skt. Mahavairochanabhisambodhivikurvitadhish-thanavaipulya-sutrendraraja-nama-dharmaparyaya).

Entrance to the Meaning of the Anuttarayoga Tantra (bla med kyi rgyud don la 'jug pa; Skt. Yoganuttaratantrarthavatara-samgraha-nama).

Entrance to the Middle Way (dbu ma la 'jug pa; Skt. Madhyamaka-avatara) by Chandrakirti.

Entrance to the Three Kayas (sku gsum la 'jug pa; Skt. Kayatrayavataramukha-nama-shastra) by Nagamitra.

Entrance to the Two Truths (bden pa gnyis la 'jug pa; Skt. Satyadvaya-avatara) by Atisha.

Equalizing Buddhahood (sangs rgyas mnyam sbyor; Skt. Sarvabuddha-samayoga).

Essence of the Crucial Meaning (gnad don snying po) by Taranatha.

Essential Meaning of the Eight Chapters (le brgyad ma'i bsdus don; Skt. Pan-chavinshatisahasrikaprajnaparamita-ashtapariccheda-samkshiptartha) by Haribhadra.

Essential Point of the Drigung ('bri gung pa'i gnad gcig).

Establishing the Reality of Other Minds (rgyud gzhan grub pa; Skt. Samtanantara-siddhi) by Dharmakirti.

Establishing the Two Systems as One (tshul gnyis gcig sgrub).

Examining Relationships ('brel pa brtag pa; Skt. Sambandha-pariksha) by Dhar-makirti.

Examining What Is Observed (dmigs pa brtag pa; Skt. Alambanapariksha) by Dignaga.

Excellent Vase Filled with Necessities (nyer mkho bum bzang).

Excellent Vase That Satisfies All Desires ('dod 'jo'i bum bzang).

Explanation of Conduct (kun spyod la ti ka).

Explanation That Clarifies the Objects of Knowledge (rnam bshad shes bya rab gsal) by Pang Lochenpo.

Explanatory Tantra (bshad rgyud).

Fifty Stanzas (lnga bcu pa; Skt. Gurupanchashika) by Aryadeva.

Fifty Verses (ka ri ka lnga bcu pa; Skt. Aryamulasarvastivadishramanerakarika) by Sanghabhadra.

Five Great Treasuries (mdzod chen po lnga) by Jamgön Kongtrul.

Five Stages (rim lnga; Skt. Panchakrama) by Nagarjuna.

Five Stages of Guhyasamaja (gsang 'dus rim lnga).

Five Teachings on the Heart Essence (snying po skor lnga) terma of Chogyur Lingpa.

Five Treatises of Maitreya (byams chos lnga).

Fivefold Profound Path of Mahamudra (phyag chen lnga ldan).

Floral Ornament of the Guhyagarbha Practice (gsang snying sgrub pa rgyan gyi me tog; Skt. Guhyagarbhasiddhipushpalamkara).

Four Branches of the Heart Essence (snying tig ya bzhi) terma of Longchenpa.

Four Collections (bsdu ba bzhi).

Four Doctrines of the Dharma Protectors (bka' srung chos bzhi) terma of Chogyur Lingpa.

Four Hundred Stanzas (bstan bcos bzhi brgya pa; Skt. Chatuhsataka-sastra-karika) by Aryadeva.

Four Vajra Seats Tantra (rdo rje gdan bzhi; Skt. Shrichatu-pitha-mahayogini-tantraraja-nama).

Further Composition, Questions and Answers (yang tshoms zhus lan).

Garland of Views (man ngag lta ba'i phreng ba) by Padmasambhava.

Gathering of Suchness (de nyid bsdus pa; Skt. Sarvatathagatatattvasamgraha-nama-mahayanasutra).

Geluk-Kagyu Tradition of Mahamudra (dge ldan bka' brgyud kyi phyag chen rgyas bshad) by Lozang Chökyi Gyaltsen.

General Secret Tantra (gsang ba spyi'i rgyud; Skt. Sarvamandalasamanyavidhi-nama-guhyatantra).

Glorious Guhyagarbha Tantra, Which Is the Net of the Magical Display of Vajrasattva (rdo rje sems dpa' sgyu 'phrul drva ba'i rgyud dpal gsang ba bnying po).

Glorious Supreme Primal Tantra (dpal mchog dang po; Skt. Shri-paramadi-tantra).

Golden Teachings (gser chos).

Golden Volume (gser po).

Gradual Path of the Wisdom Essence (lam rim ye shes snying po) terma of Jamyang Khyentse Wangpo.

Great Commentary on the Eight Thousand (brgyad stong 'grel chen; Skt. Aryaashtasahasrikaprajnaparamitavyakhyabhisamayalamkaraloka-nama) by Haribhadra.

Great Commentary on the Lamp of Wisdom (shes rab sgron ma rgya cher 'grel pa; Skt. Prajna-pradipamtika) by Avalokitavrati.

Great Compassionate One Who Embodies All the Buddhas (thugs rje chen po bde gshegs 'dus pa) by Minling Terchen Gyurme Dorje.

Great Composition of Precepts (bka' tshoms chen mo).

Great Display of Ati (a ti bkod pa chen po).

Great Essential Explanation by Rong (rong tik chen mo) by Rongtön Sheja Kunzik.

Great Explanation of the Condensed Meaning of Yoga Tantra (rnal 'byor gyi rgyud kyi bsdus pa'i don 'byung ba'i bshad pa chen mo) by Butön Rinchen Drup.

Great Explanation of Padma (rnam bshad chen mo; Skt. Brihatvritti) by Padmasambhava.

Great Exposition of Reasoning ('thad ldan chen mo; Skt. Pramanavinishchayatika) by Dharmottara.

Great Exposition of the Stages of the Path to Enlightenment (byang chub lam rin chen mo) by Tsongkhapa.

Great Exposition of the Stages of the Tantras (sngags rin chen mo) by Tsongkhapa.

Great Exposition of Valid Cognition (tshad chen; Skt. Tattvasamgrahapanjika) by Kamalashila.

Great Knot Commentary (rgya mdud 'grel; Skt. Mahamudratika or Gaganagarjitaravanameghajyotyaveshosamajasamavyajayamudragranthantantra) by Chandragomin.

Great Self-Arising Awareness Tantra (rig pa rang shar chen po'i rgyud; Skt. Vidyasvodayamahatantra).

Great Space Liberation Tantra (nam mkha' che grol ba'i rgyud).

Great Stream of Ali Kali (a li ka li chu klung chen po).

Great Translation of the Lama (bla 'gyur chen mo).

Great Treasury of Detailed Exposition (bye brag bshad mdzod chen mo; Skt. Mahavibhasha).

Great Verse (tshigs bcad chen mo).

Great Vinaya Rituals (las chog chen mo) by Butön Rinchen Drup.

Guhyagarbha Tantra (gsang ba snying po).

Guhyasamaja Mind Tantra (thugs rgyud gsang ba 'dus pa).

Guhyasamaja Tantra (gsang ba 'dus pa).

Hayagriva Supreme Practice Tantra (rta mchog rol pa'i rgyud).

Heap of Jewels Sutra (dkon mchog brtsegs pa; Skt. Ratnakuta-sutra).

Hearing the Scripture (lung gi snye ma) by Butön Rinchen Drup.

Hearing the True Meaning (nges don snye ma) by Kyorpa Dönyö Pal.

Heart Drop of the Vidyadharas (rig 'dzin thugs thig) by Minling Terchen Gyurme Dorje.

Heart Essence, Mother and Child (snying thig ma bu) by Jamgön Kongtrul.

Heart Essence of the Dakinis (mkha' 'gro snying tig) terma of Ledrel Tsal.

Heart Essence of the Great Siddhas (grub thob thugs thig) terma of Jamyang Khyentse Wangpo.

Heart Essence of Longchenpa (klong chen snying tig) terma of Jigme Lingpa.

Heart Essence of the Profound Meaning (zab don thugs gyi snying po'i gzhung).

Heart Essence of Vajrasattva (rdo sems thugs kyi snying po).

Heart Essence of Vimalamitra (*Vima Nyingtik*) (bi ma snying thig).

Heart Practice of the Wrathful Guru (thugs sgrub drag po rtsal).

Heart Practice That Dispels All Obstacles (*Barche Kunsel*) (thugs sgrub bar chad kun sel) terma of Chogyur Lingpa.

Heroic Samadhi Sutra (dpa' bar 'gro ba'i mdo'; Skt. Surangama-sutra).

Heruka Practice Tantra (he ru ka rol pa'i rgyud; Skt. Shri-herukakarunakriditatantra-guhya-gambhirottama-nama).

Hevajra Tantra (kyee rdo rje'i rgyud) (brtag gnyis).

History of the Dharma (chos 'byung) by Shechen Gyaltsap.

Illuminating the Difficult Points to Teach and Understand ('grel bshad rtogs dka'i snang ba).

Illuminating the Middle Way (bdu ma snang ba; Skt. Madhyamaka-lokanama) by Kamashila.

Informal Discussion of the View (lta ba'i 'bel gtam) by Jamgön Kongtrul.

Inner Scriptural Commentary ('grel pa khog gzhung; Skt. Vajravidarana-nama-dharanitika) by Vimalamitra.

Instruction Tantra (man ngag rgyud).

Jatakamala (skyes) by Aryashura.

Jewel Commentary (dkon mchog 'grel) by Rongzom Chökyi Zangpo.

Kalachakra Tantra (dus kyi 'khor lo).

Khandro Nyingtik (mkha' 'gro snying thig) terma of Ledrel Tsal.

Könchok Chidu (*Embodiment of the Precious Ones*) (dkon mchog spyi 'dus) terma of Jatsön Nyingpo.

Lama Gongdu (*Embodiment of the Master's Realization*) (bla ma dgongs 'dus) terma of Sangye Lingpa.

Lamp of Concise Practice (spyod bsdus; Skt. Charyamelapakapradipa) by Aryadeva.

Lamp of the Path of Awakening (byang chub lam gyi sgron ma; Skt. Bodhi-patha-pradipa) by Atisha Dipankara.

Lamp of Wisdom (shes rab sgron me'i phreng ba; Skt. Prajnapradipa-mulamadhya-maka-pritti) by Bhavaviveka.

Lankavatara Sutra (lang gshegs).

Last Meditation Tantra (bsam gtan phyi ma; Skt. Dhyanottarapatalakrama).

Last Tantra (phyi rgyud).

Last Tantra of the Ferocious Ocean of Activity (gtum po'i rgyud phyi ma; Skt. Shrichandamaharoshana-uttaratantra).

Latter Authoritative Texts (ka dpe phyi ma; Skt. Pravachanottaropama) by Naropa.

Latter Commentary (smad 'grel; Skt. Sarvatathagatatattvasamgrahamahayana-bhisamaya-nama-tantratattvalokakarinama-vyakhya) by Anandagarbha.

Life Stories of the Hundred Tertöns (gter ston brgya rtsa'i rnam thar) by Jamgön Kongtrul.

Light of Reasoning on Valid Cognition (tshad ma rig snang) by Podong Kunkhyen.

Light of Suchness (de nyid snang ba; Skt. Tattvaloka) by Bodhisattva.

Light of the Twenty Thousand (nyi khri snang ba; Skt. Arya-panchavimshatisahas-rikaprajnaparamitopadesha-shastrabhisamayalankaravritti) by Vimuktisena.

Light Rays Illuminating the Essence of the Profound Meaning (zab don snying po snang ba'i 'od zer) by Kyorpa Dönyö Pal.

Manjushri Net of Magical Display in Sixteen Thousand Stanzas ('jam dpal sgyu 'phrul drva ba khri drug stong pa; Skt. Manjushrimayajala-mahatantraraja-nama).

Mayajala Tantra (same as *Net of Magical Display*) (sgyu 'phrul drva ba).

Meaningful to Behold (mthong ba don ldan).

Medium Translation of the Lama (bla 'gyur 'bring po).

Minor Transmissions of the Vinaya ('dul ba phran tshegs; Skt. Vinaya-agama).

Mirror of Poetry in Three Chapters (snyan sngags me long le'u gsum; Skt. Kavyadarsha) by Dandi.

Mountain Pile Tantra (ri bo brtsegs pa; Skt. Sarvabuddhashayasurasamgramagirikutatantra).

Nectar Practice Tantra (bdud rtsi rol pa'i rgyud; Skt. Mahatantrarajashri-amritalalitanama).

Net of Magical Display (sgyu 'phrul drva ba; Skt. Mayajala-tantra).

Net of Magical Display, Peaceful and Wrathful (sgyu 'phrul zhi khro).

Ngagyur Kama (same as *Nyingma Kama*) (snga 'gyur bka' ma).

Ninefold Volume, the Light of the Middle Way (dbu ma snang ba bam po dgu pa; Skt. madhyamaka-lokanama) by Kamalashila.

Noble, Skillful Lasso, the Concise Lotus Garland ('phags pa thabs gyi zhags pa padmo phreng ba'i don bsdus pa; Skt. Aryapayapashapadmamala-pindarthavritti).

Nothing to Fear from Anyone (ga las 'jigs med; Skt. Mulamadhyamakavrittyakutobhaya).

Nyingma Kama (same as *Ngagyur Kama*) (rnying ma bka' ma).

Nyingtik Yabshi (snying tig ya bzhi) terma of Longchenpa.

Ocean of Dakinis of Chakrasamvara (bde mchog mkha' 'gro rgya mtsho; Skt. Shri-dakarnavamahayoginitantrarajavahikatika-nama) by Padmavajra.

Ocean of Jewels of the Lama (bla ma nor bu rgya mtsho) a terma of Padma Lingpa.

Ocean of Texts on Valid Cognition (tshad ma rig gzhung rgya mtsho) by Chödrak Gyatso.

Ocean Waves of the Meaning of the View (bzhed don rgya mtsho'i rlabs phreng) by Shakya Chogden.

Oceanlike Exposition Tantra (bshad rgyud rgya mtsho).

One-Pointed Samadhi (ting 'dzin rtse gcig).

Oral Instructions of the Lord of Secrets (gsang bdag zhal lung) by Lochen Dharma Shri.

Oral Instructions of Manjushri ('jam dpal zhal lung).

Ornament of Clear Realization (mngon par rtogs pa'i rgyan; Skt. Abhisamaya-alamkara) by Maitreya.

Ornament of the Essence of the Teachings (rnam bshad snying po rgyan) by Khedrup Gelek Palzang.

Ornament of the Mahayana Sutras (theg chen mdo sde rgyan; Skt. Mahayana-sutra-lankara) by Maitreya.

Ornament of the Middle Way (dbu ma rgyan; Skt. Madhyamaka-alankara) by Shantarakshita.

Ornament of Stainless Light (dri med 'od rgyan) by Kyorpa Dönyö Pal.

Ornament of the Wisdom Mind of the Lord of Secrets (gsang bdag dgongs rgyan) by Lochen Dharma Shri.

Path of Desire (chags lam).

Points to Remember about the View (lta ba'i brjed byang) by Rongzom Pandita Chökyi Zangpo.

Possessing the Six Transmissions (bka' babs drug ldan).

Prajnaparamita Sutra (shes rab kyi pha rol tu phyin pa'i mdo).

Prajnaparamita Sutra in Eight Thousand Stanzas (sher phyin brgyad stong pa).

Prajnaparamita Sutra in Twenty Thousand Stanzas (nyi khri).

Prajnaparamita Sutra in a Hundred Thousand Stanzas (sher phyin 'bum pa).

Pratimoksha Sutra (same as *Sutra of Individual Liberation*) (so so thar pa'i mdo).

Precious Garland (rin chen phreng ba) by Orgyen Chödrak.

Precious Source for Composing Prosody (sdeb sbyor rin 'byung).

Precious Valuable Key (rin chen gces pa'i lde'u mig) by Kyorpa Dönyö Pal.

Profound Inner Meaning (zab mo nang don) by Rangjung Dorje.

Profound Quintessence (zab mo yang tig) by Longchenpa.

Purification Tantra (sbyong rgyud).

Queen of Great Bliss (klong chen yum bka').

Quintessence of the Dakinis (mkha' 'gro yang tig) by Longchenpa.

Quintessence of the Eight Sadhana Teachings (bka' brgyad yang gsang) terma of Guru Chöwang.

Quintessence of the Lama (bla ma yang tig) by Longchenpa.

Quintessential Composition, the Root of the Dharma (nying tshoms chos kyi rtsa ba).

Rain of Whatever Is Desired ('dod rgu char 'bebs) by Könchok Yenlak.

Rampant Elephant (glang chen rab 'bog; Skt. Hastigajapradanatantra-nama).

Rays of the Sun (nyi ma'i 'od zer) by Tsonawa.

Razor Scriptures of Vajrakilaya (phur pa spu gri) terma of Guru Chöwang.

Realization of the Eighty Magical Displays (sgyu 'phrul brgyad cu pa'i mngon rtogs) by Nup Sangye Yeshe.

Red Draft (reg zeg dmar po).

Rediscovered Terma of Tri-me (dri med yang gter) terma of Jamyang Khyentse Wangpo.

Refuting Misunderstanding about the Vajrayana (sngags log sun 'byin) by Rinchen Zangpo.

Revealing the Vajra Words (rdo rje'i tshig 'byed).

Reversing Disputes (rtsod zlog; Skt. Vigrahavyavrtani) by Nagarjuna.

Rice Seedling Sutra (su lu ljang pa'i mdo; Skt. Shalistambha-sutra).

Root Tantra (rtsa rgyud).

Running Letters (nag 'jam) by Chim Tsöndru Senge.

Sadhana of the Forty-Nine Vajrabhairavas ('jigs byed zhi dgu ma'i sgrub thabs).

Sambhuti Tantra (sam bhu ti).

Scripture of the Embodiment of the Realization of All Buddhas ('dus pa 'do; mdo dgong pa 'dus pa; Skt. Mahasamajautra or Manjushri-ashayasamudayama-hatantra).

Secret Embodiment of the Lama (gsang 'dus) terma of Guru Chöwang.

Secret Essence (gsang ba snying po; Skt. Guhyagarbha).

Secret Explanation of the Forty Letters (yi ge bzhi bcu'i sbas bshad) by Tsongkhapa.

Secret Heart Essence (gsang thig) by Jamgön Kongtrul.

Secret Moon Essence (zla gsang thig le; Skt. Shri-chandraguhyatilaka-nama-mahatantraraja).

Secret Predictions (gsang ba'i lung byang).

Self-Arising Eight Sadhana Teachings (bka' brgyad rang shar).

Seven Conceptions of Vajrabhairava ('jigs byed rtog bdun).

Seven-Line Prayer (tshig bdun gsol 'debs).

Seven Profound Practices (zab pa skor bdun) terma of Chogyur Lingpa.

Seven Texts on Valid Cognition (tshad ma sde bdun; Skt. Pramanavartikadisapta-grantha-samgraha) by Dharmakirti.

Seven Treasuries (mdzod bdun) by Longchen Rabjam.

Short Exposition of the Stages of the Path to Enlightenment (byang chub lam rim chung) by Tsongkhapa.

Short Translation of the Lama (bla 'gyur chung).

Shvana Teachings (shva na'i skor) terma of Chogyur Lingpa.

Six Root Sadhanas (rtsa sgrub tshan drug) terma of Chogyur Lingpa.

Six Transmissions of the Prajnaparamita (sher phyin bka' babs drug).

Sixteen Circles of the Kadampas (thig le bcu drug).

Sixty Stanzas on Reasoning (rigs pa drug cu pa; Skt. Yuktishashthikakarika) by Nagarjuna.

Skillfully Doing Whatever One Likes (mkhas pa dga' byed) by Kyorpa Dönyö Pal.

Sky Teaching (gnam chos) terma of Migyur Dorje.

Slayer of the Lord of Death (gshin rje gshed po).

Sole Intention of Drigung ('bri gung dgongs gcig).

Sound Consequence Root Tantra (thal 'gyur rtsa ba'i rgyud; Skt. Ratnakarashab-damahaprasangatantra).

Stages of Meditation: The First Treatise, Intermediate Treatise, and Final Treatise (sgom rim thog mtha' bar gsum; Skt. Bhavanakrama) by Kamalashila.

Stages of the Vajrayana Path (gsang sngags lam rim).

Stainless Light (dri med 'od; Skt. Vimalaprabha) by Pundarika.

Sublime Basis (gzhi bla ma).

Sublime Continuum (rgyud bla ma; Skt. Uttaratantra-shastra) by Maitreya.

Sublime Medicine, the Amrita of Questions and Answers (zhus lan bdud rtsi sman mchog) by Tsongkhapa.

Sublime Teachings of the Vinaya ('dul ba gzhung dam pa; Skt. Vinaya-uttama).

Summary of Suchness (de nyid bsdus pa; Skt. Tattva-samgraha) by Shantarakshita.

Supreme Primordial Buddha (mchog gi dang po'i sangs rgyas; Skt. Paramadibuddhoddhritashrikalachakra-nama-tantraraja).

Supreme Unchanging Chapter (mchog mi 'gyur gyi le'u; Skt. Paramaksharajnana-patala).

Supreme Wishes of the Twelve Buddhas (thugs dam bde gshegs bcu gnyis) by Dampa Kunga.

Sutra of Individual Liberation (so so thar pa'i mdo; Skt. Pratimoksha-sutra).

Sutra of the King of Concentrations (mdo ting 'dzin rgyal po; Skt. Samadhiraja-sutra).

Sutra of the King of Giving Instructions (gdams ngag 'bog pa'i rgyal po).

Sutra of the Play of the River (chu klung rol pa'i mdo).

Sutra of the Recollection of the Buddha (sangs rgyas rjes su dran pa; Skt. Arya-buddhanusmriti).

Sutra of the Samadhi That Gathers All Merit (bsod nams thams cad sdud pa'i ting nge 'dzin gyi mdo; Skt. Arya-sarvapunyasamucchayasamadhi-nama-mahayanasutra).

Sutra Requested by the Naga King Madröpa (klu'i rgyal po ma dros pas zhus pa'i mdo; Skt. Arya-anavataptanagarajapariprccha-nama-mahayanasutra).

Tantra Requested by Subahu (dpung bsang; Skt. Subahupariprccha-tantra).

Teachings on Interdependence (rten 'brel gyi chos skor) by Jamgön Kongtrul.

Terma Treasury of Spontaneous Wish-Fulfilling Qualities (bsam lhun yon tan gter mdzod).

Thought Tantra of Yamantaka (gshin rje gshed kyi rgyud rtog pa; Skt. Shri-krishnayamaritantrarajatrikalpa-nama).

Three Hundred (sum brgya pa; Skt. Aryamulasarvastivadishramanerakarika) by Shakyaprabha.

Three Mothers Who Overcome Harm (yum gsum gnod 'joms; Skt. Arya-shatasaha-srikapanchavimshatisahasrikashtadashasaha-srikaprajnaparamitabrihattika) by Vasubandhu.

Torch of Pacification (zhi byed sgron ma).

Torch of the Three Methods (tshul gsum sgron ma; Skt. Nayatrayapradipa) by Tripitakamala.

Treasury of Abhidharma (mngon pa mdzod; Skt. Abhidharmakosha) by Vasubandhu.

Treasury of Instructions (gdams ngag mdzod) by Jamgön Kongtrul.

Treasury of Kagyu Vajrayana Instructions (bka' brgyud sngags mdzod) by Jamgön Kongtrul.

Treasury of Knowledge (shes bya mdzod) by Jamgön Kongtrul.

Treasury of Logic on Valid Cognition (tshad ma rig.pa'i gter) by Sakya Pandita.

Treasury of Precious Terma (rin chen gter mdzod) by Jamgön Kongtrul.

Treatise on Buddha Nature (snying po bstan pa) by Rangjung Dorje.

Treatise on Debate (rtsod pa'i rigs pa; Skt. Vadanyaya or Vadanyaya-nama-prakarana) by Dharmakirti.

Treatise on Developing a Hair's Tip of Wisdom (shes rab skra rtsa'i sa gzhung spel ba).

Trilogy of Commentaries by Bodhisattvas (sems 'grel skor gsum).

Trilogy on Natural Ease (ngal gso skor gsum) by Longchen Rabjam.

Trilogy on Purity (dag pa skor gsum).

Twelve Thousand Stanzas on Valid Cognition (tshad ma stong phrag bcu gnyis pa; Skt. Pramanavartikatika) by Devindramati.

Udanavarga (ched du brjod pa'i tshoms).

Ultimate Emptiness Sutra (don dam stong pa nyid gyi mdo; Skt. Paramarthashunyata-sutra).

Unimpeded Realization of the Great Perfection (dgongs pa zang thal) terma of Rigdzin Gödem.

Unsurpassed Quintessence of Vajrakilaya (phur pa yang gsang bla med) terma of Ratna Lingpa.

Vairochana Net of Magical Display (rnam snang sgyu 'phrul drva ba).

Vajra Bridge (snyan brgyud rdo rje zam pa).

Vajra Club (rdo rje be com) terma of Chogyur Lingpa.

Vajra Essence Commentary (rdo rje snying 'grel).

Vajra Essence Ornament Tantra (rdo rje snying po rgyan gyi rgyud; Skt. Shri-vajrahri-dayalamkara-tantra-nama).

Vajra Laugh of Scripture and Reasoning (lung rigs rdo rje'i gad rgyangs) by Minling Rabjampa Ögyen Chödrak.

Vajra Mala Tantra (rdor phreng).

Vajra Mirror Tantra (rdo rje me long; Skt. Vajradarpana).

Vajra Pinnacle (rdo rje rtse mo; Skt. Vajrashekhara-mahaguhyayogatantra).

Vajra Songs of Aspiration (smon lam gyi rdo rje'i glu).

Vajra Tent Tantra (rdo rje gur; Skt. Dakini-vajra-panjara-mahatantra).

Vajra Verses (rdo rje tshig rkang; Skt. Vajrapada or Margaphalanvitavavadaka) by Virupa.

Vajrakilaya Piece of the Root Tantra (phur pa rtsa dkum gyi rgyud).

Vajrapani Empowerment Tantra (phyag rdor dbang bskur ba'i rgyud).

Vajrapani Tantra (phyag rdor).

Vajrapani Tantra Directly Showing the Secret (phyag rdor gsang ba mngon bstan gyi rgyud; Skt. Bhagavadvajrapaniguhyabhidesha-tantra-raja).

Vast Display of the Deep Meaning (zab don thang brdal ma) by Taranatha.

Vima Nyingtik (same as *Heart Essence of Vimalamitra*) (bi ma snying thig).

Vinaya Root Discourse ('dul ba mdo rtsa; Skt. Vinayasutra) by Gunaprabha.

Vitality Practice of the Knowledge Holders (rig 'dzin srog sgrub) terma of Lhatsun Namkha Jigme.

Way of the Bodhisattva (byang chub sems dpa'i spyod pa la 'jug pa; Skt. Bodhi-charyavatara) by Shantideva.

Weapon of Speech That Cuts through Difficult Points (dka' gcod smra ba'i mtshon cha) by Nup Sangye Yeshe.

Wheel of Time (dus kyi 'khor lo; Skt. Kalachakra).

White Manifestation (dkar po rnam par 'char ba) by Palden Chökyong.

Wisdom, a Root Text of the Middle Way (dbu ma rtsa ba'i shes rap; Skt. Prajna-mulamadhyamaka-karika) by Nagarjuna.

Wisdom Essence Tantra (ye shes snying po).

Wish-Fulfilling Jewel (yid bzhin nor bu).

Yamantaka Appearance in the Mirror Tantra (pra khog snang).

Yamantaka Tantra (gshin rje gshed po).

Yamantaka Vijaya Tantra (gshin rje gshed rnam par rgyal ba'i rgyud).

Yamantaka Who Conquers the Arrogant Ones (gshin rje dregs 'joms) by Minling
    Terchen Gyurme Dorje.

Yuthok Innermost Essence (g.yu thog snying thig).

INDEX

Printed in the United States
By Bookmasters